# The Aspiring Alchemist

## JIM BRIDGEN

For Janelle

Love from Jim x

Edited by Anne Searle

Graphics by Anne Searle and Jim Bridgen

Jim was born in the village of Whittington,
near Lichfield, Staffordshire in 1937
A lifelong painter, poet and photographer,
he has led a richly varied life, ploughing his
own deep furrow in life's rich landscape.
He has worked as a lecturer in Design and
Photography at Plymouth College of Art
as well as many years as a Graphic Designer
in television.
Throughout his life Jim has kept a highly
entertaining, beautifully written account
of it all.

## 1. 'Nickel, Flint and a Venus Fly-Trap'

Change never paid homage to pimpernels or wild pansies, nor did it care tuppence for golden finches feeding in thistledown pastures. Change changed things, usually in fits and starts but always forever; hello, goodbye; hello, goodbye ad infinitum. Time itself was a continuous process of change and everything that changed was subsequently re-changed and that, constantly altered and re-arranged. 'Aspirations' and 'expectations' were poles apart even though there wasn't really that much to choose between the two of them. Ignoring any finer spiritual dimension, money was always going to be the ultimate fruit of toil, honest or otherwise; there was always 'gold in them there hills'! Alas, there was a snag; the 'toil' part of the equation wasn't in the least bit attractive to those most hotly in pursuit. It would surely be far better if 'Gold' could be persuaded or tricked into springing out from chicken-shit or something abundant and of miniscule worth. Why, dammit, if an 'oyster' of all lowly creatures could concoct a pearl from an ill-considered ablution in a 'small-room' part of its digestion, then, what was there to prevent 'Gold' from being made by a creature aspiring not to be that low down in the order of things?

The answer sad to say, lay in time-old deserts of forgotten questions that'd once stood up mountainously mighty, leafy forested and alive, now blown to dust along with their answers and their secrets, making 'Time' itself the most impossibly hard concept upon which to find purchase for the mind. It was plain to see that a limit had been placed around that which we actually were, or could aspire to be, similarly and separately as infinitely variably ultimate limits had been placed around every other species upon the planet, thus making it impossible for one species to look inside the mind of another. The only single thing to set 'Homo Sapiens' apart from all other species was its absolute dependence on a contrived 'magic', the self-proscribed, make-believe brainwash of 'Religion' in all its gruesome manifestations and made-to-measure conveniences designed to provide 'the' answer; where no questions were permitted to be asked and for the male of the species to go about his bigoted and bullying ways, believing himself to be the divinely 'chosen one' from that which he had contrived; thence to go contorting, distorting, concocting, enforcing a bully's ways over the ways of those simpletons that harboured thoughts of 'wealth' to be pimpernels and wild pansies, golden finches in thistledown pastures and all surrounding, abounding richness of Reason ever available ... if only!

The past had passed, was still passing; new ways were muscling-in upon old remedies and an invisible method of running with Hares whilst simultaneously hunting with Hounds was sought by those aspiring to Alchemy and acquiring Authority as the vitally essential first rung of the ladder.

Change was such a virulent irritation that there wasn't an arse anywhere that knew where or what an elbow was, as out from the confusion of a darkness devoid of moon and stars, a rabble-rousing band of rebellious hopefuls came invisibly chanting; "We're gonna change the world, gonna change the world; we're gonna gonna, gonna gonna, gonna change the world! There'll be no Government, be no Government; be no, be no, be no be no, be no Government! We'll manufacture Gold, manu...." "Bugger off, yer noisy bastards ... aint yer got no 'omes to go to!" A haggard shadow of a father-again for the umpteenth time, bawled out into the droopy dark, starless night from a bedroom window amidst squawking babies, howling and growling dogs and an entire fidgety twitching of curtains as the poor, mithered stump of a man bellowed out again ... "Bugger off the lot of yer or yo'll be feelin' my clog up yer arses!" The 'opium of the people' had extended to now include, 'College Education' and there were more budding Chiefs than Indians as a result!

Before I had reached the age of fourteen I found myself attending Lichfield School of Art on two afternoons, two evenings and on Saturday mornings, having been instructed to abandon any remaining 'normal' education and to concentrate on Art. All of this somewhat radical thinking resulted from the arrival of a new Headmaster, replacing the tobacco-smelling, worn out and fighting for breath disciplinarian, 'Monkey' Miller. Our new man, Mister Nichols, was a desperately needed breath of fresh air, as much a revolution as a revelation; a baggy tan-corduroyed, mustachioed and strong-minded, wickedly straightforward sort of man. He took me to one side and told me in plain terms that I was wasting my talent doing History, Geography and 'other' stuff, and that he was going to see to it that, from now on, I would be doing Art all of the time. That I would be provided with the very barest of materials and a place to work, with an assurance that he would coach me himself whenever possible.

This decision of his had, to a large part, been influenced by the fact that I had just won first prize in a 'Road Safety Poster Competition', one which had covered the whole West Midlands area. A beaming, immensely proud Mister Nichols made the announcement at assembly one morning when, luck would have it, that I was hidden away in the back row and paying no attention to what was being said as my malingering best pal, Jeff Farnsworth, whispered a very rude joke deafeningly down my ear. Somewhat to my surprise, the whole class started to applaud, and so just to be on the safe side I joined in as too did Jeff, neither of us wanting to be seen inattentive, even though we hadn't a clue about what we were clapping about. To my further consternation my name was called; my head was still clumsily full of the rude image which Jeff had just left me with, that of a bloke kissing his girlfriend goodnight whereupon, she crossed her legs and busted his glasses! I was still tittering over this in little uncontrollable fluttering outbursts and was blushing furiously, when my name was called out yet again. All my mates started to cheer as I stood up guiltily and was summoned to the front of the class. I was squirming with embarrassment as I faced my comeuppance. My shirt was open down to my belly-button due to it having no buttons, and on my feet I had wellies with their tops rolled down and, worst of all, shabby short trousers because Mom and Dad still stubbornly refused either to submit or admit to my beginning to look like a man and allow me to wear long trousers like all the other lads were wearing. In my dithering state of confusion and fear I was presented with, not the clip round the ear that I expected but a Prize of all things, a small gift-wrapped box in which was the most unbelievably beautiful fountain pen all prettily marbled in red, black and gold. Then Mister Nichols proudly placed his arm across my shoulder and told everyone that I had worked extremely hard and was a credit to the school and that this proud achievement had helped put 'Whittington School' on the map. It still hadn't dawned on me as to what this was all about having long since forgotten all about the Poster Competition. I was applauded all the way back to where my disgusting friend was now sprawled hidden from the Headmaster's view, cross-eyed and with his big dribbling tongue sticking out sideways and with a pair of busted spectacles crookedly straddling his nose.

Lichfield Art School was a, 'plaster-still-wet', brand new purpose-built building situated on the south bank of a deep sandstoned-cliffed railway ravine in an area prettily named 'Cherry Orchard'. The Principal was a most amazing, larger-than-life, somewhat tyrannical extrovert by the name of Ethel Mary Flint; when she wasn't within earshot they called her 'Emma' for short. She, like Mister Nichols, had recognised a particular, even peculiar brand of 'something' which I apparently possessed, a certain resemblance to 'base-metal' which, through a mysterious, ambiguous medieval chemistry and a goodly amount of devotional tinkering and tampering, could be persuaded into becoming 'Gold'!

I was soon in the thick of unimagined things; jewellery making, coppersmithing and letter-carving in wood by day, still-life painting and costume life-drawing in the evenings Wednesday and Fridays and with botanical water-colouring on Saturday mornings. It was all a bit of a sudden shock to my system and I felt like some insignificant dot in a sea of overfed, dilettante ladies of leisure with waxed and gaudily distempered smiles; all of them barnacled and adorned in their own hand-made jewellery and with ear-rings that hung glittering in an opulence bordering on vulgarity. There were small thin men also, almost all of them with sharp pointed noses, pin-striped waistcoated suits and receding hair flattened under icing-sugar thick Brylcreem, all of them preciously tending to hobbies, their aspirations having long since withered on the ever-changing vine of rambling time. A man in a white coat and sporting a monumental 'Your Country Needs You' moustache the size of a yard broom, taught me to work with copper, softening it with nitric acid and then, pummelling it into shape over a last with a round-ended fine hammer, before finally silver-plating it. The ladies set diamonds, rubies and emeralds into silver and gold, watching in fascination my virginal enthusiasm, like as though watching a spaniel having its first pups.

By this time Dad had reluctantly been obliged to provide me with a bike of sorts, a 'gift-horse' as it turned out, a dead man's bike, one which the grieving widow had been glad to see the back of. It was a huge black, rupturously heavy 'Raleigh' with a substantial chain-guard, dynamo, large saddlebag and four-speed 'Sturmey Archer' hub gears. Size-wise it surely had to be the biggest of the range as well as the heaviest; even with the seat down as low as it would go, my feet still barely touched the pedals. The slightest of slips from either pedals or saddle and its crossbar would surely castrate me without even blinking! What I'd wanted most of all and had been pleading for, was a racing bike, I wanted one more than ever now and I felt myself becoming wilder, more isolated and forgotten by the hour. I didn't want a dead man's bike any more than I wanted a dead man's jock-strap and I cursed Dad for disregarding my essentially youthful feelings over this. I was becoming a rebel, a R.E.B.B.L.E, so beware! Dad remained unmoved, like a four-inch thick book of blank pages and he never even twitched a single leaf, turning my intended gale into a whisper.

Dad's own 'axe-to-grind', was deep, far deeper than normal axes went and he watched with a certain reserved timidity, my emergence as a free-thinking, mind-of-my-own sort of person, reckoning my chances of succeeding in the 'Art' world like that of being a solitary balloon in an ocean-skyful of pins. His attitude stemmed from a loathing mistrust of the world in which 'Art' was situated, rather than a lack of belief in the one following in his pained footsteps. Time for him had cruelly turned hopes into despairs, dreams into nightmares; better the nightmare you knew and trusted than the dream you only ever dreamed at its best.

He was invited to a meeting with Miss Flint, taking me with him, to discuss my future. He told her that he had given the matter a lot of thought and, after weighing things up and, in the light of experience, was rather of the opinion that it might be best if I pursued a career in the Royal Navy. At which point Miss Flint became highly unstable and promptly erupted all over him. I sat and watched as Dad's big red balloon deflated into a crinkled and wrinkled, withered-to-nothing currant at her feet. "I've never heard anything so preposterous in all my life! You should jolly well be ashamed of yourself, Mr. Bridgen! Are you telling me that you are prepared to see your son's unique artistic talent go to waste ... in the 'NAVY' of all things? Shame on you, man; you must be out of your mind!"

Poor Dad, he hadn't been prepared for her ebullient bombardment and he'd certainly got more than he'd bargained for as he capitulated with as much dignity as his shamed embarrassment would allow. Ethel Mary Flint was a dreadnought and would have done well had she herself chosen to follow a career in the Royal Navy! What she didn't know or appreciate though, was the fact that Dad was an artist too and, brilliant though Ethel Flint was, Dad was at least her equal and, to my mind, her superior.

This solitary event marked the most significant moment of my entire life; this very moment was the one and only one that changed all things beyond the point of no-return, changed it all forever.

Destiny precariously resolved, I looked at Dad and felt ashamedly sorry for putting him through this when I knew that, deep down he really did want me to be the artist that he himself had been denied and I felt that it was I who was to blame for the ill-considered nonsense about my joining the Navy. Truth was, I'd earlier in my life taken a liking to the way Uncle George looked in his sailor's uniform and was taken-in, hook, line and sinker by the yarns he told and with the romantic notion of seeing the world and the wilder, even more romantic lure of having a sweetheart in every port. It had all really blinded me and, instead of Dad putting me straight and telling me the military life was nothing like that at all, as he should have so done, he just went along with it. He complacently reckoned it to be one major worry off his mind now that he had a new daughter to focus his affections and attentions on, especially so with my having what he and Mom referred to with a certain revulsion and disdain as being, an 'Artistic Temperament'.

My having been appointed 'Head Boy' in my final year was something of an embarrassment to them both, raising the family profile a touch too much for comfort; success in their minds was never intended for the likes of us. They'd got me believing that too, failure was preferable; ideally being somewhere lost out of sight in the middle was best of all, if that could be achieved. Being made Head Boy was something which I didn't feel comfortable with, it made me feel a bit of a prick wearing a badge with that printed on it; it was bad enough earlier having to wear one with 'Prefect' printed on it ... they'd even spelt 'Perfect' wrong! 'Head Boy' really was a bit pompous and divisive, so I knew how Mom and Dad must have felt; it wasn't my fault that I'd been mistaken for a Chief instead of a good old-fashioned, honest, working Indian.

I settled into the routine of attending Lichfield Art School, coming to terms with the various, rather obscure disciplines till I felt a degree or two less self-conscious. It was all beginning to come along nicely and my confidence was gradually starting to show signs of life; it was something which I'd never before known, these frail, first trembling moments of self-belief. Then out of the blue, I got the shock of my young life at one Friday evenings Costume-Life class; Miss Flint had by now really taken me under her wing and was treating me like a Princely Son. She gave me a strangely cheeky, rather wistful wisp of a smile as she had her customary discussion with the model over working out the pose or poses for the evening. Then she marched briskly across the studio announcing; "I've got something a little different for you tonight, Bridgen!" and she gave the model a nod indicating for her to take up her pose. My mouth fell agape and my enraged eyes ballooned, boiled and fell twitching all jellified on the floor. I was trembling and couldn't even hold my pencil; the model was stark naked in all her short and curly glory and I couldn't look at her for fear of the Almighty striking me dead with a lightning flash from his forefinger. I could hear lots of little throat-clearing noises and a sudden clatter of shuffling activity as the pointed-nosed little men became all glinty-eyed, bushy-tailed and ferrety as they discreetly concealed their newly erected trouser-wigwams beneath their drawing boards. I could sense the eyes of all the women pressing down on me in a kind of judgmental, rather disapproving curiosity, making it impossible for me to feel at ease and I thought to myself about what would happen if Mom or Dad were to know about this ... I'd be in the Navy like a shot, double-quick, no messing!

I was in a most unexpected nightmarish dilemma; I couldn't do anything, same as I couldn't do nothing. Something far mightier than Miss Flint was bearing down on me and stopping me from looking at the model's special 'female bits' but I knew more crucially still that the formidable Miss Flint was a very much 'in-the-flesh', real manifestation and, at this moment of time, a whole lot bigger than any pie-in-the-sky God and I had to very quickly decide which of the two I most feared right now. The answer was as easy as diarrhoea, Miss Flint won by a mile. I ditheringly attempted to wobble my first marks upon the paper, knowing that my mentor would soon be descending on me, her loud enthusiastic voice showing no respect whatsoever for my agonising embarrassment. I had to have something worthy of comment on the paper, otherwise I'd be publicly humiliated; old 'Emma' didn't suffer fools, full-stop!

My moment of truth duly arrived and, like it or not, I was in at the deep end and those 'special' private bits which I'd so vehemently avoided were now starkly conspicuous by their absence from my drawing and I was blushingly forced into closely examining and addressing those very 'prohibited' parts. "Frightened of a 'mound of Venus' and two breasts are we, Bridgen!" Miss Flint scolded in her no-nonsense sort of way, making me cringe almost to the point of spontaneous combustion with the ferocity of my blushes. Everyone else had stopped what they were doing and were all now tuned-in to the 'master class' with demonstrations which I was being given. "Come on now, Bridgen; without the beautiful forms of breasts, bottoms and Venuses, Classical Art wouldn't exist!" She went further into raptures extolling the beauty of breasts in all their sculptural glory, waxing lyrical over those other intimate, out-of-bounds-to-my-eyes parts which had suffocated me in shyness. She went on to conclude that nothing, absolutely nothing, was nearly so beautiful as the human body and insisting on me that I must look at it, examine it closely, even to go up and touch it if I felt it necessary for a better understanding, making everyone laugh by adding that the model wouldn't bite me. Even the model was smiling as our eyes briefly collided; I sensed a sigh of relief in her attractive face now that my embarrassment-bubble had been pricked.

I was in no hurry as I slowly pedalled back to the village. The nerve-racking experience had left me in a state of shock, half excited in a very nervous sort of way, half ashamed and wanting to talk about it but was afraid to even breath a word lest it pack me off into the Navy. As I lay in my bed unable to sleep, the experience lay awkward and heavy throughout my mind in a 'trespassing' sort of way that still had the taste of guilt about it. I needed to get this 'carnal' thing out from me, trivialise it in some way, make it naughty and set me free from the thought that I had sinned. The sudden image of her grown-up nudity had really scared me stiff; things like that were meant best to be seen through keyholes, flimsily wrapped in wickedness, stolen and fondled and never made ordinary in any way, shape or form. It were as though the 'sin' of it was that I needed to have undressed her myself with no-one looking, just her and me, then being able to touch her all over with my worshipping fingers and to rub noses and things, instead of having to sit amongst well-to-do adults and just 'look'. I hadn't been prepared for this huge step that I had just taken.

By repetitious degrees I got used to the new experience and time blew the days by like leaves from the trees and birds from the skies, severing me from the village school and distancing me from hosts of other things in this palpitational turning of time. I could smell 'Gold' in a thousand places, the land around was ripe with it, all ready for harvesting, a flowing currency aspiring to feed the world and line its pockets with 'currency-buns'. At long last I'd reaped my longed-for long trousers. They were big and baggy and made of a thick coarse tweed intended more for the upholstering of palatial sofas than they were for my skinny legs. Dad's demob trousers, a suit in fact, one which would see me over the next five years at the Art College in Stafford, a numbing prospect to say the least. Whether this gesture of Dad's was a self-sacrificial, or maybe a miserly one, I couldn't really tell, he'd only ever worn the suit on the solitary occasion of his demobilisation from the Army; he hadn't chosen it, it was just 'Army Issue', no questions asked and no measurements taken..."Next one!" It completely swamped me but, as he persuasively pointed out, I'd grow into it with time; one thing for certain, it most certainly wasn't going to wear out and would no doubt last me through till I was a father myself and could then hand it down to one of Dad's grandsons.

I wasn't the only village migrant. My cousin Gordon had already flown off like an old pigeon, away south to a farm in Berkshire from where he wrote letters describing the vast rolling landscapes with so much more sky than ever we'd been allocated here in the village. The fields near Wantage where his farm was situated he said were like prairies, most corn-growing, some sheep and with white horses carved into the chalk hills by our early ancestors. There were also plagues of rabbits which he readily caught, gutted, parcelled-up and sent through the post back home to Aunty Hilda. I'd often hear Mom ask Aunty ... "Have you heard from Gordon?" and Aunty would reply ... "Yes, I had a rabbit in the post from him only this mornin'!"

Another migration was happening all around as a result of a boom in Council House building which had really altered the face of things, gobbling up gardens, allotments, orchards and seemingly whatever fell in its path. We'd been re-housed in a brand new 'box' down Blacksmith Lane while other neighbours migrated to boxes further afield, some to Shenstone, others out towards Burton, Tamworth and Lichfield. The new fledglings adults-to-be that'd left the nest with me were all now learning to fly, working in shops, offices, hospitals, serving apprenticeships operating machines in factories, labouring on farms and on building-sites. Others of us had hit the college trail, hooked on the lure of eventual gold gleaned from a ruralist, primaeval sludge which may or may not have been mercurial. My sister Fay, having survived Polio had also plugged for the new 'gold-rush' and had dreams of becoming a secretary in some posh office in Lichfield, preferable a solicitors where men wore ties, suits and braces and polished shoes. We were the ones that would have to wait another three to five years before getting our first sniff of a wage-packet but at least we'd have certificates, magic bits of paper that kept us true to the trail of this new 'Klondike'-thinking, Fay to her Pitmans' Commercial College in Walsall and me to my arty-farty one in Stafford, double-decker bussing it the pair of us.

The thought of starting at the Art College was turning me into a bag of nerves. There wouldn't be a single person there that I knew and, worse still, I was scared stiff of big towns and had never set foot in Stafford before so didn't have a clue as to where the Art College was. "You've got a bloomin' tongue in yer head!" Dad groaned frustratedly over my whinging, offering me a begrudging morsel of irritated support as he re-reminded me of the offer of his six-sizes-too-big demob-suit which he appeared to misguidedly believe, as though by magic, would dispel any notion of my being of pauper-stock and would safeguard me by making me look like landed gentry. If they saw the dead-man's bike that I was riding, they'd have no such wild misconceptions! I was still struggling on with the cumbersome monstrosity despite my constant mitherings for a second-hand racer, one with a bit of style, one that I could really fly on. Such mithering fell on stony ground; weighing more heavily on Dad's mind was the vexing issue of bus fares and money for cups of tea and other such niggling things which constituted my 'upkeep'. I had apparently been awarded what he referred to as a 'piddling-little' grant, but I wasn't allowed to know how much this was. "'That aint your business!" was the answer I got when I asked. "'Taint nearly enough for what it's gonna cost to keep you at that bloomin' college I can tell you, straight up!" If ever there was a time for discovering what the magic ingredient was that could be mixed with chicken-shit to produce Gold, that time was now!

## 2. 'Pigments of the Imagination'

Meanwhile, the new Council House in Blacksmith Lane was proving to be quite a novelty; to our reckoning it was a bit 'posh' and had an outside lavatory all of its own and a separate one upstairs in the little bathroom, for Mom, Fay and Rosie. That wasn't all, it also had a tap with the word, 'hot' next to one saying 'cold', and there were two radiators running off a 'Rayburn' stove, which Mom found to be a bit on the 'new-fangled' side and which she didn't seem to be able to get the hang of, making her start to yearn for the old open range back in Bevans Row. Ours was the very last Council House down the lane, which suited Mom and Dad because it meant that we only had neighbours on one side, the other side was just a neglected and overgrown jungle with a sagging old red-brick shed hidden amongst towering nettles, hogweeds and willowherbs. Further over stood the tumbledown remains of a longish cottage which appeared to have suffered bomb-damage with part of its roof blown-in, a couple of windows and part of a wall missing yet, somewhat scarily, was still being lived in by a very old, wizened and wild woman that nobody ever saw, 'Meg Bagley', rumoured to be a witch! There were rats everywhere over beyond that bit of fencing, the old ruin must have been riddled with them and they'd even started showing up in our brand new garden. I was given strict instructions never to go anywhere near the place; apart from it being dangerous, it was said to be haunted, weird shrieks having been heard coming from there.

Not having to share a bedroom with Fay and Rosemary any more, Dad had sprung into uncharacteristic jolly fervour of tilling the soil. He wasn't noted for vocal utterances of a musical kind, he couldn't even whistle but, by golly, he was giving it both barrels now; he'd certainly got bitten by some bug or other. Fay looked at me and I looked at Fay in despairing resignation, at least he wasn't trying to remember or even attempt Words! Mom seemed pretty perky too, despite the new-fangled Rayburn and, while she sang "Trallallallalla" interspersed with a good deal of bee noises, he went on his merry way with a "Riddledee Diddledee, Hiddledee Piddledee, Dabba dabbadoo; Dipperty dapperty, Ripperty rapperty, Doodle doodle dee!" Fay shook her head and vanished as I leaned back watching this singing donkey of a Dad in a pre, pre-autumnal dig in impatient readiness for next year's potatoes, broad beans and beetroot by the ton. Further along towards the front of the garden he'd had another burst of celebratory energy and had demolished an ivy-covered wall, cleared away piles of earth rubble and bushes and had created a gravelled parking place for his motor-bike and sidebox, with additional space for his ladder-rack.

While he went about his jolly-gardener thing, I gazed lustily at this forbidden, forgotten corner of the world. An odorous, alchemic witchcraft wafting its cats' piss and lavender signature upon the air and a mediaeval veiled stench of decomposing ghosts and forgotten time darkly turning to poison in the blackest of magics; an Alchemist's dream.

Foreboding and forbidden as this sinister and mysterious corner was, I was intrigued by it and felt its power irresistibly drawing me ever closer and I fought with a failing resolve until I could fight it no longer. There was something in that old shed that wouldn't let go of me and was beckoning as treacle to a wasp. I glanced across at Dad and could see that his pre-occupation was intense to the point of intoxication with the mysterious black soil, feeling it and smelling it, resisting to the limit an urge to taste it. He was unaware of my surreptitious side-stepping to the motorbike and then silently out into a short dark alley and into that forbidden tangle of demonic intrigue. Once there I felt encapsulated by its terrible stillness; nothing stirred, just a timeless silence at death everywhere. Heavily drooping and anciently cobwebbed, rotting lace curtains hung behind filthied broken glass in a window and I felt myself held in a sinister, time-warped rigor-mortis-like torment and I wondered if there were evil eyes stalking me. It was the old shed that had intrigued me most of all; someone, sometime had built it, an alive mind here in this very space. A mind full of brightly coloured dreams while the old-world was still in black and white, long before Grandad was born.

I hardly dared move lest I attracted Dad and so I summoned a degree of stealth to surpass any I'd ever known and, inch by silent inch I made my way into the terrible invitation of the half-open, or half-closed door, I didn't know which. I was here caught between past and future, one of which had left marks where it had been, the other yet in wait. Old sheds were treasure-chests, gold from galleons sunk by storms or by warrior madness and here lying at the bottom of the sea where I walked. Once inside I'd be safe from Dad and be able to relax and absorb the stillness that time had forgotten, satisfy my greedy curiosity that'd got the better of me, much to my un-admitted shame.

I was inside at last, feasting my eyes and mind in an insatiable fascination. As well as being treasure-chests, old sheds were the abandoned and forgotten birds nests of a people that'd flown and I stood in solemn reverence gazing at the age-bended shelves, the grey-laced webs cast like ancient nets for long gone shoals, the handmade iron nails wedged between the crumbling bricks, through which the daylight stole, still with old garden forks, hoes, sickles and busted rakes hanging there all skeletal and stark, long after the gardener had turned to soil. There were baskets, boxes and tins, twine that'd rotted, sieves that'd broken; there were skulls of rats, petrified starling corpses, an owl's feather in a dusty web, rosebriars floundering for the light that spilled from where tiles had fallen through, rusted buckets with no bottoms, remains of a black pram with all its scriptures blown to dust.. Very slowly I turned around, half expecting to see a silhouetted ghost standing in the doorway but my eyes were magnetically pulled to the shelf behind the door. I couldn't believe what I was looking at ... a shelf weighed-down with unexploded incendiary bombs left over from the war!

I gasped, like as though sucking in a ton of burning iron-dust, as a wickedly silent dream of genocide by burning was silently sleeping all about me and I was but a tiptoe from turning it into an awakened nightmare. I hardly dared breath, terror had petrified me to the spot as I wondered how or why these terrible things had come to be here; in this insignificant shed of all places. By degrees my rigid fear slackened and squirmed into a morbid fascination and I dared to venture an inch closer, my confounded curiosity not in any way satisfied by just looking. My fingers had started itching like a disease, telling me that I had to touch them ... hold one of them, feel its weight, examine it, touch it with my nose and cheek and be this perilously close in questioning this fiendish invention and intention of mankind to wreak such unimaginable terror upon another. I couldn't help being this close, the moment had already been chosen for me. I couldn't, couldn't no matter what, understand the madness behind it, the warped and twisted-to-scrap mentality that chose entirely Man-made 'Gods' over the overwhelming beautiful logical balance and justice of 'Nature', whatever that was.

'Control' was the difference and I was now touching a deathly heavy artifact of that diseased thinking. Little shits shouting in streets used sticks; bigger bastards booming from belfries used bombs! These bombs here, all nine of them, had come all the way from Germany; they had been dropped in good faith and murderous intention but had failed to explode, possibly as a result of Anti-War Sabotage in the bomb factory; either that, or nine pieces of poor workmanship, ending up here in my hands.

I could still hear Dad 'singing' in the garden as I confronted this grave life or death, freedom or slavery issue. Slowly and carefully I reached up until the cruel, cold iron met the living warmth of my fingers ... I was touching it. Not satisfied with this, I clasped my fingers around it and took firm hold, immediately being struck by the wretched thing's weight; it was entirely evil, like a miniature torpedo, four stabilizing fins and sugary corrosions all over it's wretched skin. It felt like death itself, sending a horrid shiver through me, a backwards picture of being born dead and to grow down into being an infant and, finally a new-died. I eased it gently from the shelf, immediately struck by how heavy it was for all its smallness when, the sudden displacement of weight sent the remaining eight bombs see-sawing down the collapsing shelf in an instantaneous nightmare of a moment, crashing them into a terrible pile at my feet! I died too fast for either my brain or body to have noticed; I was dumbstruck, one bomb in my hand and eight more apparently 'dud' ones still fast asleep on the ground where I stood. "Shit!", I gasped in a thousandth of a second, weirdly wondering what a thousand and a half pieces of shrapnel would feel like lacerating my simple human body ... but nothing happened. Curiosity had killed the cat and I'd been spared, more aware than ever before that this moment now was the closest I'd ever come to the 'war' which had occupied almost the entire of my life to this point.

I made a feeble mee-owing sound to trick Dad into thinking the clatter had been caused by a cat hunting a rat, it seemed to have worked because the pregnant silence of hanging seconds gave birth to a spade going about its work, plus a few vigorous notelets from his golden 'song-without-words'. I stood for a merciful age counting my blessings and wondering what to do next. The shed had outlived its usefulness and had suddenly become a treacherous minefield out of which I had to somehow pick my way.

Still clutching the dud bomb, I gave a huge sigh of relief and very stealthily emerged into the sunlight, thankful and silent as I gulped the marvellous air, the lovely image of Dad with his back to me, still hard at it. I stood there concealed amongst the drying umbrellas of hogweed, almost smug with relief at being free of that terrible infatuation. Spiders webs across my skin felt like gluey elastic, invisible and fine as nerves, while my thankful heart bubbled in a whole devilment of rejoicing. Dad's garbled symphony in the key of 'Z' wasn't entirely unbearable, but it was getting close to it! The bomb in my hand was growing heavier by the second and it occurred to me, somewhat playfully, that I could share my amazing discovery with him; play a trick on him and give him a bit of a fright, just like Uncle Bill would have done to Uncle George back in the old days up on the Common. I chuckled to myself, confident in the knowledge that the unexploded bombs were in fact simply duds, probably made that way by saboteurs back in the bomb factory.

Gripping my bomb, I sneaked back the same way as I had come and I stood nonchalantly by the garden fence, unseen by Dad, then gathering together all my strength, I tossed the bomb towards him, at the same time shouting, "Ay-up, Dad; It's an Air Raid!" He spun round just as the bomb thudded its nose into the soft, newly turned soil beside him. I never saw him move so fast or leap so high in all my life; not even Hitler himself had brought him this close to shitting himself. Words failed him when he needed them most, 'diddledeedee' wasn't any use, but it made little difference because he took up his measuring-stick, with string wound around it, and he spoke in seventeen languages across my arse with it, then back-handed me across my mouth whenever I tried to speak eventually finding his voice, which brought our crippled old new neighbour, Mister Grant, hobbling on sturdy sticks to the dividing fence, anxious to know what on earth was happening. On seeing me wiping the blood from my mouth and trying my hardest not to cry, he looked condemningly at Dad and slowly shook his head. Mom came running to the scene and poor Dad was almost wishing now that the thing had exploded. He didn't dare for the life of him pick the evil, most terrifying thing up whilst at the same time being at a loss to find credibility in claiming that I had 'bombed' him, he simply couldn't win.

My own dilemma was that of letting him know, as a matter of great urgency that the situation was many times worse, knowing that my punishment for disobedience would be that many times more painful for me. I had no choice, I had to tell him about what I had found in the shed. It was like 'God' telling me that I must come clean, either that or something I had already learned about the way I wanted to be in my own life. There was no forgiving what I had done but, if I hadn't done it we'd be living next to a nightmare never realising it until it was too late. I thought about this for a while, wondering perhaps that my misdemeanour might yet provide me with a pat on the back and a whole lot of gratitude rather than kicked-arse condemnation. Dad was no fool, he could read my thinking and wasn't about to give me strawberries and cream. My disobedience and stupidity were separate issues and so, when Mister Grant had shuffled off the scene and Mom had gone back to boiling beetroot in the kitchen, he gave me an extra wallop for good measure and promptly put an end to gardening until next Spring ... if not forever. The village policeman was summoned to investigate this secret arsenal and, after the briefest of glances, fled and fetched the Army bomb-disposal squad, who very gingerly took them away and disposed of them over by the firing ranges somewhere. The ground shook for miles around, they weren't so 'dud' after all!

In the last days before starting college, the bombs incident had done its rounds with no-one able to discover where the bombs had come from or who had put them there. It remained a mystery with talk of witches, warlocks and secret agents, making it all seem a bit spooky at night-time, especially so with there being rats about the place as well. These days were the dismembered precious last of a remembered village life; ahead lay towns sprawling and consuming, commerce in the robes of dark chemistry and with aspirations hidden in tapestries of knotted jargon. I was thoughtful over where the pathway ahead might take me; would I remain alone or would there be a shoulder when I needed one. I knew a thing or two about fear, life had thus far taught me well but I didn't pretend to know it all, exciting though the subject may have been at times. Fear was a mysterious abstraction and sprang unexpectedly from ordinary things that'd somehow strayed from predictability. Sometimes it lingered like toothache, other times it hid behind things laying in wait to leap out unexpectedly. There were times when it pretended to be predictable and delighted in concealing a far worse fear behind another lesser one, as this so proved one sunny morning whilst attending to an urgent call of nature. It wasn't the rat in the lav' that scared me half as much as the confounded beetroot I'd forgotten having eaten the night before! Defecation in a glowing crimson lake made rats seem like teddy bears and could drastically shorten a life if they played that trick too often!

Time made another indelible mark upon the sprawling ordinariness and brought on the morning that I'd feared. I looked like a poorly restored reproduction antique sofa standing there in Dad's demob-suit; the material was so thick it snapped my cycle-clips, forcing me to stuff my trouser bottoms inside my socks when I cycled to Lichfield. My jacket-pockets bulged with sandwiches and my bus-fare and tea-money jingled in an animated lump in my trouser pocket; I wasn't even remotely excited, just scared stiff, that's all! I was heading for a coalshed in Sandford Street, fifty yards from the Regal Cinema and all it's golden 'ABC Minors" fame, where an arrangement had been made for me to park my bike in an old lady's coalshed, next door to Uncle Tom and Aunty Mary. It would be quite safe there, well out of sight at the far end of a long, dark alley ... not that there was much of a risk of there being anyone daft enough to want to steal it!

I made my way along the early morning Lichfield streets to the bus station where a big 'Midland Red' double-decker was parked with, 'Stafford via Rugeley' displayed on the front. I could see the driver and conductress sitting in the cafe enjoying a good laugh over a cup of tea and a bacon sandwich and I envied them their apparent hilarious simplicity, knowing deeper down that all that glittered wasn't necessarily gold. It just seemed like it to me this morning as I begrudgingly boarded their big jolly bus for the first time, choosing to go upstairs in the hope that seeing the world all spread out would help take my mind off the ordeal ahead.

I wanted a front seat but 'regulars' had already claimed them, 'cock-of-the-roost' being a 'snazzy' little spiv of a man wearing the most rancid aftershave and sporting a goat-beard and a designer moustache curled and waxed at the ends. On his head he wore the latest of flat corduroy caps with its peak stitched down and, under his whiskery chin-curl, a gaudy dickie-bow while he gripped between his gold-capped teeth, a huge porcelain and gold cigarette-holder with a black, gold-filtered and foul-smelling cigarette filling the bus with its clouds of writhing stink. He sprawled back with lavish disregard for his immaculate pin-stripes as he crossed his suede shoes up on the front window ledge and nonchalantly browsed through 'The Times', giving preferential treatment to its pink pages. What with having this vast acreage of transformed wood-pulp in his outstretched fists, an obese briefcase and a very large umbrella in close attendance; it denied anyone else the chance of the seat next to him. It occurred to me that I was back in the regime of 'pecking-orders', back down at the very bottom of this particular one. The driver and conductress came jalloping out from the cafe, both of them laughing, both of them displaying love-bites and squeezing their arms about each other; 'sweethearts' I thought, with my first trace of a smile all morning. The bus pulled out, my hour-long journey had started, this solitary one of which would be the one I'd remember most; 'morning one' of five long years of mornings and evenings in sun, rain, wind, snow, ice and fog; another beginning.

## 3. 'Ologies, Isms and Rainbows from Prisms'

A week weird and wild took me and shook me, blew me whither it willed; a dead leaf from a tree, an empty snail-shell blown in a gale, lonely lost emptinesses placeless and far. First impressions were surreal, anarchic and isolating in alchemic disarray. It was all a fragmented primeval confetti puked into an hallucinatory market-pageant, circus-like with unicorns pulling pretty milk-floats and glamorous mermaids lying waiting to be filleted on fishmongers' slabs. Embryonic firsts were knee-deep everywhere, overlapping, interchanging; nothing connected to anything else and time gaining no purchase upon any of it. Everywhere there were gnomes, goblins, pixies and elves, albatrosses, hyenas, nightingales, crocodiles, priests and parrots; wheels inside wheels within other wheels all revolving, some fast some slow, some going backwards mining yesterdays to turn into tomorrows. Below, the sky was lying wrecked and drowning in a river where two swans fought to the death of one of them which could be me. 'Hello's' had no eyes or ears to hold them in any care, while cranes, trains and aeroplanes, blocked drains, fused mains, strains, assorted pains and confused brains gawped at gargoyles face-pulling and chortling with pea-shooters on churches over dead words breathed with chisels in stone beneath an owl asleep in a beech tree, waiting for the darkness to see by as fairies in duffel-coats and sandals of leather paraded all rubber-ducked and bouncily prancing with elephantile ivoried smiles and hair. The pageant proceeded with mad march-hares and heiresses shadow-boxing in brash bead-necklaces, all cultivated, cuticled, correct, careful and calculated in a scruffiness measured to the last paint-splash and with butter-fingered mouths drooping the best bone-china names in decibels and being seen with '2B' 'Venus' or 'Royal Sovereign' pencils and brushes still wet with stinking turpentine somewhere about them. Huge portfolios full of nothing, massive drawing-boards full of nob-pin holes and gum-strip fragments, while filthy-fingeredly describing in dripping terms, new dazzling light and the eiderdowns of delight of artistic thought and simply being seen, seen simply to be.

I proceeded particled, promiscuously naive and fragmented even further as bare-chested, fag-smoking, hob-nailed workmen dismantled all the rainbows of my life into separate colours, grinding them all to dust and telling me that, from now on, if I wanted a rainbow I'd have to invent one and make one myself. I threw my befuddled head back and stared at the sky where a large, round cake was castled, marzipan and icing on the top ... the Art College! The five dreary floors beneath it was just thousands upon thousands of red bricks with cement holding them into an authoritative integrity and with a hundred windows intended more for letting in light than for seeing out of; the 'Technical College'. A hauntingly unimpressive Cathedral of 'Ology' with other

'Ologies' of sobering variety, each one normal, straightforward and perfectly useful for everyday life. Apprentices came smartly overalled, brisk and eager from every corner of the county, with screwdrivers in their pockets, cement in their hair, feeler-gauges, spark-plugs, pens, rulers, ready-reckoners, trowels, penknives, fuse-wire, string and 'Woodbines' in their briefcases. All of them come to gain certificates in technical stuff such as; buildingology, electricology, domestic scienceology, plumbingology, carpentryology, engineeringology and just plain ology. It was an education factory no less, right here under us, tradesman's gold in the making. Nothing at all like this Art College thing that I'd been sucked into and was fast becoming obliged and advised into going somewhere quiet and re-contemplating my navel and trying to work out whether or not I really wanted or needed to be part of the 'Human Race' after all. Failing this, I could risk a disc in the contemplation of my anus with the view to becoming a farm-worker!

There was not just an 'Artistic' streak in me but a confoundedly obstinate, cussed one also; even though sometimes on saying 'no', I wavered into 'yes-like' interpretations of the word's meaning, but when I committed myself to a 'yes', I meant it with all my heart. If I said I'd do something, I'd do it no matter what! This wasn't so much a glittering praiseworthy gift from heaven, but more a 'do-it-or-die' incurable disease from my village upbringing. I wasn't at Art College merely to make up the numbers and hang on as a survivor, no way; I was there with honour, dignity and all the fury of my insatiable artistic hunger.

Another five-portioned wafer of days scattered names like ice-creams into an oven with persistence itself allowing them to settle with blurred faces slowly coming into focus, all of them concealing the caged-up colours of themselves, reticent over letting those caged-birds sing or fly to a perch. There were shadows being constantly cast from careful calculations as loud, blousy jackets stalked studiously diseased in self-desire. 'Art' was alluring, intoxicatingly seductive and with no apparent measuring of its worth when weighed against Gold; the thrill was thrilling when the will was willing.

The great leveller lurked unseen and unexpected like a wart-in-waiting to disfigure narcissoid delusions within conceited mirrors. The ultimate measure was drawing nigh, was an unarguable, inescapable and unforgiving expectation of there being a river of gold flowing from the mind to the eye and with the glorious fiery orb of glowing grace and ultramarine electricity combined, permitting frail fingers to see as eyes and to speak as choirs, to fondle and feel as lovers and to make invisibility visible and hugely more valuable than gold, richer than riches, lovely as love; the great leveller was 'drawing' itself.

I felt a gradual growing sense of pride punctuating my skin and making me grow an inch in less than half an inch of time. I couldn't explain how it was all going when asked because, what I was feeling was largely abstract and mysterious beyond my ability to communicate to Mom and Dad. Germination was complex, it was the 'Blackout' all over again and could prove foul, if not fatal, at a whim. "It's coming on okay ... I'm getting to like it," was all that I could really say, apart from comforting their minds by adding how smashing and 'ordinary' were my new friends; 'ordinariness' being a 'God' to them both. I tried to explain that the group I was in were mostly those of us who, for one reason or another, had no educational qualifications, no 'O' or 'A' levels and, as a result, being channelled into an almost ‘apologetic’ course which was supposedly designed to give us the ‘basics’ of making-it in the world of Commercial Art. I further tried explaining to them what a restriction the decision not to allow me to go to the Grammar School was now proving to be and how a few ‘O’ levels would now open those doors which were closed to me. The loss was mine; for Mom and Dad, a partial success in keeping with our social status was preferable to a full-blown success, one which took us all into the deep-end; we were ‘dog-paddlers’ not text-book ‘crawlers’, we were survivors, not achievers.

Gordon came home for a long weekend. The village was deeply rooted in his veins whereas, for me it was beginning to give distinct feelings of slipping away, being transitory and inadequate in some incomplete and inexplicable way; proof to Gordon that I was becoming lost and in need of being found before it was too late. His reasoning brain was like that of a witch doctor, with an arsenal-cum-dispensary of ever-ready cures, whether the problem be pigeon lice, sleep-walking outdoors, unhealing wounds caused by being beaten with a garden rake, watering eyes or whatever. He rapidly deduced that my symptoms would be best treated with a good old fashioned dose of pike fishing ... up the canal; a deft touch of the self-medication in his prognosis.

Gold had darkened to a peaty bronze in fallow fields, where skylarks and partridges found food and shelter amongst the stubble. Fogs were veiling villages, jewelling the white embroidery of webs in solemn stillness far beneath the reach of the wind; time waited for nothing, even in a stillness resembling death. Its pace remained unaffected and cussedly more abstract than Art, more invisible than music in all its hurting of ears and wetting of eyes; ‘time’ was cowboy over everything, never close enough to be kissed, always too close, too fast, fickle and fairy-like, too maddeningly impossible for the simplest of liaisons by virtue of its being less by light-years than simple.

There was nothing complicated about Gordon, he wore his soul on the outside in a 'take-it-or-leave' sort of way which kept me sane when lunacy was beckoning with the lure of false measures of worth. His leaving the village had broken Aunty Hilda's heart, as too had his brief return and would do so again on his departure. As prescribed, he and I walked the canal towpath to Huddlesford Junction and, in the wide triangle where barges in the past had manoeuvred and where Uncle Ady had seen a monster pike with another large pike in its mouth, not fussy over a bit of cannibalism in the same way that humans thought of it. With the authoritative, licencing-power of paper having no persuasion over him, Gordon, bureaucracy and petty law had no place in the same bed; anyone challenging him for proof of a right to hold a rod to fish, ran the stark risk of an unscheduled swim with a bloody nose and miserably aching testicles. Gordon's integrity was Holy, he could so easily have become a Lay-preacher ... hard to say of what persuasion but, he most certainly had an obscure brand of Christian-dynamite, stacks of sticks of it at his very command.

Gordon was an artist lacking the 'obvious' ability, pure and simple; he and I had the same Sargasso elvers swimming in our veins, same trusty old blood from the same trusty old fountain. What he could do, I couldn't; what I could do, he couldn't. Same difference distanced only by the fact that we were cousins when, in all anthropological truth we were more like brothers. His Dad and my Dad had marinated in the same garlicky and honeyed, onioned and blackberried concoction prior to stinking in separate cradles. My Uncle and his Uncle, Adrian and Albert together had lain like a pair of onions deep in onion-thought over eye-watering time, Gordon and I the two, too-hot-to-handle shallots of the different unions.

A swirl in the water told us that a pike had just made a strike at something; they were still here, big and hungry. Without the working barges anymore and with the adjoining Black Country section of the canal having been breached and drained as a result of a catastrophic lock-collapse half a mile back along at 'Cappers', the huge triangular barge-turning area had as a result, become overgrown with dense weed. It was an aquatic jungle now, virtually impossible for a 'spinner' to operate in its water, providing a sanctuary for a big old pike whose only effective predator now was other pike. Gordon changed all that, albeit very briefly, when he hooked two whopping pike in rapid succession before the weed forced him to pack up spinning and give it up as a bad job.

New-fangled as the Rayburn stove was for Mom, a hefty pike roasting in its oven very soon brought it back down to earth, making the house smell like old times again. Stuffed with thyme and parsley, a bay-leaf and an onion, the very least we expected when it was taken from the oven was for there to be a perfectly-formed pearl there cradled in the delicious stuffing ... either that or a solid gold nugget. Our expectations, extravagant as they may have been, were real enough and the search went on regardless. For me it meant scrumptious pike sandwiches for a whole week, a blessing brought about by Dad referring to the pike as a 'canal' crocodile', enough to restrict its pinky brown flesh to just Mom and me ... Yippee!

My sandwiches prompted a certain intrusive curiosity and questioning of my sanity by those around me with strawberry jam on theirs. Laugh as they may, I felt a sense of immense pride filling me almost to bursting; I was even getting a glow from Dad's demob-suit which had also caused a few titters. They could laugh and snigger as much as they liked, I was the one properly laughing, knowing that ordinariness held no attraction for me anymore whatsoever, whether this was about my person or about the marks I made on paper. The very word 'Ordinary' made me sick after having served an entire growing-up in service to it. If all that I could aspire to be was 'ordinary', then I was a waste of space, a parasite, feeding off the unsuspecting soft underbelly of convention!

'Art' was a tantalisingly elusive, non-existent mystery; it was shapeless like the air and had no artificial bulk that could be weighed or measured; any such material evidences were as headstones, life alone had been the most precious art. Just a journey, that's all it was; it could never be a destination, for to arrive was equal to being buried in a box in the ground. I'll say it again ... the thrill was thrilling when the will was willing!

To define the shape of Air one had to focus on all the things that were in it; to understand Light it was necessary to know and understand the darkness, because only from darkness could Light exist at all. As for the shape of Light, this was more or less what Art was ... the eternal search for the shape of Light.

Answers forever killed questions in a meddlesome chemistry contrivedly dispensed in convenience-sized doses. Answers were dark, static, opinionated and final; a book of answers was a block of stone, a library of answers was a weighty wall which time eventually would grind back to dust from which new questions would grow. 'Time' itself was shapeless like the 'Light, like the Air. Light and Air in the care of cool kisses of Darkness was what 'Time' was; eternal, having no beginning or ending; for there to have been a beginning or ending, 'Time' could never have existed.Eternity was all that there was, nothing else, just Eternity, the shape of Light with a myriad, trilliad, billionad beautiful things making endless journeys all inter-related, all interlocked and interwoven in faultless planned pattern. The search for Origins was fruitless, far more fruitful to search for oranges!

Back down on Mother Earth I had been channelled, faceted, herded, pigeon-holed and most probably sluiced, into a cramped-up looking object, a 'Commercial Art' course and the new label now stitched to my brain had branded me and already had been shortened to 'Commercial'. Being one of these lowly 'Commercials' by now both felt and looked as that of an ingredient-part of an eventual cake. The luxurious time which I had mistakenly thought was fine gold dust, was in fact, self-raising flour here being mixed with margarine in a bowl, gradually to have dried fruit, sugar, salt water and eggs added and thoroughly mixed-in prior to my being stuffed into a wickedly hot oven thence to hopefully emerge as a 'qualified' cake, never to eat, but always to be eaten.

This was the closest that the Art College ever came to earthly functionalism; its very predictability made it 'ordinary', frowned on by an elite, who were pretending with their magic 'O' and 'A' level passports to Nurvana, levitating high and higher yet into the nowhere ether where I aspired to go day-tripping but, because of a lack of magic paper of my own, couldn't. There was no such drearily ordinary and predictable end-product planned for these high-fliers. They were destined to emerge eventually, most of them with their brains uproariously aching from the constant traffic and relentless grand processional passage of 'Art' in all its gaudy, gaseous, chemistried vibrations, hugely unqualified but in possession of a presumptuous, wizardly paper certificate signed by the Minister of Education himself and granting letters after their names, to be framed and hung on some ordinary wall where its ordinariness could go on growing, or perhaps shrinking, till eventually being eaten by moths. Certificates were like that, a finality more resembling a death certificate than a seed-packet and with a value diminishing faster than that of a ten-bob note.

It seemed to me as being too simplistic and somewhat crude for 'value' to be measured solely in monetary terms and I dreamed outrageously of suddenly being blessed with the knowledge of how to manufacture gold, thence to devalue the entire world currency by flooding the markets with my home-made gold, making way for onions and oats, potatoes, cabbages and hens eggs to be the new world currency. I'd go cycling to Lichfield on a solid gold bike, which I'd leave slumped in the coalshed and the only thing about me likely to attract the attention of a thief would be the pike sandwiches in my jacket pocket. The dream did, however, have its own down-to-earth wake-up call when it reminded me that my dream wouldn't change anything and that the rich would still be the fattest and the poor would remain the thinnest; status quo being more deeply rooted than the Pope was to Catholicism.

The existence of dreams was a questionable fascination, their only evidence being a kind of remembered film-show in the privacy of darkness; often visually livid and convincingly unhinged in a complete surrealism, yet with only a rapidly bleaching memory to recall them by. Dreams and Imagination were plucked from the same proud peacock's tail and with daydreams forming fleeting rainbows linking the two. Art was, at best, a dream; once it awakened and became all dictatorial, official and serious about itself, it ceased to be Art anymore.

As for 'Commercial Art', this wasn't 'Art' at all, simply because it was functional and consisted of recognisable images. Be that as it may, it pretended to be Art in a way that didn't require bare-buttocked, bare-breasted women or muscly males with lumpy jock-straps concealing that which male-dominance forbad from being seen. Commercial Art, an 'Applied-Art' so-called, was the marinating of dream-effluent with the dictatorial, alchemic and downright dishonest. It was that very alluring scent on a whore that could make piss on a blanket smell like Champagne on a mink coat, or vomit on the wet lips of a kiss seem as like toffee on an onion in a darkened room. I found myself somewhat deliciously slipping away from this Venus-flytrap, espionaged 'Art' so-called. I wasn't ready for 'function', I knew nothing, nothing at all, not a damned thing about life. My mind, eyes and fingers were not intended for any latter-day workhouse, not when I could feel 'Art' itself, all tingly and invisible, miserably evaluated and subsidised in a state of non-being and with no other purpose other than that of serving itself. A state of journey and not of arrival. 'Art' being the most ultimate in travel, a never-ending journey to somewheres that were nowheres. No, it was 'Fiction' that I needed, not function; try telling that to your Mom and Dad, Granny and Grandad!

Whilst it was Turner that distempered the sunsets, using grease from the roadway where rainbows had bled a scum across the puddles, it was Samuel Palmer that really painted the weariness into the ageing year, into a tired and magical eternity under the watchful eyes of evening with dull moons, upside-down moons, half-moons, full moons sadder and larger than cows'-eyes and with steeples and stars and a people stumbling out from churches into stillness beneath praying trees and the raptures of thrushes and nightingales. The year had tuned again from golden ochre to sepia and from sepia to bleeding and staining into a russety Van Dyke brown before the surgical bandage of Paynes grey came soothing with indigo smudges and flake white smears, all murky and misty bringing choking fogs and sulphuric Christmas, bronchial with wishes and dreams to drive nightmares away.

'Down-to-earth' was the sudden jolt of a 'real place', a reawakening to what had never gone to sleep anyway. It was the ghost-figures in it that were sleeping an inherited treasury of darkness within the confines of a lavishly gilt-framed confinement outside of which it was perilous to venture. Distance was never more distant than Christmas now and I sat straight-jacketed in Yuletide quietude, adrift with my doors all bolted from intrusive affections. Art College had already buggered me away from the only life I had ever known and I was caught-up in a warp of some sort, fearful and tired of the past, hopeful and deep-secretly excited about the future. There were still more questions than there were answers. Madness was never so very far away, I refer to 'The War', the inexplicable nightmared lunacy of witnessing an old and beautiful city, Exeter, flattened to rubble by young boys in aeroplanes. Watching them being shot down over the sea, their beautiful lives reduced to the unimaginable terror of being trapped and the experiencing of their last living moments before the price of madness was paid on behalf of those that'd dreamed-up the madness in the first place.

It was old Ethel Flint in Lichfield who had sown the seed; she was the one who'd taken me as a weed from the strong nurturing green fingers of the fatherly Mister Nichols back at the village school, and had cultivated me up to that of a dandelion and had blown my seeding head into a million nowhere places where to produce gold each time that one of me flowered. Adrift was a nowhere state without the comfort of a somewhere place and I felt bereft in all this pretend electricity, in dire need of a harbour of sorts to earth, that which wasn't electricity but a yawningly haunting pain of non-being, transient and temporary, more in-exact than the length of a piece of string.

It was that tyrannical old water-colourist, Ethel, together with the strong-minded Mister Nichols who, between them, gave my walnut-shell of a coracle its irreversible push with me and all my remaining life there nestled aboard it, pushed it out into the huge, tumultuous colourwash drawing of an eternity of troubled ocean, fully knowing that it was the loneliest of imaginable places, the very kind that was best prescribed for murderers and other despicable cretins. 'Art' was that jolly fine place cosily situated somewhere between Heaven and Dartmoor prison, far too in-exact for it to be within the reach of Ordnance Survey Maps, or of any Biblical reference or recognition.

A certifiable eccentricity was the expected norm for all those pedalling the 'Art' creed; if they weren't ninety per cent mad, something was most seriously wrong. Even a ten percent margin for apparent normality was questionably over-generous, making the challenge of any aspiring Artist one of remaining sane, whilst those others plainly weren't but were faking it; just like young anarchists so readily faked their intellectual orgasms and a pestilence of 'Culture-vultures' revealed themselves not to be of an ornithological species of scavenging birds, more to the pity. For a raptor to be rapturous in this way would elevate bird-watching to an academia hitherto unknown and having the potential to remove the glittering, bejeweled crown from a Monarch's head and replacing it with an old bird's nest.

## 4. 'Smudges and Smears'

Terms came and went like double-decker buses; no sooner had one pulled out than another pulled in. I was now getting to be really hooked on Art College, not only was it becoming a growing fascination but, more of an infatuation, one that had seized upon my mercurial base-metal and was hell-bent on turning it into Gold. It bore no resemblance to those oh, so faraway schooldays which had preceded it, indeed, this seemed more like a fun-factory, an old wizardly paintbox that rattled with hidden secrets, the discovering of which was the reason for our being here.

Our Principal struck me as an escapee from 'A Christmas Carol', ponderously Dickensian and lots more besides. I had a sneaking suspicion that he was part turkey-cock and very large part elephant-seal and he grunted, hissed and puffed more rupturedly than a terminally ill and totally knackered steam railway locomotive. Bald as a jug, whiskery sideburned and of a purply underpainting thinly overglazed with vermilion throughout his dangling blubbery bits; he never smiled, grimacing whilst passing wind was the nearest he ever came to it. He was utterly unapproachable ... so we never approached him, or he us. Someone gave him the nickname 'Bong' out of indifferent affection and we forgot about him, praying never to incur his wrath.

I didn't know of a single person that disliked being part of the Art College; it was fast becoming a kind of 'upstairs, downstairs' family, brothers and sisters all of us. By grim contrast, the Technical College housed on all the floors beneath us, had a certain hostile, intimidatory aura about it, with occasional rowdy, loutish scuffles on the stair and with the odd bloody nose and black-eye showing up, displaying too a kind of ill-disguised loathing of Art students, those 'poncey twats' in dickie-bows, sandals, beads, black suspenders and laddered fishnets, even an old demob-suit; all so carefree, so very happy. Rather surprisingly, within the Technical College's agenda, that formidable old 'Fourth 'R' was still in evidence, like a dinosaur amongst all the presumptuous 'ologies' in the form of a Morning Assembly of all things. With hymns being pompously plonked on the upright piano, together with prayers boomed out across the large hall outside of which our 'Dress-design', Textile and other of our students patiently waited for these conscripted 'Masonic' Christians to pack up and go and allow them, already half-an-hour late, to laboriously re-assemble worktables and equipment before being able to resume artistic studies. It was a most unexpected and bizarre kind of arrangement for these virtual adults to be daily subjected to, especially so when, those being indoctrinated were aspiring tradesmen and women in hot pursuit of certificates in all sorts of 'ologies', in the rebuilding of England after the mess that 'Jerry' had left.

My fascination broadened and deepened and it both intrigued and amused me just to observe how others made their very own visual sense of things. Not one person was even remotely similar to the next in the expressing of this most diverse and magical of universal languages. Being part of the less prestigious, 'downstairs' 'Commercial group, we were not expected to dazzle or to display anything out-of-the-ordinary. I wasn't happy with this state of affairs and I felt determined to do my best in making 'Commercial Art' an eye-catching, provocative, intriguing if not outrageous theatre of artistic fervour which would no longer remain ignored by the 'upstairs' arty-farties; those prematurely-bearded, gushingly effervescent designer-scruffs who strained-out cultured 'pearls' as though giving birth to red-hot potatoes. I knew in my deeper mind that, if I was a true artist, it didn't really matter if I was a 'Commercial', I'd have all my life to prove this and for it to emerge from me in the most natural way possible. The thought made me feel slightly better about my situation, although I would have preferred for it to show sooner rather than later.

The more I looked about me, the more it became apparent that the ability to draw was not as much in evidence as I had expected it to be, in fact it was harder to disguise this than it was to admit to it. I became rather tickled by the glib assumption by some of the more extreme 'arty-farties' that they could conceal their lack of ability behind lavish waffle while still having the convenient and highly ambiguous 'Abstract' concept as a bolt-hole with emergency ration-packs of gimmicks and fragmentary plagiarism's thrown-in to complete their dillusionary disguise. There was no such hiding place for a lowly 'Commercial' who, it seemed, was only here to make up the numbers anyway. Just a two-year mad dash for a piddling little and utterly worthless passport to designing fish-paste labels, and this only for the successful ones; for the remainder of us, we all knew that with no 'O' or 'A' levels, we'd be more than lucky to end up as bus-conductors!

Losing the proud family heirloom of an inferiority complex was virtually impossible to monitor, being neither measurable or predictable. It was largely this which had kept me away from Grammar School, ignoring any ability I may have had to absorb the sort of stuff which was considered not to be for the likes of us. While family confidence was down in the gutter, mine rather surprisingly was trespassing up in the giddy heights at the other end of the scale. I took my ability to draw for granted, same as with painting, it all seemed as easy as piddling up a wall, something I could do with my eyes closed ... not that I made a habit of piddling up walls! The confidence that it was providing was making my lowly 'Commercial' status that much more acceptable and a degree enjoyable and I persevered in a kind of euphoria, feeling that Dad's drab old demob-suit was becoming as Joseph's coat of many colours and was setting me apart from others by virtue of its excessive bagginess and total absence of any definable form. Truth was, it didn't possess a recognisable colour at all and felt more like a shed than a suit. It was in fact, that very rainbow that'd been ground to dust by workmen and had ended up as a puzzling shade of grey; slightly pinky, slightly bluey, slightly yellowy, browny, pucey, ordinary, greyish grey. That's what I'd got enveloping me; you could prop a bike, even motorbike against it without denting it! I was stomping about in a pigmentedly, particled dustcloud of a rainbow which had been woven into a suit and with a pike-sandwich in its jacket pocket. I felt a glow of pride and I knew that, before discovering the ordinary ingredients that made Gold, I would first set about reconstructing the Rainbow ... and what better place to do it!

While colour was intoxicating my mind, unbeknown to me, moves were afoot to make the world bigger, for both me and my 'coat of many colours'. Apparently, there was a special clause hidden away in the system, no relation to Santa Claus, but one which specifically addressed the hypothetical issue whereby any student who had demonstrated what could be termed, 'outstanding ability' and hadn't attained the necessary general education 'O' or 'A' level requirements then that student should be permitted to bypass existing rules, and be allowed to progress along the lines of his or her appropriate academic study right up to the point of 'National Diploma of Design'. The very top award for an Art College. It appeared that I had satisfied this criteria and plans were being made for me to be transferred on to the course, ultimately leading to the 'National Diploma' Bloody hell! I gulped so hard that I was in grave danger of spitting out my underpants!

Mom and Dad were duly informed of the proposals which, if agreeable, would mean my being at Art College for fully five years. Dad was marvellous and gave the matter his deep down nod of approval, regardless of the fact that he was hoping to see me bringing in a bit of money to help pay the bills. I could tell that he was really very proud, it was as though he wanted me to be living the life that he had been denied; not an easy thing for him to confront. It must have been like rubbing salt into an unbelievably painful old wound.

It still hadn't properly dawned on me what was happening; the moment 'Now' being far more blinding than any of those yet in waiting. What I did vaguely recall being parroted into me by a whole perchful of Lecturers was that I'd soon be joining a two-year 'Intermediate' course which was demanding and was already a year old; a kind of kick-up-the-arse warning that I'd got loads of catching-up to do before the crucial Final Examinations. Whilst all this 'parrot-chatter' was squawking, I did my obstinate-ostrich impersonation and determined myself to enjoy my last days in the 'Commercials', the formerly insignificant 'nobodies' who by now, were transforming into a very popular, lively, outrageously comical and modestly talented group of 'somebodies', primary colours emerging and slowly mixing into more colourful possibilities.

It no longer seemed so vitally dependent on one having the ability to draw, as I had so vehemently believed ... well not entirely anyway; there were other elements now more widely dispensing into my chemistried understanding which made 'Art' a whole lot more fascinating. 'Art' could enter into dull things and make them alive in brand new ways, yet remaining indefinable, as well as invisible and impossible to equate or evaluate in mere 'inside-leg' or 'hat-size' measuremental terms of reckoning. 'Art' was half of all things wherever the germ of artistic thought existed; the only missing balancing element necessary for the germination of 'Inspiration' being 'Perspiration'. Without this there could be no Conception and no Birth; one of the basic raw facts of life artistically!

Cuckoos were not writing books but were adequately punctuating those written by others, like a triangle player in an orchestra with only two notes to play in the entire massive symphony. It was the time of music everywhere, bringing my heart to tremble; sweet fleeting moments when little things could be heard before being swallowed by something bigger; there was always something bigger.

Up in the crow's-nest of the marvellous red double-decker, Arthur Tomkins, fellow 'Commercial', and I, luxuriated in these very transient, priceless moments of discourse with a fleeting landscape which was briefer than a dog-end's fire. Milford Hills, all up and down and winding at the northernmost reach of Cannock Chase; heathery, scrubby, wildly contoured and with evergreens vanishing away beyond. I was never freer in all my days than here, held now in the breeze-blown moments with the window as far open as it would go, trying to catch the tinkling triangle of a cuckoo beyond the wild roar of the air. Arthur, 'Art' as he was nicknamed', stank rancidly of his big brothers aftershave, while other art students babbled blissfully away all down the bus. I was in no hurry for the rest of my life to come swallowing me up like the final movements in the great symphony. I just wanted these Art College days to go on forever and ever and ever. Only indefinable art, not Arthur, could make me feel this way; arithmetic and carpentry couldn't, neither could electricity, painting and decorating, plumbing or building, nothing, not even farming, was more beautiful than Art.

'Art' Tomkins took his nickname from his initials and that was more or less as close as he ever got to it; he really couldn't draw to save his life. For all that there was something meticulous and steely about him; he was more of a technician and could accurately paint an eight-point typeface with a number one brush, no trouble at all. A true Advertising Agency man in the making. We were really good mates, he and I, opposites in almost every way, yet balanced because of this. He was an 'Indian-ink', hard-edged, dark charcoal-grey character with a blinding white, starched and cut-away collared shirt, the narrowest of black ties triple-knotted and appearing to be at the point of choking him. His long and slightly bandy legs were intimately adorned in 'drainpipe' trousers with creases like scythes, charcoal-grey of course, and he wore black slip-on silver-buckled shoes, so highly polished that you could see your face in them. He was gaunt and good-looking, very proud of his angular chin and close crew-cut hair that he'd cut himself with his sister's scissors. His approach to Art and Design was similarly meticulous although dreadfully overshadowed by his attentions always being magnetically drawn elsewhere, namely everywhere and anywhere that a slinky woman slinked ... or slunk. He was, in his narcissoid eyes, an object of sex and sexual desire; competitive and oozing musty confidence to this end. He'd roll his sleeves up to show off his polished muscles, drop his trousers to flex his leg muscles, assuming that the rest of us had nothing up our trousers to show. He really loved his own body and considered himself to be the answer to a woman's prayers.

While the rest of us just bumped and shuffled about like dusty old bumble bees, 'Art' strutted like a black and white peacock with a 'click', 'clack', 'click', 'clack' rhythm, that left one in no doubt that he was abroad on one of his scent-marking look-abouts; nothing at all like my other, non-too-tall mate from Uttoxeter, 'Midge' Kelly. This dappled moss-green, leaf-rustling grass-nibbling, elfish, Jack-in-the-box, weasel of a pal. His wily eyes didn't miss a thing, he knew everything that went on, absolutely every little thing; nothing was safe from 'Midge'. He was very studious and capable, a really smashing and highly entertaining colleague with interests very close to my own. In fact we were even closer than 'Art' and I in that we were both born-naturalists with the words, 'Staffordshire-Rock' written all the way down through our 'sticks-of-rocks' bones. 'Art' by contrast had arrived here since the war from down South, London way; a pearly-kinged, squawking-ravened, jellied-eeled kingdom of concrete and electricity, throbbing with engines. With these two, I had the very best mates I could ever wish for, two real brothers.

Even at this dangerously late stage, it still hadn't properly registered in my mind as to the enormity of what was about to transform my life and thrust me beyond the reach of the last vestiges of usefulness and on to a higher grade of uselessness yet. I was still a village boy, still with dreams of having a racing-bike between my legs and becoming a racing cyclist in my spare time, winning the Tour de France during my holidays. 'Art' Tomkins dreamed of almost identical things, topping mine by virtue of there being an engine on his bike. He dreamed of winning the Isle of Man TT having contracted the disease from his big brother Ted, a chain-smoking, 'International Norton' man, nicknamed 'TT', a human rocket if ever there was; he was awesome in his black leathers and 'Art' had caught the disease good and proper.

We all had our dreams and we clowned, trying to keep them hidden, fully knowing that our colleagues were jackals, all eager, hungry and wild, and would make mincemeat of any dream that went astray. Electricity in a rubber-gloved fist was never far away from blowing the fuses and our Lecturers just stood back in a dilemma of not knowing whether to be part of this lively banter of sparks or, just to play cool and stay a safe distance away. Not being quite in tune with those making the rules, 'Art' Tomkins and I decided to make a 'statement' of our own. To this end, we made a few 'modifications' to the Technical College's upright piano which to our aggrieved opinions, was out-of-bounds being situated in our Design Studio, resulting in our classes always being half-an-hour late. We carefully pressed brass drawing pins into the felt hammers that struck the strings inside it, not many, just a few positioned here and there, it needed no more than that. There was a spontaneous riot as the first piously-plonked hymn fell foul of the drawing pins. We'd taken the smug step or organising an audience for this performance and they were not disappointed; the assembly was aborted amidst a thunder of laughter which could be heard throughout the college. It was the kind of juvenile prank that bordered on the 'artistic', a simple yet powerful statement, hilarious beyond measure and it popularised our small group still further, albeit in a slightly notorious way and permitted our confidence to steal out somewhat cheekily still further into the open.

Our studio was situated in a busy thoroughfare linking the metalwork room and its adjoining 'Intermediate' Life Drawing studio at one end, and at the other end, a doorway with a short passage to the College Secretary's office at the top of a clatteringly noisy, ornate and spiraling staircase with a convergence of corridors mysteriously leading away. This was where my own future was laying in wait with its Pottery and Ceramics, the main National Diploma of Fine Art studios, Sculpture, Life Drawing, Lithography, Etching, Screen-printing, Bookbinding and, darkly secret like a rat-hole, the Principal's Official Residence. So, we had more than our share of through-traffic to contend with ... including mice, some of which didn't wear the seemingly obligatory dickie-bows and sandals!

I had another mate in the 'Commercials', 'Big Mick', a very tall quietly spoken youth, tweed-jacketed, all whiskery and in rusty shades of brown. He had a nose like two bowed steps up to a cottage door and a temperament just like the quaint and peaceful, hollyhocked and rosed cottage itself. Nothing could ever provoke him into straying from his gentleness, his response to anything and everything was simply a smile; the ultimate conclusion. He was very shy and, like so many others, found drawing to be aggravatingly unlearnable if it wasn't there in the first place. He really wanted most of all to have drawing flowing from his fingers, but was sadly deficient of that most vital and precious of links between that which he aspired to and that which he actually was. Apart from that single flaw, he was fairly average in other artistic ways and always seemed to enjoy making visual logic of things, especially where colour was concerned. Overnight, it seemed, his sow's ear was more resembling a silk purse. He'd suddenly started 'method' drawing by use of dots, not tiny pinprick ones like the grains on a photograph, but neatly considered and perfectly round blobby ones, after which he would meticulously join them up with neatly drawn lines until a vague 'form' emerged that was somehow safe from the usual accepted critical scrutiny where rules of drawing were concerned. This gentle giant without any trace of fire in his belly and only dove-grey velvety blood in his veins, was here suddenly ... exactly the same as he'd always been, with one exception, that of a cripple having found a crutch. He'd concluded that, if ability didn't work, a 'formula' might just possibly do the trick ... and it was working! What he was now producing was pleasantly eye-catching in a 'diagrammatic' sort of way which seemed to benefit from use of colour, his only real strength. It all seemed so convincing, despite the fact only yesterday he didn't know a pencil from a toothpick!

'Art' Tomkins, meanwhile, pressed on with his insistence that drawing was best when restricted to being between consenting adults, done with a ruler, compass, spirit-level, feeler-gauge and an '8 H' pencil marinated in aftershave. 'Midge' Kelly just impishly clowned, safe now in the knowledge that he could adequately design labels for fish-paste jars and wasn't in any way daunted by wider aspects of 'Commercial Art'. His confidence bordered on conceit, always doing just enough to get by and never venturing further, for fear of hidden icebergs in the mysteriously deep, unfathomable art world that encapsulated us like a grub-skin. The only girl in our group, the freckled, plump and pimply Mavis Spooner, 'Speckly' as she was fondly known, was a heavily-bosomed, gypsy-like girl with rings on her legs, not of gold or silver but from where her wellies had rubbed. Style-less and excessively ordinary, she cruised on into yet deeper oceans of glorious mediocrity and, with her new found confidence, had taken to wearing lipstick, making her mouth more a place for posting letters than for kissing. She was wonderful in all her cluttered clumsiness and valiantly did her best in keeping our flame from dying in these, my final days with the 'Commercials'.

It was whilst browsing through a Graphic Design Annual that I spotted something which looked strikingly similar to something else that's recently taken my eye. I looked again and smiled; I had inadvertently stumbled across the very goose that'd laid 'Big Mick's' Golden Egg. More to the pity, so too had 'Midge' spotted it and Big Mick's goose alas, was now well and truly cooked, arse-up and legs in the air. All that remained now was for the devilish 'Midge' to take centre stage and to extract the stuffing, an exercise which he performed to cruel perfection, entertainingly slowly, bringing burning blushes to the victim's cheeks and the entire studio to a cacophony of raucous laughter, occasioning the mighty 'Bong' himself to darken the doorway and stand there, flippers on hips, hissing and grunting. He didn't approve of laughter in any way, shape or form; corporal- punishment-induced tears were far and away preferable; he could smell a rat and hadn't forgotten the 'jangly-piano' incident. He glared at us with burning veiled eyes, furious that his formidable presence had not commanded the silence that he'd expected it to. He hissed again and tittering broke out in the ranks, obliging him to swallow his pride and back-off, mindful of the fact that we were none other than the 'bums-on-seats' that were helping him keep in his highly salaried job.

He hadn't frightened 'Art' Tomkins who, throughout the entire noisy episode was hidden away under the table practicing a bit of advanced juggling and a spot of tittering of his own, with 'Speckly' Mavis's newly liberated and enormous, bare and bouncy breasts, her only protestations being low mutterings of ..."Oh, Arthur, you're wicked you are!" They were there under the pretext of looking for stuff that'd supposedly got knocked off during the commotion. I looked across at 'Midge' and his eyes were flaring like an owl's, he hadn't missed a trick; his ears were twitching and his mouth agape, gasping beyond words. I could read his astonished mind, it said, "Oh, no. Don't say he's gonna give her one under the table!" I shook my head in despair, not daring for a moment to believe my colleague here within touching distance of a whole sea of knees, would be so bold as to go that far. I'd never known 'Midge' to be so comprehensively lost for words and he stared at me in shocked belief. I shook my head again in hopeless resignation knowing that 'Art' was simply keeping his hand in, a bit of fortuitous practice that's all, having himself come to know, that the thrill was always thrilling when the will was ever willing! 'Midge' gasped and rattled a hugely relieved snigger as 'Art' emerged from under the table, all smiling and surprisingly still quite immaculate, albeit with his trouser-buttons undone and his white shirt sticking out through the indiscreet gap. A minute later, Mavis, with the complexion of a freshly boiled lobster, made a brief appearance before vanishing away to the 'Ladies'!

'Midge' had taken note of something else which was getting his ears, nose and eyes all glowing and his juices all getting in the way of each other. This was really hot stuff this time and it involved one of our lecturers, Miss Murphy, 'Spud' as she was affectionately known out of respectful memory of the Irish potato famine. "Well?" I sighed tediously ... "Cough it up for Christ's sake!" He glared at me in astonishment and slowly shook his head. "D'you mean to tell me that you don't know?" "Know what?" I sighed impatiently. "Know who the 'other' person is!" I shook my head, prompting him to spit out the words ... "YOU, you prat! You that's WHO!" "Don't talk so bloody soft!" I sighed, gulping furiously in a growing embarrassment that was making my cheeks burn and bringing my roses into bloom.

'Spud' Murphy was an object of the most ultimate of animal desire; a walking palette of oozing, crazily mixed pigments and with all the most alluring of scents imaginable wafting from the slightest movement of her brash, translucent butterfly wings. 'Midge' shook his head in woeful dismay at my inability to see what he and all the rest of them could. "She's on heat for you, you prat ... can't you see that? Get IN there!" 'Spud', was in fact I did concede, giving me rather more of her attention than appeared fair and did, I had to further admit, seem to be forever stooping intimately close over me, allowing her beautifully ripe and heavy bosoms to brush my head over and over as she involved herself in what I was doing. I pretended not to notice as she went on touching me in the tenderest of ways and with only whispered words, thoughtful and encouraging. She made me feel like a real person and not imply a student and we talked of Art in a way that seemed to make it ours and nobody else's. It was this and this reason alone that made her seem so close, I was too scared to think otherwise. I tried hard to conceal and deny having 'other' feelings about her physically, I was no different from any of the others in this respect; it was just that I could never consider the possibility of anyone thinking of me in this way ... certainly not Miss Murphy!

My embarrassment turned to irritation. Such intrusive scrutiny was entirely without regard for my feelings and I shared with nobody the fact that I dreamed of her in a way that scared the hell out of me. Having an angered hornet's nest in my trousers was proving to be a nightmare and never a dream and was proving harder to conceal than pike sandwiches in my coat pocket ever did. Whenever I looked up, mischievous eyes were watching, grins were grinning and I really started to think of this as being the smallest, most poisonous village that I'd ever known. I felt glad at last that I'd be moving on to more demanding things; away from 'naughty prankster' attitudes, good fun though most of it had been until now. Embarrassed as I was, I marvelled at 'Spuds' slender arm all silky and reaching away down to my paper, where her brightly nail-varnished fingers sweetly demonstrated how marvellously colours related to others in so many variable ways different from the next. Her fascination with colour was matched only by my own and she made me tremble with excitement in a wanting to please her. Her soft breath was all cool and feathery and I blushed and shivered at the same time as it brushed my ear and moistened my cheek; I could both hear and feel her heart beating. I stole a glance across to 'Midge' and we exchanged cross-eyed squints and stuck our dribbly tongues out sideways in the most desperate life-or-death heat dispersal therapy prior to my hornets nest exploding. When she popped out of the room, I slumped down exhausted and 'Midge' leaned over and whispered, "You lucky bugger, she don't do that to me ... nor to no bugger else neither! I don't know what you're waiting for, I really don't ... you bloody idiot!"

The very suggestion frightened the living hell out of me. It was preposterous beyond belief for anyone to be thinking in terms of a 'Her' and 'Me', what's more she was seven years older than me, a proper woman while I was a village virgin, solidly destined to remain that way over the foreseeable future, even longer than that if I could hold out. My naivety was so thickly fatted about me that it would take ten full-grown men to carve even the thinnest sliver of it. I was more naive than naive, so solidly, cussedly naive that I didn't know the difference between a leg-over and a pullover! All those past childhood adventures into touching games when no-one was looking, all had been 'play', 'naughty-learning' but 'play' all the same. It had vaguely taught me, in the sketchiest of ways, that I had been given, apparently by 'God', a kind of had-grenade arrangement in my trousers which, should the safety-pin ever get pulled, would bring about an explosion of babies. What more did I need to frighten the living daylight out of me!

'Art' Tomkins was smarting with both envy and disbelief; he couldn't figure out why his big brother's aftershave, his razor-sharp pressed charcoal-grey drainpipes, blinding white shirt and dazzling shoes had failed him so absolutely. What he hadn't learned was that, the currency into which he was placing his entire aspirations and expectations, wasn't to everyone's liking. 'Spud' knew all too well what made him tick and really found him tiresome and lacking, to say the least. It was Art and the exciting prospect of Artistic fusion that lit her candle and gave me a glow, that's why she and I had come so close. Falling in love, whatever it was, had never been part of the plan and was something that I'd never, ever admit to and would slip silently away from.

'Summer vacation' was a strangely lawless outback, a wild and weird melting pot, so full of its swishing self as to erase all that's gone before into minute crumbs of rubber. Student friends had all melted back into the scruffy shadows of villages and shapeless sprawled suburbs. Lecturers had sneaked away and broken themselves back down to being normal brothers and sisters once more, and picking peas in gardens, and in leather sandals going to Rome to lick ice-cream on a barge pushed by an Italian with a stick, then throwing their small aluminium change into a pond, before getting brown feet and coming back home full of ultramarine and viridian dreams with pointed, spiralling evergreen trees.

In the midst of mad commerce, our family moved from Blacksmith Lane to a bay-windowed house on the village green, opposite the 'Bell Inn' where, as though by magic, Dad presented me with a red racing-bike, a 'Norman Invader' with Derailleur gears. I helped him paint the ivy-covered Waterworks Pumping Station on the Walsall Road, by way of paying him back. Poor Dad had needs and priorities of his own and right now he desperately wanted for our new house to be connected by telephone, just as other tradesmen were finding it necessary to do in the nurturing of their businesses. Alas, phones were fangled as fridges, flush loos and stoves with boilers in their bums. Just a voice without a face and with just a bell that sprang out of the quiet and made you rush to the mirror and tidy-up, powder the nose and brush the hair before tip-toeing to answer it an a whisper. No! Mum put her foot down firmly and forbad any such sordidly fangled gadget from entering our home, arguing with Dad that his handwriting was sufficient for him to run a business by ... and that was that!

The 'Common' was all at peace now. Sundays were Sundays, all bright and belling once more with Uncles, skylarks galore, aunties with lipstick, cousins in clusters and rabbits with fleas; a leathery tough shoulder of mutton from a pensioner-sheep and waddling Elsie Snape with her stockings rolled down making Sunday all so very far from Art, asleep in the breakneck stratospheric madness of moments wasting their shoulders away on time racing recklessly in the opposite direction with its eyes shut. The future had gone and the tin that it had been in, thrown away. The past lay strewn ahead where tomorrows had for years been yesterdays, before Art had climbed all coloured onto paper and technology porcelained like gold balls, up poles with wires galore for swallows to congregate upon and chatter about vacations. The whole crazy summer had more fields of corn that it had measured minutes tick-tocking in dark rooms, and there were not roads enough for my new spoked wheels to speak and take me to places of different tasting winds; even though by now I knew the horizon by its smell. My sketchbook begged for my fingers to break its silence and I could hear above the din listening of dire consequences of there being nothing to show for all the horizontal days that'd licked the paper pages bare.

## 5. 'Fools Gold in an Allotment Shed'

Few things were ever what they seemed, grand illusions and grander yet delusions of self-worth more blinding than lorry headlights in the dark, especially in others. How heavy, just how light would I weigh if I could be weighed without my dreams. Would I float away like a blown dandelion umbrella and make my own Gold somewhere simple and quiet, on an allotment perhaps, or beside a stream. I was weighed down by my own worthless worry, lost in Art and trying to shine my way free from its black, clawing fingers. I envied the starling on the chimney pot, not 'singing' but texturing the air with iridescent rainbows of montage-like percussive tongues of joyful meaning that had no measurement of musical worth, beyond being just a noisy, greedy bloody starling! That's all I ever heard, said of the starling, bird of rainbowed colour and of music beyond comprehension; what was a mouth-organ in my pocket compared with that which he'd got like a volcano in his shimmering throat! Fewer things still were ever what they seemed and I knew that, if I could have a wish to be one single thing other than a human, it'd be a starling.

Mid-summer seemed like a strange time for one year to end and another one to start, but there was a discernible lethargy crawling through the wearisome moments. This was especially noticeable on one particular afternoon when, breaking the yawning hazy silence, half-a-dozen bedraggled hands languidly clapped Summer's sleepy-slow cricket along on its way down Charlie Mann's field. Swallows skimmed low over the sward and others, newly-hatched in the pavilion, crapped on the dainty white bread triangles of cucumber and fish-paste, as the village's secret Sunday weapon, Sandy Morris, with his deathly slow left arm spinners, got mercilessly hammered all about the cow-pats by farmhands from other villages, one mighty six clearing the pavilion and landing in a pram with a baby asleep inside. No-one dared believe their eyes when they saw God's miracle with the hard red ball rested beside the still slumbering baby's head; so near yet so far from whatever else may have happened to influence the path of destiny.

Precarious days with too much peace running to waste for any good to come of it, as students with determinedly nothing to do beyond daisy-chains, were self-appointed chiefs, not Indians, while the dream lasted. It couldn't last much longer though. Already the haws were turning crimson and rose-hips glowed like tangerines, long after their frail pink cotton frocks twirled and were disrobed like hearts by seductive breezes, where purring doves laid pearls on firewood bushels and nothing, absolutely nothing stood still. Who could any longer trust anything when memories were still wet from a time of lunacy and savagery beyond sense. There was not a single lad of my age who could trust in 'Peace' having a meaning when, whatever their dreams, the Motherland was lying in wait to pounce and steal us away, put rifles in our hands, bullets and grenades about our frail bodies and a suit of cow-shit green in the University of War, whether we liked it or not. There'd be no escape and we'd be held prisoners for two long years; it didn't bear thinking about. It made whatever we were doing with our dreams a worthless waste of time because, only after it had released us from its prison could we begin to think of life as being Ours to do something worthwhile with.

The blood-red double-decker buses still pulsated along the time-worn artery necklacing the towns and concocting commerce like nurturing jet-black tulips from things like onions that were fit only for slugs to eat; carting fountain-pens to paper like rams to ewes, wet tongues to stamps, faraway addresses to envelopes, bells to tills and electricity making every telegraph pole buzz and hum like orchestras, splintering our confounded ears as we listened in amazement.

Somewhere amongst all this, English Art spoke with its very own accent and with a poetry and a music like none other; it was far too romantic for it to be fallen in love with, coming closest of all in the form of a damp dream, never closer than that. It climbed out from nothing, no cement, no nuts or bolts, no whips, no artificial weighing or measuring of worth, absolutely nothing. An angel's egg hatching in a nest somewhere in a secret paradise. It was no more than a unsung song and an un-coloured rainbow asleep in a starling's egg and it couldn't be forced, only encouraged because it came from nothing, absolutely nothing. What made it so magical was that which artists did with that 'nothing'; drawing out from somewhere that was everywhere and nowhere at the same time, something of themselves that was personal and uniquely different from any other's private perception and understanding, or evaluation or worth, where any worth of this kind was forever worthless. A robin's song rippling on a frosty dawn had no worth; golden glory at break of day and fiery grandeur at eventide had no worth, criss-crossed circular drawings of rain on water or icy ferns growing on windows had no worth. Not the same as saw-mills making furniture and fence-posts had, or typewriters click-clacking words on paper, irons smelting into lorry-chassis and farmers leaning on gates counting sheep had. For me, the most worthwhile things were those that were worthless, a prescription for a life of poverty if ever there was but, a life without Art was a nightmare too far. If you had the disease you'd got it for life; if it could be cured, the disease had been wrongly diagnosed in the first instance.

My second year was underway as binders and combines bared the corns leaving oceans of stubble reaching away into other counties. It was my birthday month, Mom's and Rosemary's too all of us September's children emerging into our lives as golden harvests fell from theirs. It felt strange no longer being one of the 'Commercials', stranger still seeing the remote figure of Miss Murphy always from a distance now, our paths never crossing and glances unrevealing of any dust of what may or may not have once been. I was amongst different sorts of people now, a self-assured and almost pompously confident brand of individuals, each one with an unashamed eagerness to demonstrate their worth. The difference that confidence made was breathtaking and I knew for sure that I had to acquire a bit more of it myself if I wasn't to be suffocated by their intellectual hooliganism, even though I believed I knew that it was always best if 'Art' itself be allowed to do the talking. No amount of cleverly calculated words could argue with that.

This was a most vibrantly interesting and stimulating group of people to be part of. Every single one of them had an enthusiasm bordering on being intimidating, one which fairly buzzed and rubbed off till we were all twitching with an electricity, if not separating us, bonding us instead into a kind of wayward pack. The work started to flow and I was catching up in leaps and bounds while becoming intoxicated by the thrill of the chase; the demands being enormous with no time for slacking. The days were flying by too fast to keep much of a record of and with so much having to be learned in the catching-up process, with a broader sphere of Art History, plus illustrated essays on a variety of aspects on Art. The sketchbook emerged as being the most effective and fool-proof measuring stick, there were no short-cuts where this 'Bible' of a thing was concerned. What went into it was essentially self-motivated, a measure of one's ability, speaking volumes about attitudes and values and stripping one down to a nakedness, beyond even the most convincing bullshit; the sketchbook revealed all.

I knew that I was in at the deep end alright and I knew for sure now what those earlier warnings had referred to. Making up for a lost year was a tall order to say the least, and I'd be glad to see the finishing straight coming into view, knowing deep down that I'd get there by hook or by crook. Nothing was going to stop me now because I was very secretly loving every exhilarating minute of it and was turning it all into fun. I was doing what I loved doing best of all and I felt that I had a growing advantage by virtue of it all beginning to feel like downhill. My appetite was insatiable and, without knowing it, I had started to write a 'poetry' of sorts in the form of scribbling urgent, very basic descriptions of things onto my unfinished drawings. A form of poor man's shorthand so as to enable me to take up the work later and to complete it convincingly and at leisure, like cheating, after which I'd rub all traces away; a kind of survival tactic, no more than that. Periodically sketchbooks were gathered-in for random assessment and, catching me somewhat off-balance, one of my Lecturers took me to one side and inquired about these 'word-things' that I'd not had time to erase from my drawings. I apologised, fearing that they were evidence of a lack of ability to finish a drawing on time. To my utter surprise he laughed at my naive apology and instead insisted that I wrote them all out clearly on separate paper so that he could then let his literary friend take a look at them, and to possibly offer me encouragement. I was gob-smacked, embarrassed beyond belief at the very suggestion, wishing that I'd never started the slovenly practice in the first place. He persisted despite my protestation and eventually succeeded in getting his way. Heaven only knows why I felt so ashamed, possibly because the words had exposed more of my inner privacy than I had been aware of; something that made me feel shy and self-conscious as well as ashamed. It was because I'd never done English or written anything much beyond my name in my life before; I simply wasn't supposed or even remotely entitled to be a writer or anything near to that. I was an imposter pure and simple, a village duffer, that just happened to be able to draw.

My senior Lecturer, Mister Bedwell, changed all that and he opened a door to another world for me. It was one where I had never entered into before, almost like being able to fly, so different were its sensations and possibilities. It did however require some getting used to. The difficult part being actually believing that I could do it with the overwhelmingly persistent feeling that I was trespassing in a world where I had no earthly right to be; it wasn't easy to come to terms with this. Duncan Bedwell viewed it all with concerned amusement and incredible patience. His literary friend had by now responded to the handful of scribbled words which I had sent him and he offered praise and encouragement beyond my wildest dreams. He went so far as to make constructive proposals as to how I should proceed under his guidance, both of them stressing upon me the importance of reading, naming selected literary works, something which I'd never done before. I had to admit, with some degree of shame, as to never having read a single book in my life. What's more, the likelihood of my starting to do that now was a virtual nonstarter because I couldn't even keep up with the overwhelming eruption of stuff that was bursting out of me; there simply wasn't room in me for other peoples' words!

Time just kept rushing by, whirlpooled, treacherous and far too dangerous to go paddling in. There were seemingly no islands or harbours of safety, the water ran far too deep and fast for any comfort of that kind, now that the day of reckoning was within our sights. Nerves had started jangling and showing signs of fraying at the edges, poorly veiled under brave un-humerous and insincere laughter. So much was at stake with the 'Intermediate' exam, it was the doorway to the National Diploma, the alchemist's ultimate dream. Those fortunate to have rich parents always had the option of sitting the exam again if they failed; no such luxury for the likes of me though, all my eggs were here in this one basket and I'd be an omelette for sure if I failed!

Camaraderie ran strong whether it be true or false, much to the amusement of those loftier scruffs, the Diploma first years who were putting on the style and pulling a little rank, the unhurried luxury of having three years to go before their shit hit the final fan. Above them, years two and three Diploma students were above all this puerile stuff and looked down on our floundering as though we were ducklings on a pond in the park; not even donating a crumb of recognition, let alone a morsel of comfort in our direction. As for us, we looked up to the First Year Diploma students, albeit with a certain guarded reservation and a questionable doubt as to the likelihood of miracles. The fact that they were there where we aspired to be, was enough to 'wax our lyricals' in a way that made them feel important. In truth, the majority of them came across as being really smashing people, brazenly extrovert whilst in the subtle cultivation of a brand of sham introversion known only to themselves. It all looked like an exciting place to be and I was wishing that my having a good sound and solid sketchbook was adequate on its own to pass this confounded 'Intermediate' exam. Alas, this wasn't the case and so I joined those ranks with bleeding nibbled nails and diarrhoea and waited patiently at the door forever marked 'Engaged'!

In disorientating timeless bedlam, an entire year had somehow stolen past into unremembered history. An avalanche of black confetti in the owl-flying, soundless, bat-swooping amnesia of regrets; unbreathed and outwardly imploding to other centres beyond experiences deeper than myself, nearer than never and further than ever. There was no avoiding this laceration of outward waste whilst attempting to stand motionless, calm within to count to ten, safe from the mind's scythe making empty pages to pasture dreams yet undreamed.

Vanished without trace the terracotta and alabaster Winter fields, the Arts Ball in the Borough Hall, with a plump, suspendered leg sticking through the towering, lavishly chandeliered and ornately plastered ceiling where 'Speckly' Mavis had almost fallen through, cheating death by a whisker and now all black-confettied in the dancing dark days sunken from memory. The repetitiously stitched to's and fro's of bus-rides and mile upon mile of pencil lines forgotten on paper, kisses stolen in lost dreams where no-one ever knew they were being kissed and I had forgotten the person I used to be, or probably never was. A stranger now, having only ever lightly touched things and only ever being lightly touched, never to have wholly eaten or to have been wholly eaten; not until now, an orphan three times eaten and cast by convention into despair at the failure to remember ever having been a starling. Now, having to proceed, laboured and leaden, amongst black confetti, striving to find the wedding of light and lighter still and to see the dark-stained shadows bleeding from the blinding light, telling me that I was precisely still here dynamically poised upon the Genesis pin-prick between where light and dark held hands.

The first exam day had arrived amidst a panicked melee of officialdom, with clerks and clocks twitching and ticking and our places already labelled and laid at long tables. It was more resembling a Maternity Ward than an examination room, with invigilators like midwives burdened with responsibility which froze us from our ease, leaving us statued-stiff and quaking in our shoes. The question-papers were a tightly kept secret, guarded by a grunting, sneezing musketeer with snuff in his bullets, waiting for the fingers of the clock to decide our fate and spit-out the hour like a fish bone from its gullet, summoning the first of the labour-pains to plague the deathly silence that accompanied the first raw sight of the cruel questions to be undressed.

Silence had always been a stranger here but, that tall dark stranger was here now, clip-clopping in plimpsoles, marching up the wall and across the ceiling, in and out of nostrils and ears, mouth and other orifices. It was an eerie kind of silence, not light-years from death itself, almost but not quite denying me a stolen dialogue of caressing glances at Miss Murphy invigilating like a corpse there on a chair. Tight black skirt, dark green stockings, mustard, magenta and turquoise blouse, beads and silken scarf and looking cosmetically tanned about her nose and cheeks. I'd married her the night before but no-one had informed her, leaving consummation to telepathy alone, whilst I proceeded deeper into the recipe for making Gold adorn her ears and make her listen, band her finger and make her mine.

The silence worsened when the pencils started to scratch and rubbers squeaked like mice while floundering, heavily breathed whispers of foreboding were ruled out-of-order or disqualified from the hostile air, as wearisome fingers began their marathon round the large Roman-numeralled running-track of the clock which sounded exactly like Granny's grandfather timepiece in the living room up on The Common. Students were looking over each others shoulders in a sharing, caring, for some a despairing, sort of way; everyone comradely willing each other on, even though we were each and every one of us on our own now. It was 'do or die', only we, our solitary selves now, that could shape these destined moments and make them bless us and become as wind in our sails. A break for a tea or a pause for a pee came soothingly, relieving tensions in a babble of bravado. The worst bit, the first bit, was over in that our nerves had by now calmed allowing us not to panic too much in the confronting and repairing of whatever damage may have initially resulted. The trouble was, there wasn't time, provision or material, for completely starting again, leaving some having to make the best of a bad job and to keep their fingers crossed that subsequent subjects in the ongoing series of exams would better favour them in a 'swings-and-roundabouts' sort of way.

At the crucial hour when the clock's big finger had crossed the finishing line, an audible cacophony of relief and flatulent resignation erupted in an amazing outpouring and we all stood up, stretched our arms and legs and hungrily scoffed over what each other had done. Artwork was in most cases still wet and, impatiently eager as dictatorial hands were to snatch everything up and whoosh it away to somewhere sinisterly private, nothing could be touched lest it become instantly ruined. We made sure of that and guarded our work stalwartly as stoats until it was all completely dry. During the wait, an invading tribe of Diploma students came bursting in like unruly hyenas to feast their ravenous eyes, turning the previously templed silence into an anarchic zoo. In the kerfuffle that ensued, I noticed how my own efforts were attracting a good deal of favourable attention, helping me feel that I hadn't let anyone down and for my confidence to emerge once more. I knew that Dad's old demob-suit had served me well, even though my own earlier attempts at amorous telepathy in it had proven sterile and totally impotent!

The first of the exams had taken the pressure out of the situation and had made it easier for us to confront the remaining exams in a kind of philosophical resignation. What was to be would be and there was nothing that we could do about anything now, apart from just getting on with it and doing our best. The week took over a month to pass. So many peripheral nonentities had fallen foul of anaesthesia caused by the presumptuously attempted measuring of artistic worth, provoking artistic temperaments to come ghosting out and revealing their most unpleasant fraying at the edges. This was the most difficult time that I had know since starting at the Art College and focused my thoughts on the nature of insecurity and the great castles and palaces which were hopes and dreams of our own making, and which could crumble in an instance, plunging us into hopeless despair. The daft thing was that, even the healthiest confidence couldn't offer protection or shed any light on what the Examining Body had ultimately decided was to be our fate ... we had to wait. Only in the midst of the approaching long Summer vacation would it cough-up this most crucial of pellets and ease our battered nerves, allowing us to become 'normal' once more.

In the immediate aftermath there was a numb straggle of seemingly empty days, ours to fill with meaningful reflection and a much-needed letting off of steam. Final Year Diploma students had now grown beyond their laughing days, part-time was over for them and the thought of failure was unbearable and virtually impossible to ignore. Some of these most senior individuals would, if successful, be going on to do their Art Teachers Diploma at some other specializing college somewhere, while other, males that'd either failed or had chosen not to teach, would have the agonising wait to be 'called-up' to do their National Service. Had they chosen farmwork or coalmining instead of Art, they'd be exempt; let's face it, who in their right mind needed Art anyway?

It was really quite a sad time. The 'Commercials' were preparing for their voyage into the unknown, with their portfolios lined with assorted fish-paste label designs and other iconic graphickery which was hoped would wizard its way beyond stubborn prejudice somewhere. They'd all sat their own exams and had impressive certificates to bolster their credibility; I knew that I was really going to miss them, no matter what my own fate had in store. 'Art' Tomkins had however, boldly decided to do the last year again in the hope of sorting out his priorities this time and getting something worthwhile in his portfolio to show for his efforts. Assuming that I'd be back here at college myself, I was glad of this decision of his. He and I, having already joined the Lichfield Cycling Club, were becoming somewhat notorious on the Sunday Club-runs when a pedalling mass of upwards of fifty varyingly sexed, aged and sized specimens clogged the roads, all gobbling away like turkeys and leaving the stink of embrocation lacing the air, causing all the Yellowhammers in the hedges to cough themselves blue beyond recognition. We were getting to be the 'fast boys' on the long return journeys, which invariably turned into races back to 'Carol's Cafe' which was to become our base. I really loved it and couldn't bear the thought of our becoming split up because of college, bringing an effective end to all this cycling hysteria, especially at a time when we were fancying our chances in 'time-trials' and had grander ideas of forming a team and getting onto the road-racing circuit.

Impertinent dreams indeed for two aspiring lads with bikes built of solid lead and with fat town and country tyres, instead of the finger-thin tubular, ultra-lightweight jobs that proper racing cyclists had. True, we'd stripped our machines of their mudguards and dynamos, heavy bells and saddlebags and we spent long hours polishing them so that they'd be slippery through the air. We were laughed at by the prima-donnas in the club who had specially hand-built, lightweight racing bikes which had cost the earth and which 'Art' and I hadn't a hope in hell of owning. Laugh as they may, they didn't like it too much when we started to make a habit of being the first two back at 'Carol's Cafe', even more so when our 25 mile time trial times impressively started to speak for themselves; making others in the club to take note. It came as something of a surprise when, an ex-racing cyclist in the village told me that I'd had a mention in the 'Cycling Weekly' after a recent time-trial. They'd apparently said that I showed promise, no doubt being impressed by my ‘roadster’ which was almost twice the weight of all the other hand-built flying machines.

The last days before the solitary Summer vigil were like Summer playgrounds had been back at school, when it was too hot to even think and the playground itself was too hot to sit on. Around us, lecturers were all like bits of paper in a wind, all beavering away under the self-blinding shepherdship of the Principal; even their bits of paper were whispering as they scurried this way and that, fragmentedly debating in over the shoulder discourses. ‘Bong’ himself, was in his element as smartly dressed parents filed in and out of appointments with their offsprings all eager to take up Art as a career, being duly lied to and made to believe that life begged for art and lavishly rewarded it accordingly. We were all made to keep well out of the way, to go off with our sketchbooks or to study paintings in the Art Gallery, anything so long as we didn’t look like scruffy, loudmouthed, melodramatic Art students with nothing to do.

Being a bit of a loner, I took my sketchbook and watercolours and followed a little river to the north. I seated myself in a sea of yellow Irises and painted an old flour-mill which stood like an elegant ghost amongst white, turbulent water which had large fishes gliding amongst it as in some mysterious aquatic ballet.

A pretty golden-haired girl that I’d never seen before came and sat nearby and watched me with inquisitive fascination, spilling from her pale, slightly thin face. She smiled at me and I smiled back as, very stealthily, she inched nearer so as to see more clearly what I was doing. I didn't feel unduly invaded or pressured by her presence, on the contrary I found it to be quite beautiful and sweetly innocent. It was probably the first time she’d ever watched a painting being painted and the experience plainly delighted her. “Do you like it?” I asked and she nodded approvingly as a blush brushed her cheeks. Very carefully I removed the page from my sketchbook and held out the picture for her to take. “There, you can have it ... it’s for you.”

We sat side by side watching the fishes, which I now recognised as being 'Chub', and we idled an hour away before two inquisitive swans with their four cygnets came across to us, with the cob hissing a warning for us to get off his territory. At this point I felt the girl’s thin fingers clasp tensely about my own and we slowly got to our feet and strolled easily away hand in hand, sweethearts for an afternoon. Before parting, I asked her what her name was and she whispered, “Rita,” then, as I was writing ‘for Rita’ above my signature, she gave a slight frown and whispered ... “Can I see you again?” “Same time, same place tomorrow?” I suggested and she smiled, then tip-toed up close and kissed me on the lips for what seemed a suffocating age, before hurrying away towards a suburbia which was foreign to me. I watched, as a shaft of sunlight illuminated her hair and made it glow more golden than summer itself; I’d found my Gold and my knees were knocking like loose tappets as I made my way rather clumsily back to college.

Everything about me was tying itself in nervous knots; my inside was all effervescing with bubbles bursting, and a whole feeling of being scared out of my wits never being far from breaking the surface. I was half wishing that I’d not been alone up there along the river but, walking distances of even that modest sort wasn’t to the liking of any of the others and would have been more likely to end in illegal fishing or swimming than in watercolour painting. Even though what had happened had been so very quaint, simple and lovely, I was still afraid, just like I had been with Miss Murphy; life hadn’t prepared me for strides to suddenly lengthen and for bigger things to happen that much faster. This was where having a 'running-mate', someone like 'Art' Tomkins, would have come in handy ... although on reflection, that may not have been the most ideal of solutions!

The following day started off bright and dazzly but, clouds didn't take long to appear and our things-to-do options were drastically reduced as rain started to fall. By this time I was already along that little river, still feeling nervous and quite afraid. I had made an attempt to do another watercolour sketch of the mill for myself when, my sweet new friend appeared some distance away, rather rat's-tailed as she sheltered under a high hedge from where she beckoned me to join her. I strolled over and we stood looking rather bashfully at each other. "It would rain today of all days!" I groaned miserably and she came up close and smiled. "I know where we can go that's dry ... the allotments. We've got a plot with a shed on it, it's dry in there; c'mon follow me!"

By this time the rain was coming down heavily and I followed her at a brisk, skipping sort of gait for about half a mile before coming to a horticultural jigsaw-puzzle of allotment plots. A beautiful shanty town of sheds of all shapes and sizes, with monumental rows of runner-beans, fruit bushes, sub-tropical jungles of rhubarb, avenues of peas, cabbages galore, all sorts there in the grey, driving rain. The entire 'rain-forest' of it all was deserted as we hurried on through and down a pathway leading to a ramshackle shed. Somewhat to my surprise, I could see now that she had actually planned all this when she suddenly produced a key from her bag and hurriedly fumbled the shed door open, then dragged me inside and bolted the door behind us. I was suddenly a quaking bag of nerves, caught in a cosy trap and stricken with a bewildering sudden flooding disillusionment on witnessing what I had naively believed was sweet innocence, rabidly becoming something entirely different, all calculating and reckless in a passionately greedy sort of way. She was clinging all over me, kissing furiously and panting feverishly in a lusting determination to have me abandon control and to take her in the 'lock-stock-and-barrel' way that she was blatantly begging and expecting of me. "Come on," she hotly urged, tearing away her pretty wet cotton dress, tossing it over an untidy clutter of boxes and sacks. "Come on, John Constable, what are you waiting for?"

Helplessly boiling over and my body scalding the turgid moments, a voice inside was booming, "NO!" It was either Grandad or God, I couldn't tell which in all this steam, both of them had silver whiskers and jowly double-chins. The voice boomed again and I felt myself being manhandled by a hefty no-nonsense Angel sent with a heavy-duty needle and strong cobblers-thread to stitch up my demob-suit trouser flyholes and to then unceremoniously stitch the trousers to my body. The Angel needn't have gone to all this devotional trouble, my pounding heart was already aching and breaking with tormenting sadness on realising that this wasn't the pure, 'virginal' sweetheart-thing and, more sadly still, that this angelic-looking girl here, hell-bent on stripping me of all traces of my own virginity, had most certainly already lost hers somewhere along the way, most probably in this very shed!

Glitter as she may have done, she wasn't the Gold of my searching and the rain beat down on the roof like handfuls of gravel being thrown. It should have made it all feel so cosy here inside but, instead it added to my feeling of being ensnared and in a miserable confusion of part-wanting and a greater part still of not wanting! I was absolutely terrified lest the cobblers-thread give way projecting me into the reproductory minefield of her plotting. The threads miraculously held and I stubbornly refused to be drawn any further into the trap, causing her to lose both patience and temper in a most alarming personality change. “You’re too damn slow for me, you are; you aint normal like other lads I know!” “That’s the trouble,” I replied. “I don’t even know you or anything about you and you don’t know anything about me either, so we shouldn’t even be thinking of going this far, not until we’ve got to know, love and trust each other ... ‘stands to reason!” “You’ve got summat wrong with you ... you’re mad!” she scolded, sliding back the bolt, showing me the door and pointing out into the driving rain. “Goodbye, Rita,” I said in a low thud of a voice and headed disconsolately out into the grey monsoon afternoon, dishevelled but still in one piece.

## 6. ‘Muses in Solace’

The student world of waiting was like Russian roulette, starving incentive of any clear purpose or enthusiasm. It was proving to be a dangerous world out there and with a stinging nettle somewhere lurking in every bunch of flowers, warning to be wary and not over-generous in my trusting. Determining that which was not wanted was proving to be rather more important than identifying that which was actually wanted. If the unwanted could be clarified and singled out it was, despite it being of a negative consideration, something that could provide a protection of sorts; things that were wanted were sometimes subject to error of a change of mind, thence to fall through into the basket of the unwanted. In reality, both the wanted and the unwanted existed in pairs, they were the counter-balancing forces in each other, as I had already discovered to my scratched and love-bitten cost; making me far more aware now of the weight of things that I didn't know, rather than of those which I did know. Short of being chaperoned, there wasn't a fat lot that I could actually do to make the emerging adult world a place of dependable safety.

We'd all slipped away into our hiding places from where to watch and wait for the postman. It wasn't only a watched kettle that never boiled, but similarly, a waited-for postman never called either and the days thus dawdled like lingering diseases that responded to no initiatives whatsoever. 'Art' Tomkins and I spent what was left of the evenings and weekends burning up the miles on our bikes, he wasn't waiting for the postman like I was and had no immediate worries ageing him. As for the remainder of the week, Dad was making sure that he got his pound of flesh and had me sand-papering and priming doors and windows, just making sure that, if Art failed, painting and decorating wouldn't!

Eventually the postman materialised with, quivering in his fist, the dreaded envelope, which neither Dad nor I was brave enough to open. We knew all too well what it was; my sister Fay had already successfully received hers from the Pitman's Commercial College, so we harboured no doubts when we saw the words Staffordshire Education Committee printed on the envelope. "Well, there it is, it's what you've been waiting for ... aint you gonna open it and see what it says?" His sham casual attitude was irritating and I very gingerly took hold of the white envelope and stood, still too afraid to open it. Losing her patience, Fay rushed up and snatched it from my hand and clumsily tore it open, frowning as she scrutinised it. "James blaa blaa blaa ...

Intermediate Examination in Art, blaa blaa ... PASS! " 'ere, let's have a look at that!" Dad snapped and a cheer went up. "I think this calls for a nice cup of tea!" Mom glowed, she was every bit as relieved as I was.

I felt quite delirious and bubbling with excitement on knowing that I really would now be doing my National Diploma, having already chosen 'Illustration' as my main subject. Dad was doing his special celebratory whistle and I was fondling the sheet of paper, drooling over it just so's to be sure that it was real and feeling smugly proud for having accomplished it in half the normal time; justifying the faith shown in me by my lecturers. Dad could see the state I was in and he very thoughtfully suggested that I spent my time now in getting back on with my art-work in readiness for the approaching new 'Diploma' regime of things; the very word diploma not seeming to nestle comfortably in his mouth. I didn't need telling twice and I wasted no time in gathering together my recently acquired ex-army haversack with sketchbook and other materials stuffed inside. I cycled off to Lichfield where I parked my bike in my usual shed and then strolled along Dam Street to the pool by the Cathedral and settled myself down amongst the trees and painted.

When I'd finished, I wandered over into the opposite park beside where the Art Gallery was situated and I sauntered under the shade-splashing lime trees and amongst the flowerbeds and benches. I caught sight of a familiar figure a little way ahead sitting on a bench watching two girls playing tennis. I grinned, it was 'Art' Tomkins, busy keeping his eye in and trying to come to terms with a sudden passion for the game of tennis. He had his bike thrown on the grass beside him, having been doing a few reckless laps on the remains of the banked cycle-racing track which surrounded the tennis courts. He was most surprised to see me suddenly sitting myself down beside him and I asked "Which one is it that's taken your fancy then?" He laughed, "The dark-haired one ... just you look at them legs on her!" "That leaves me with the blonde one!" I joked and joined him in acquainting myself with the fascinating new game. It became apparent that our presence was putting them off their stroke and their game thus fell into disarray, with giggling fits and blushes galore, as they made mistake after mistake. I had by now taken a fancy to the one with the longish blonde hair and it struck me that she had taken a bit of a shine to me as well, causing me to forget to tell 'Art' about my exam results. Our involvement in their game intensified and we were now applauding every stroke and gasping at every stumble they made, careful not to overdo it lest they take it as mockery and write us off as being yobs.

Unpredictably 'hairy' as 'Art's' company occasionally was, I felt really rather good in it and I could tell that he felt good in my company too, we really were 'running-mates', each looking after the others' well-being, with an unlimited agenda over every conceivable worldly commodity. The refreshing thing was that we held no secrets from each other, and not from anyone else for that matter, a kind of liberating, wide open freedom to be able to re-examine all previous habit-learning. I'd never known this kind of attitude-thinking before, all previous friendships in my life had been a somewhat greedy, selfish 'just-you-and-me' kind of inwardly self-consuming nature. With 'Art' it included his parents and family, my own parents and family and it was really unbarred to anyone of genuine openness, a resultant new-age chemistry from the mixing together of each other's attitudes and longings.

Right now, however, we had other fish to fry ... a bit of name-dropping, charmed behaviour and inspired good manners with a safety net to catch the small-fry rude words which sometimes unavoidably popped up like fish bubbles in the pool. With 'Art' taking the lead, as I knew he would, introductions were made, 'Julie' turning out to be the blonde one, 'Yvonne' the brunette with the legs. For me, not for the first time in my life, it was 'love at first sight' and I found myself properly bitten and caught-up in a fluttering sea of pink petals; unable to take my eyes off her, as also appeared to be the case with Julie too. I hadn't a clue as to how 'Art's' side of things was progressing, so blinding was this first-love fever which I was caught up in. Dad's demob suit was certainly back in business.

By the Art Gallery we sauntered to a halt prior to going our separate ways; Yvonne and Julie lived at opposite ends of the city and I was determined to remain glued to Julie's side and to accompany her back to her door. 'Art's' thinking was likewise and so, he walked with brunette, tennis racket and racing bike proudly down the Trent Valley Road, while I walked Julie down 'Gaia Lane, as far as her cottage. We loitered there for almost an hour admiring the hollyhocks which towered higher than the downstairs windows, the blossoming creeper bandaging the upstairs windows and then fussing over her new Welsh Collie puppy. We exchanged full names and addresses and promised that we'd stay in touch and meet again, the tennis courts seemed to be the most appropriate venue at this rather delicate stage. I felt like a bashful bundle of nerves, more so than ever when her mother suddenly appeared with a watering can. Julie introduced me to her as a 'budding artist' and I felt myself being very subtly and thoroughly scrutinised as to my suitability to be associated with her darling daughter. While she was looking me over, I was looking absorbingly at both of them, coming to the conclusion that I was amongst exceptionally nice people, her mother was lovely and I could tell that her smile was genuine by the very warmth of her nature itself. Julie then, reading the situation with consideration, pointed to a little pathway opposite, pointing out that it was a short-cut into town. It went downhill behind the Cathedral and then along to where, in earlier times, I had attended an annexe of Lichfield Art School to do 'silver-smithing' of all things. I said goodbye to them both and slipped off down the pathway and out of sight, glowing with elation almost to the point of floating up high over the rooftops and to have all the birds rejoicingly accompanying me safely back to earth.

I was ironically back in a situation where I was looking out for the postman, slightly more than half expecting a letter or perhaps a card from Julie. I dearly wanted to send her a note of some sort but I was afraid to for fear of her thinking I was coming-on a bit too fast. So, I left the initiative with her, I'd know it was for real then and I wouldn't have risked spoiling it; the postman called on neither of us!

On the other front, I was keen to keep 'Art' informed of developments. I still hadn't told him of my exam success, in fact, it seemed a bit odd that he hadn't come blasting over to update me on 'things' like I had expected him to, making me think that he was too caught up in the same stalemate indecision. I decided to break the deadlock and tore off on my bike leaving rubber on the tight corners in my reckless haste to catch up on events. Dribbling with sweat, I arrived at the council house where the big black and white 'Norton' was blocking the path with big Ted, 'Art's' brother squatting down, fag in mouth, beside it. Oil and grease plastered his hands and arms as he stripped the engine down and laid out the various parts lovingly on a large sheet. "He's out at the back doin' summat to his bike," he informed me and I squeezed past and found 'Art' similarly up to his ears in his machine, studiously fitting new handlebars, alloy brakes and racier new tyres. "Oho; sneaking an advantage over your racing partner, hey!" I joked, giving him a bit of a surprise and he stopped what he was doing and came grinning and stood beside me. "She looks good, don't you agree?" he said, referring to his randy-looking bike and presenting me with a slender window of opportunity to check to see if he'd got love-bites on his neck. I couldn't see any, which explained why he hadn't already beaten me to raising the subject of Yvonne. "Didn't it go very well, you and your leggy brunette?" I asked. His face remained unilluminated and I could tell that he hadn't gone his way. "Not bad," he tried unenthusiastically, ..."how did you get on with yours?" I gave him a cross-eyed crazy look and sighed ... "I think I'm in love, I even met her mother!" "That's nothin', I met mine's ... didn't make any difference though. Yvonne wasn't really my sort ... they're high school girls, both of them!" "What difference does that make, they're only a year or so younger than us ... now't wrong with that," I pointed out in defence of my new high school sweetheart, and he shrugged his shoulders and muttered, "I suppose not." I got off the subject and told him about my exam success, prompting him to suggest a celebratory piece of Cheddar cheese and some pickled onions with his Mom and Dad.

On my way back I decided to stop off by the Art Gallery and wheeled my bike through the park in the hope of seeing Julie; I wasn't disappointed, finding her there playing tennis with another girl, there was no sign of Yvonne. I was most relieved to catch sight of her sudden radiant smile and the eager wave which seemed to say what I'd been waiting for. We exchanged hello's and I seated myself on a bench and waited, wishing that I had my sketch book to make me feel less like some love-smitten lump of helplessness.

Fortunately I didn't have long to wait and soon found myself being introduced to Julie's friend, her neighbour Cath. We all strolled along to the Art Gallery where Cath tactfully decided that three wasn't company and suddenly remembered that she had to meet somebody, leaving Julie and I to stroll the other, longer way back to her house. I wanted desperately to hold her hand but I was too bashful by a mile and became nervously clumsy and tried to hide it by acting the fool in the hope that she'd take this as being more a 'strength of character' sort of thing than a maggot impersonation.

The subject eventually got round to Yvonne and 'Art' and, most revealing it was in an unsurprising sort of way, with my running-mate predictably proving himself rather too hot to handle. After walking her home and politely being asked in for a refreshing drink, and with no-one else in the house, 'Art' decided to turn on his hot tap and make himself irresistible to her. He was apparently doing moderately well despite stiff resistance, but Yvonne's mother suddenly returned and caught them tangled like spider-crabs in a basket. 'Art's' hands were everywhere where they were not wanted and he was dispatched on his way forthwith and told never to darken their door again. This explained it all and left me fearing that she may think that I, being his mate, was tarred with the same brush. Before I could utter a sound, Julie asked me ... "You're not like that I hope, are you James?" I gulped, shaking my head as I choked, "No way!" hurriedly going on to explain that 'Art' was a really nice bloke, despite the belief that he was God's gift to women and that furthermore; nobody was perfect. At this point I felt her soft, warm hand take hold of mine and we went hand-in-hand along the narrow, shady pathway; it felt like heaven.

Assurances of two years earlier that I'd grow into my inherited demob-suit were slowly coming true; I'd grown an inch or two since then and it was not making me resemble a sack of cauliflowers quite so much when I wore it. Getting drenched through to the skin in it on umpteen occasions had assisted too, shrinking it a fraction and freshening it up somewhat, giving me a more 'normal' appearance. So, with a degree more self-assurance and with the comforting new glow of having a sweetheart back at home, I joined the 'elite' on the National Diploma course as the Art College reopened its Fool's-G'old doors once more to a ravenous tide of reinvigorated aspiring alchemists.

It all seemed like a lavish banquet laid out before us on a three-year long table, a promised feast as well as a mysterious journey into a world of strange etiquettes and species obscure. The thrill was certainly thrilling as we clamoured full of willing to plunge-in and to suffocate, choke and drown like lemmings in the most inexplicable, excruciatingly delicious, bewildering extravaganza.

I was glad to have chosen 'Illustration' as my main Diploma subject, something with an essentially unambiguous 'function'. One which boiled down to simply being, 'saying something' in pictures, in a kind of literal way as opposed to the rather blurred, smudgy, somewhat vague intellectuality which seemed to be the case where Art College Painting was concerned. The idea of actually communicating and expressing something through a generously broad palette of techniques and disciplines was a most appetising carrot to have dangling from my donkey's nose, even though, in all honesty, I could see no compelling reason for there to be any division between painting and illustration when so much fine painting was born of illustration anyway, just as illustration was born of drawing.

Any such dividing line was always going to be a difficult one to draw and didn't really appear to serve any useful purpose beyond that of being a bit of cultivated snobbery and light-hearted rivalry.

I'd never had such a diverse assortment of colleagues before and they all looked bigger, older and much, much bolder now. New doors were opening all around allowing cautious access to the more advanced Diploma students, ability itself very tentatively emerging as being the determining factor where associations and friendships were concerned. It was becoming apparent that there existed, rivalries apart, a broader underlying fellowship, a kind of clanship of respect here amongst the 'elite'. A somewhat surprising yet comforting discovery, one which was giving me a more 'adult' feeling and providing the basic nutrients for my emerging stature although, at the same time distancing me painfully further from my still-attached wild roots and far deeper still into that seemingly shoreless, ever expanding ocean, the Ocean of Art.

No matter what, I was always vulnerable to spontaneous realisations of being alone, lost of reason and adrift with only illusions providing me with the blinkers to help me see the way forward. At times like this I retreated into my shell and sought solace in thought and quietly broke things down into crumb-sized morsels which would keep me alive and kicking. No matter how else it may have seemed, there were still only twenty-four hours in a day and but seven of those in a week after which the lumps got too big, too cumbersome to handle. Within it all I was still only me, there was no escape from this prison-truth which I returned to unfailingly from exploratory thinking-missions tethered to an elastic dog-lead. I had no magic fire in my breath that I could exhale to light the way when each night I was bludgeoned into recognising and forced to admit to my solitariness down the pitch-black bed where my legs were even lonelier than my brain. Tender, pale, frail and not boasting to be so strong now, my legs reached blindly away to my lost feet which had, from that faraway Genesis grave of a womb of a cradle of a seed-shell upon a lark-whistling heavened health, never failed me for one single feather of a second, and sixty more of these in every tangible hour of my twenty-four-hour days of existence. Now here, flush to these jet-black lonely realisations before sleep carried me in her arms to where my secret dreams grazed in waiting, themselves to be rasped from my begging memory's need by the light of new days relentlessly rising up ... or falling down.

From the house at awakening; my blood's blood emerging to the light, the soft arising and softer still passing-by of a Mother's, Father's, Sister's Brother's separate secretly flying birds of thoughts caged within. I could see them all as strangers because they were only themselves and nobody else besides; they were strangers even to themselves, we to ourselves. Sharing the same tastes maybe when talking of tea and bacon, but not sharing the same preferences where wider opinions separately sprouted. We were all adrift on seas of sorts, seas that had no shores, each of us having lost a priceless nature to a thief back in time, somewhere thence made to follow concocted rules instead and never to know who we really were, or what or why.

From the village in long early shadows dancing their stains, past breathed breath on windows leaving tears on panes, amongst cattle in mourning and along wandering lanes, through soft sparkling dew and tyre-patterned remains, I went pedalling my way through a stillness bordering on sanity unknown, starling like a greased parcel of secrets on my bike, between hedges and beneath leafy trees. What on earth was the reason for being me in all this sea so dwarfing to my knowledge and to all things pretended? The sky was the biggest thing, the hugest, mightiest place and it was there, right there, emptier than a shed, scratched and scrawped by light and dark, pocked-marked from where stars had scabbed and wandering moons had languished in their death-throes. There it was, a topless, bottomless basket that couldn't even hold apples!

From the last cottage; the cool, licked kiss of air sugared by trumpeting honeysuckle in fanfared silence, the dear lark had stolen from beneath the turf and was already a mile invisible where clouds had not yet dared to slipper, and he sang. He poured from his tiny heart, the most colossal beauty, the most gargantuan statement that the sky had ever known, and he remained the only one in all this creation everywhere who knew the reason why. Keeping me smaller than I ever knew small could be and offering no reason anymore for my racing wheels taking me chasing certificates unknown to larks and now, quite meaningless to me.

From the hilltop with all the thorns of Lichfield's spires peeping over other gentler hills, I free-wheeled down into a valley of partridges and on beyond a quiet farm to the scar, where a canal had once been, leaving its humped-backed bridge like a gold ring left on a dead woman's finger. My body, yet full of a rush to nowhere, all reason and reasons hidden from me in the first breeze-whispered leaves of the morning and in the fading enraptured song in the sky, trying still to tell me what it was that I needed to know. Apart from 'love', something else which I could feel yet couldn't explain, nothing, not anything was larger than what that little lark was 'being'. Very little, even 'nothing' else could fill me so awe-inspiringly full with something which, in all my life's learning could ever be explained in the way I needed to understand.

Only Art could ever aspire to be so ethereal a teacher; only she could even dare to be the wondrous wings to carry me even remotely near to finding out what that magic was. The more I thought, the more I set myself off wondering if, just maybe perhaps, it was the 'not knowing' that was the elusive magical factor. Some things, by their very miraculous nature, having to remain forever a mystery, reminding us all that it was only our questions that could help us to fly, and that too many stock answers always ran the risk of keeping us too heavy on the ground.

From the coalshed where I kept my bike, an old worn face hello-ing from around the corner of an even older lace curtain and smearing the wet breath away with a pain-distorted hand tied with dark stringy veins. Down streets full of shop-windows still asleep, someone's cat lying run-over close by a drain; vans, bikes and wagons and nobody talking, just smoking; nobody singing, just yawning; nobody laughing, just coughing. Dog-piss at every pole betraying a human condition that'd long-lost its purpose as I rushed for my bus along with the lost. Along into sunlight and an opening flower as memory held a sweetheart's face close to mine and I gazed across at her High School where soon she'd be treading, me on my bus dreaming of a wedding.

From the red double-decker and the world slipping by; nothing was perfect but some things were better than others, the better they were, the better, even better was the best. I soon got lost in this tin box with a staircase as it stuffed full with the bodies of students, apprentices, clerks, cleaners and businessmen, who never carried carrier-bags and never spoke either in this enveloping game of Commerce that was so big that it was running out of telegraph poles and the wire to string them with. Simplicity had soon soured in the mad blindness and I wanted the good Goddess of Art to come rushing and be my saviour but, the only 'Art' aboard this hurtling bus was 'Art' Tomkins, more rancid than a jasmine-farm and as resplendent as a knife-blade, not speaking but quietly clocking things prior to making a strike. I was as repaired as I was ever likely to be and so resigned myself to fortune and returned to the fold.

## 7. 'Forthwith and Fifthwith to a Weekend in Armageddon'

Wherever there were groups of people working together, invisible factors soon set to work into dividing them into smaller groupings, usually into pairs; the process took time because no-one was over-willing to reveal their true colours too soon. I had already spent a year with this group of people back in the 'Intermediates' but, that all seemed so long ago when we were all like hatchlings fighting for crumbs whilst at the same time, contriving our 'best-behaviour' disguises of sorts. We'd all undergone a notable spurt in our growing-up since then, the girls looked more like women now and previous scruffy mates were suddenly smart young men, some even attempting their first pathetic beards, all of us having aged into seriousness about the new Diploma Course.

Slowly, the invisible dividing factor went about its work and I found myself becoming naturally drawn into enjoying the company of one of my last year's more remote 'Intermediate' mates, John Burton. 'Burto', as he was known, was a Stafford born-and-bred member of the group, a thoughtful, extremely casual sort of bloke, who left me in no doubt whatsoever about his being a 'Stafford lad'. He strutted about as though the town belonged to him personally and he made me feel like I was an outsider from the 'country', a place which in his mind was a mythical concoction of cows and grass-roofed cottages and where joined-up writing still hadn't arrived, or worse still, had, but had been rejected.

'Burto' was known in Stafford's cricketing circles for his prowess as a seam-bowler and he had a cricketer's kind of pin-toed gait, all sort of stuttery and hunched as he shuffled the long footpaths, as though just getting into his bowler's run-up. God only knows what it was that suddenly made us get along so well, we had nothing in common that I could think of ... apart from an easy going nature, a feature which he took to the limit. He was so unhurried, so cussedly far laid-back that I'd swear he had dogshit in his hair at the back! Punctuality for him didn't exist; he was never on time for anything, always at least half-an-hour late in the morning and unfailingly with his breath smelling of sherry, swearing by raw egg and sherry as being the most ideal breakfast for him. If there happened to be a Test Match on the Television, the newly established electronic plague-gadget to have swept the nation, he'd come into college as normal, develop a sudden passion for his sketchbook, either that or having sprung a headache, and at lunchtime slope off back home coaxing me to go with him, our sketchbooks as alibis and we'd spend the afternoon with our eyes glued to the screen.

When the teams went off for tea, his long-suffering Mother kicked the pair of us out from under her feet and we meandered idly out through the back kitchen door and into the miniscule, cat-crapped patch at the back, where we sprawled on the crudely nibbled bit of lawn and consulted our sketchbooks at long last. This was where I was given a rare privilege insight into 'Burto's' unique, half-cock, 'minimal' approach to visual art, likening him to that of a woman avidly knitting whilst watching television at the same time, as he obliviously dipped his pen into a jar of green ink and proceeded to dreamily fill a page with randomly-angled, half-inch scrawled pen lines. What amazed me more was the fact that he considered it to be a serious piece of work with the title 'Grass Cuttings', signed and dated. It was the kind of doodle he could have done with his eyes shut and really exemplified his attitude to the artistic process, one of over-caution and a reluctance to break sweat when there might be a crafty, 'intellectualish' alternative available instead. He always somehow managed to give the impression that he was just 'ticking over', never ever having to rev his 'powerful' engine and to show what it could really do. It bordered on being a confidence trick perpetrated to a large extent upon himself, yet he would have you believing in him, eating out of his hands even. Always tantilising you with minimalist scraps and scribbles, none of which ever came close to being completed or resembled anything in particular yet, vaguely intriguing in an aggravating sort of way. Ideally, he should have been in with the painters in the Fine Art section where he could woffle and play at 'Artists', plenty of name-dropping and getting up onto pedestals where obnoxiousness could be muck-spread more lavishly. Whatever it was that 'Burto' had, it couldn't be dismissed so easily; there was 'something' there somewhere, hard as it was to winkle out into visible and generous abundance.

The old saying that 'birds of a feather flocked together', simply wasn't the explanation for our getting along so well together, because we really were unlike each other in so many ways; whilst I was a straw-in-the-hair nature boy, he was a streetwise townie. He didn't know a Bluetit from a cow and was no way disadvantaged by this because he more than made up for it by having the ability to deduce from the clouds and determine from the barometric feel of the air, whether or not the ball was going to 'swing' or 'turn' on the cricket field; something that I couldn't do, but didn't feel disadvantaged by either. The plain simple truth was that we found each other okay, full stop!

I wasn't the only one that liked 'Burto', everyone did; he was just simply a smashing bloke, courteous and clean-minded and with never a bad thing to say about anyone or anything. His laid-backness made you want to shake him out of his cussedly aggravating cocoon, an impossibility to say the least; one just had to accept him, warts and all, nothing was ever going to change 'Burto'!

One girl who was trying her hardest to do just that was a beautifully wild, clumsily lanky, National Health bespectacled, tousled glossy black-haired girl with a most infectiously engaging personality. Alison Thorne was the most abundantly talented artist and she'd got the 'love-thing' really bad over 'Burto'; we could all see this lovely romance struggling to flower, only to repeatedly come up against this cussed, immovable object lovingly known as, 'Burto'. Try as she may poor Alison couldn't find any purchase on him, he was mercurial and couldn't be managed, only willing to go part of the way and then becoming his old stubborn mule of an animal, facing a thousand other directions and refusing to be budged into treading even one of them.

Feeling sorry for Alison and knowing how she must be feeling despite putting a brave face on it, I somewhat fortuitously found a few moments alone with 'Burto' and I decided to broach the subject; after all, that's what friends were supposed to be for. Thinking the water to be only ankle-deep, I waded-in and asked him why he was showing her such reticence, when she was so plainly in love with him. His face suddenly tensed up as an expression of grave seriousness swept over him, making me realise too late that I was in it up to my neck, and none too good a swimmer either. He hadn't expected my untimely invasion of his privacy and was caught somewhat pants-down and temporarily unguarded as he floundered in my bow-wave, grasping at anything that might roughly make a raft; one which he would have preferred never to have needed crafting in the first place. "She ... she's a Catholic" he stammered at last, "'s.s ... staunch Roman Catholic, that's why!"

A stunned silence smarted about us and I was now the one that was taken by surprise, I simply hadn't expected an answer to come from this particular direction. In my astonishment I grunted in a low voice ... "You daft sod!" and shook my head in quiet disbelief. "What kind of excuse do you call that! You can't use that as a reason ... it's no different to you being a Church of England 'Prottydog'. What's it matter when you loves somebody!" My words were the first of this kind that he'd ever had to deal with and he shuffled uneasily as he attempted to regain his composure. It was obvious that I'd touched on something that'd skirmished in his private mind for some while now and this was a fence that his mule was adamantly refused to jump over. He felt compelled to continue ... "I couldn't cope with all that Pope-grovelling stuff ... all those 'dripping Cardinals strutting about like peacocks clamouring around him as though he was God himself. All those shifty little priests and nuns pretending not to be normal, all making their little flocks go into sinister confession-boxes and cough-up their sordid secrets, while all those other bigots kept theirs. I couldn't cope with all that stuff ... could you?" I was speechless; I hadn't gone to Grammar School, thank the Lord or whoever it was back in the village that influenced the decision. “Surely love’s bigger than all that stuff, ‘Burto’!” I sighed with a clarity that’d cut more corners than a baby crocodile had cut teeth, and I sensed that he was feeling better now that he’d got it all off his chest. Then wanting to have the last word on the subject he added caustically, “Love’s one thing ... it’s what you love most that worries me, James boy!” I laughed at this, relieved no end to be back out in the open with my mule-friend as I sneaked in and stole the last word on the subject from him. “Ar, I know what You love Most, Mister Burto ... cricket, bloody cricket!"

Poor Alison went on tearing her hair out over him and that’s the way it stayed as other social structures emerged about the place now that ‘best behaviour’ had reverted to ‘bog-standard’ behaviour and all disguises had by now perished, permitting the pair of them to merge their problematical romance into the background.

Whilst life was inexorably ramshackling on amongst its ecstatic catastrophes, I came somewhat soothingly upon evidence of a time when dawn-choruses must have sounded more rejoicingly deafening than at any time since. The pages of the book of Thomas Bewick’s wood engravings, through which I was reverently browsing, held only silent memories now, with no-one left to remember, save for perhaps the odd ‘stepping-stone’ ancient who once knew people, who once knew people who once knew people, each one handing on tiny pebbles from the mighty volcano that once was. Here was a most prolific genius of an illustrator sharing with me something of his life and time; an observed natural history rich and varied. A pageant of more domestic animals, mad bulls, cocks and hens, pigs and horses as well as simple moments recording how life went on, the ordinary things that people did. Treasured things and sometimes things of a more frightening nature, like bird-nesting boys tumbling from trees as dead branches gave way; an entire world long before the advent of the camera to provide endless snapshots to document the passage of time. What I was looking at wasn't so much 'Art' but 'Life' itself, all beautifully engraved, a most meticulously demanding and, occasionally rather dangerous medium when in unpracticed hands. I relate to my very first attempt at wood engraving which resulted in the 'graver' suddenly skidding off the wooden block and sinking into my inner left wrist; it caused a few horrified gasps about the place when they caught sight of blood.

Drawing was 'positive' and involved making dark lines upon a light background; engraving, by contrast was 'negative' and involved making lines of light against a dark background. Of the two, nothing could be simpler or more straightforward than drawing; whereas, wood engraving was a medium where technique always presented a restriction over spontaneous, fluid freedom of line. For all that, Bewick's miraculous white on black vignettes ached with a timeless charm, telling stories that glowed with life, elevating wood engraving to a higher Art and the role of the illustrator to a nobler place of importance in the world of artistic expression.

Bewick's recorded images wandered at will throughout my mind, like a Sunday stroll. I couldn't stop thinking about them, they were breathing and alive within me now, it was the very same air that I was breathing, just as it was the self-same sun providing identical light and warmth. Sure, the air had been sucked-in and blown-out a few countless zillions of time by everything that had ever lived, including all the things in those wonderful engravings. I could hardly grasp the magnitude of what it was that I was coming to realise; everything, every single thing had touched and breathed the same basic, vehicular body of air, taking from it and adding to it. I realised also that, the word 'always' meant precisely that, just as 'forever' was likewise; 'always and forever', this moment NOW, having no ending or beginning, 'Eternity' in other words.

Birth was the bursting moment of the sparkling fish leaping from the water. Life was the duration of that wondrous leap. Death was the splash of the fish re-entering the water ... always though, the water ... always and forever, the water. It was all a circle, one unimaginably marvellous golden, glowing circle, deep and mysterious, sustenance for our mithered souls.

Feeling somewhat spiritually ravaged from having stumbled across this long-lost secret of divine alchemy, I determined myself that I must now attempt to spend some of its newly acquired wealth of Gold. Strangely however, Dad's old demob-suit didn't recognise the obscure currency and its pockets remained stolidly empty, informing me that 'Wealth' wasn't money at all and, neither was 'Gold'; furthermore it was spelling it out to me that 'Wealth' was simply, the 'Light of Knowing' and that, that most precious of all things which we had lost and that which the Skylark hadn't, was none other than the very 'Light' itself, something that had to be shared, not traded. Identifying what it was that's blinded us from the 'Light of Knowing', was easier to see now and wasn't the 'Guiding Light' that it'd pretended to be after all, but a sinister, calculated and prescribed enslaving 'Darkness'. The knowledge of which began to frighten me because it left me feeling isolated, like a tiny ant adrift from the colony and looking up at a colossal mountain blocking the way; one which had vanished up high and away beyond the dark enormous clouds, too much by far for a mere antling to attempt to eat its way through.

I sought comfort in thoughts of my sweetheart back in Lichfield. I wanted more than ever to be with her, see her nose crinkle when she smiled and how her eyes lit-up when we were glued just looking at each other. I wanted to share with her my newfound 'Gold', but afraid lest the noise of my words prove too clumsy and frighten their 'Light' back into the shadows once more. She and I had so much to learn in our growing closer to one other; it wasn't noises we should be making, but learning to listen to the very silence of our being together. Becoming aware of each other's innermost feelings and never to presume upon anything. It was all so delicate, exciting, so delightful; we could make noises any old time; dammit ... we'd still not attempted our first kiss, the very thought of which was tying my legs in knots and making my eyeballs rattle!

With rapidly shortening days, the last fading 'Samuel Palmer' eventides had left bronze and golden leaves all crinkled and a-sail in the breezes, beneath flickering constellations, somersaulting sideways, swirling like late haphazard moths amongst owls and moons while, hand in hand, Julie and I there, kicking the drifted leaves into showers around us as we timorously cavorted into that clumsy firework of our first kiss. Not Palmer, Turner or even William Blake in all this bloodstained dusk could come anywhere near the beauty of this sweet, frail 'First Love'. It didn't matter that our preciously awaited 'First Kiss' more resembled a collision between passing cyclists in the dark than it did an 'expression of love'; the second kiss made up for debris left from the first and the third was better still and I knew, beyond any trace of doubt here in these very trembling moments that I had never, not even remotely ever, been in love before. This here Now was unmistakably... Gold!

Nothing in my entire life had ever done to me what this was doing. I'd never been taught that an erection could quite suddenly become a terminal illness, forcing me to stoop doubled-over like some crippled agricultural rustic in an old sepia photograph, wrestling and contorting with embarrassment trying to conceal it prior to it striking me dead. Never before had I known my brain to turn instantly to pulp and my breathing shatter into chaotic flounderings, or my fingers to groveling stumps and my heart into a red-hot biscuit tin full of grasshoppers! My only, only comfort in all this pyre of ecstatic misery, if any comfort there could be at all, came from the plain undisguisable fact that Julie too had joined 'death-row-without-a-lawyer' and was out of control and about to explode into delicious death throes of her own; thus enabling us to leave this mortal coil together, blissfully happy here in the dark field where the grim shapes of once stately trees dimly showed their bared skeletons against the misting over navy-blue canopy of our brand-new, ferociously burning Love.

A state of numbness subdued the world; I'd never known anything to possess such inexplicable power over me before, it defied description with the added mystery of 'it', whatever 'it' was, remaining invisible. The only clearly defined thing that stood out any more was Julie herself, all else just faded to ghost-forms in the background. There was a strange unnerving magic in the air, all sort of electric and tingly as though every web on every wayside parsley was a silken, high-voltage pheromone love-thread, connecting our two plagued, palpitating hearts. Changing what had formerly been a delicately honeyed and fairylike love into a gluttonous, cannibalistic, raging monster of a thing.

Such was the dark alchemy of that 'first kiss' which had turned old iron keys and opened new doors to where golden roaring lions lurked, with emerald serpents amongst lush rubied vetches and somehow managed to remain hidden both from view and expectation. It reminded me of that most ancient of ancient, infamous old allotment plot the 'Garden of Eden' that Id heard so much about back at the village school. It wasn't 'Adam and Eve' anymore, but 'Julie and Jim' along with a Cox's Orange Pippin that we'd been ordered not to eat; a really desirable red, gold and green beauty it was too and we resisted it despite the overwhelming temptation. All we'd done was drool over it, stroke it and lick it a bit, but never once did we take a bite of it. The couple back in the real story apparently were not as strong as Julie and me and succumbed to the temptation and did what any other spoilt brats would have done ... ate the bloomin' thing and then tossed the core down for the serpent to eat! For so doing, they were punished for the rest of time, no second chance given, resulting in every single one of us to follow thereafter to suffer the same uncompromising fate. It didn't seem fair to me back at the village school, and even now it didn't seem to be the most reasonable way of going about things.

The five days separating the weekends dawdled now that we were effectively fuses at either end of this high-voltage, pheromone love-thread. Darker evenings and longer nights were adding to the dawdling process, while the year inexorably shuffled to its conclusion with the added hiccup of a Christmas thrown in, to provide me with the embarrassing ordeal of being expected to accompany Julie to her annual High School Christmas dance. Dancing for me, being a thing which only others were afflicted by. I didn't much relish the prospect of prancing about under glaring, tinseled lights in my ferociously flat-ironed demob-suit and a borrowed obligatory 'Tootal' tie, all done up like a dog's dinner while being watched over by matronly, be-spectacled strangers roped-up in pearl necklaces and blue-rinsed perms. I blushed and tottered about amongst floral evening-gowned, sparkling-eyed girls in daring lipstick and amongst a hundred and more 'Errol Flynn' look-alikes from the nearby Grammar School for Boys. The highly polished wooded floor wasn't helping matters, it was an obstacle course upon which I hadn't a clue in the world as to what my feet were supposed to be doing.

Somehow I managed to survive the ordeal and I kept my fingers crossed that such occasions didn't crop up too often because this one had left me singularly unimpressed to say the least. Glad now for any old excuse for us both to go up to her bedroom, Julie seized on the opportunity to suggest to her parents that she gave me dancing lessons up there as a matter of urgency in preparation for a New Year Ball which I'd also be expected to accompany her to. When she borrowed a record-player and a pile of Victor Sylvester dance-records from her friend Cath, it seemed like a perfectly reasonable request, and her parents even found it quaintly amusing that I, being from a village, didn't have a clue about dancing.

Once old Victor's orchestra was all hot and throbbing away full blast and with 'Testosterone' on draught at the hand-pump, we cannibalised on her little bed in a raging fanfare eruption of multiple explosions and implosions that'd make Armageddon seem like a cosy place for spending a quiet weekend. Miraculously and I have to admit, downright infuriatingly, our virginities somehow stayed intact. This was no doubt assisted by the repeated sudden explosions of silence when the wretched record came too quickly to its end, projecting us both into mid-air collisions in our panicked desperation to get the damned thing started again, and for us to resume our dancing lesson forthwith ... fifthwith, sixthwith, seventh, eight, ninth and tenthwith; we lost count!

## 8. 'Pointillist Snow and the Subterranean Black'

After both Christmas and the New Year had been duly disinfected out of sight for another year, things settled down into a kind of surrender to inevitability. Winter wasn't about to break the habit of a lifetime and to spare anyone anything. I didn't mind what it did to me, in fact the worse it got the better I liked it; a purely selfish attitude I know, but there was nothing that I could do about it either one way or another. Arguably snow was one of the most beautiful things in nature, it wasn't just the stunning white patchworked fields and the finger-fronded branches all turned into a lacelike fairyland of something more different from anything else. It wasn't just these more obvious things but, the actual textured falling snowflakes themselves in their indescribable dance in the air; a most mesmerizing ballet in both the light and the dark. It was something I'd never seen sufficiently captured in painting. Turner's efforts were rather more dramatic than balletic and were supplementary to a far broader canvas, incredibly beautiful nonetheless. Once the snow had fallen and the skies were blue again, artists like Breughel painted the snowy landscape itself in a somewhat sedate and poetic kind of way as in his 'Hunting Scene'. For me though, probably my favourite snow-painting of all was by Monet, a tenderly virgin snow-scene with a single magpie sitting on a little gate ... absolute perfection.

Snowflakes themselves were a challenge apart, a 'Pointillist's' dream in fact; essentially they were just moving dots, textural animation in a chaotic modesty of white against white; probably closer to Music and Ballet than to anything else. Whiteness was like sound, the nearer it was the whiter it was; the further away it was the paler it became; bright white and pale white with yet paler, tinier textured whites even further away still. A blizzard was like a dawn chorus; near birds and far birds, sound in movement creating patterns in the air. I liked the idea of this kind of abstract perspective as opposed to the more obvious, rulered, mathematical, architectural perspective which had been drummed into me. I could see these other perspectives very clearly and delighted over the prospect of exploring them in all of their forms and varieties, especially with colour, where some colours seemed to leap off the canvas into your face when applied over other colours, just as the other colours receded into the distance. Because snow was entirely consisting of white dots on white dots, nobody bothered painting it. I could imagine every student turning up with a picture of snowflakes falling; a hundred pictures side by side, every single one of them looking more or less the same as the next. I was rather surprised that 'Burto' hadn't come up with something to match his last summer's 'Grass-cuttings', but on reflection knowing him, he'd make his statement with a whitewash brush ... and that'd be in his sketchbook!

'Isms' in Art were as bad as 'Ologies' in Science. Painting in dots was for me, quite a natural variation from time to time as the subject demanded or, in my own case, 'persuaded'. There was a great clanking, 'out-of-the-ark' labelling-machine that stitched 'isms' and 'ologies' onto things. It was archaic to say the least and betrayed a human characteristical flaw of sorts; a need for everything to be identifiable and accountable with minefields of laws and licensing requirements, suggesting to me that the rest of my life was likely to be dominated and dictated by accountants and verminious plagues of clerks accountable to them. Whatever the future, right now I was a 'Pointillist', yesterday an 'Impressionist', the day before that a 'Surrealist', while always to the painting students an 'Illustrator'!

Art College was really getting to feel quite an enthralling place to be; it felt like I was getting a thorough grounding in probably the second oldest profession known to man. There were odd occasions when it felt like the first and remoter ones when it came third or fourth, as with most things, the more you were prepared to put in, the more you could expect to get out. It really was a fine place to be prior to becoming ground to pulp by the monster beyond, wherever or whatever that was ... but it was there alright and in many guises too. Still being a bit young seemed to offer a flimsy, perishing skin of protection and, while it lasted, I was determined to indulge to my gluttonous limits.

Art was as old as the hills, history was littered with 'picture-makers', ordinary everyday people with something in their hand that'd leave a mark on something. It could have been on the wall of a cave, on rough fabric, animal-skins, on crude paper or even the human body itself, anything in fact. These visual statements conveyed something for a variety of purposes, decoration, celebration or education and could even venture into more spiritual dimensions; surely one of the earliest forms of sophistication in the world of communication, something that was to far outlast its creators, a powerful medicine that could even make silk purses out of sows' ears and vice versa. It told stories which could just as easily be false as they could be true and, for this reason appealed to the vanities of those wielding power. Such a powerful taskmaster was the 'Church' who hi-jacked art most greedily in order for itself to be portrayed through rose-tinted spectacles and be made to look like something which it most certainly wasn't, and to have all its old stories to have pictures put to them, faces put to myths, credibility to make visible miracles of ancient fairytales. Powerful medicine indeed, giving artists new powers and a living as well, provided they did what their bigoted master told them, effectively stopping them from remaining artists in the purely creative sense.

Coming across Hogarth brought me back down to earth; here was an artist drawn apparently, more to what he loathed rather than to that which he loved, although not quite entirely. He seemed to be caught-up in the somewhat ambiguous web cast between Religion and Immorality, with an emphasis on Morality not exactly being divine province of the Church. I sensed a kind of antagonism in his work, a 'warts-and-all' attitude which could just as easily had been a determination on his part to show truth in a kind of over-compensatory way. He most certainly called a spade a spade and didn't appear to suffer fools gladly either, making imbeciles of the rich, giving cross-eyes and scabs to Lords and Ladies and a variety of poxes to their offspring and lots more besides. I took a kind of artistic nourishment from his 'Modern Moral Subjects' and I wandered thoughtfully down his 'Gin Street' and 'Beer Lane', noting how nothing, absolutely nothing had changed. His, 'O the Roast Beef of Old England' was really rather 'comic', almost like a one-act farce; too bad he preceded the camera and cinematography in particular. I felt that I wanted to recreate some of these pictures, not in paint but by using real, live people, all of them dressed exactly as they appeared in his paintings, bring them to life three dimensionally, an accurate re-enactment no less, right down to the last blemish.

In a morbid eloquence he had actually dared to touch on the vulgarities of opulence and of excesses in general and to contrast this with its moral opposite; using Religion like a jock-strap to support his rapturous ruptures. He intrigued me in that he perched himself finely balanced somewhere between Preacher and Joker, not quite wholly either but sufficient of both to be taken seriously as Moralist and Satirist. Whilst most other artists were steering clear of dictating what people should or shouldn't do, Hogarth just indulged in the whole circus-like cabaret of debauchery, conveniently finding some sort of spiritual cleansing through his moralistic condemnation of a morality which had festered into grossness. Beneath it all I could see that he had a wicked sense of humour as well as a burning radical streak running through him. A storyteller through and through and I had a sneaking suspicion that, deep down he was a bit of a 'lad', a trait which I'm sure he would never have admitted to.

February's relentless rain thawed puddles, ponds and pools again before March came marching in with strident gait rattling windows, doors, unfastening the gate. Spring was springing, bringing flowers to flower and birds to singing. Sometimes the wind was soft on my back, other times hard in my face altering my tack and slowing my pace; sending white clouds sailing and rabbled rooks like tea-leaves trailing way beyond the bending air. I wanted to fly, it wasn't fair.

The difference that Julie had made to my life was really quite remarkable. It was as though I had found a spiritual harbour, an island of repose, comforting simply by the knowledge of it dependably being there when we were both separated by our other commitments. The comfort of just knowing and trusting was worth its weight in bread and marge, even butter when we could get it, and kept us ravenously hungry for each other; eager for our two selves to become the best sandwich imaginable when we eventually met. 'Burto's' miserly 'romance' with Alison had by now exhausted me of any further tolerance, he plainly wasn't a 'lovey-touchy' sort of person, beyond that of bat and ball. Similarly, I had lost patience with 'Art' Tomkins idea of love being a 'knickers off first, then we'll talk business' kind of arrangement. Julie and I had miraculously got it right, we had somehow survived early calamity and weathered the inferno, even though we'd had to endure a melting of our wax when we had flown too close to the sun on the odd occasion. We had come to learn that 'love' was our servant and not necessarily our master, hard as this was to grasp, eventually coming to see it as being like as though one of us was trying to hold a pig while the other attempted to clip a viciously sharp ring into its nose; just as kissing was like tossing ten gallons of petrol on sparks to get the fire started in the hearth. We just had to get used to this 'love' thing, familiarize ourselves with our rearranged biological body behaviour and to respect where the dividing lines were being drawn, and to recognise the consequences of over-stepping the ultimate 'STOP' line. Smug as bugs in rugs as we may have given the impression of being, we secretly desired with chronically concealed desperation, to make babies by the pramful whenever we set eyes on each other; realisation of which made the rest of life a sobering, unfathomable maze of trepidation.

So many things had the unnerving habit of bringing me back down to earth with a rude bump. Observing people about their work doing seriously hard and extremely unpleasant jobs while I just went back and forth on a bus to sit drawing nudes in a warm studio, and then to drink tea and eat currant buns in a subsidised refectory, was one such wickedly honest mirror that I occasionally looked into.

Surely, what I was doing was frivolous by comparison, it was a charmed life I was living and I felt the need to compensate in some way or other. Working doubly hard was the nearest I could ever seem to get to achieving any such anaesthetizing that'd help me feel better about myself. The week I spent at Cannock Chase Colliery really rubbed salt into this troublesome wound when, a small group of us had been granted permission to go there and capture the atmosphere and to record in our sketchbooks the human involvement with this most dangerous of professions in the whole of industry. I stood gobsmacked in awe as I watched these men toiling like termites in a subterranean termite's nest of unimaginable fervent bedlam and hell.

After life's previous pleasantries of cosy allotments, the sweet birds-egg of my soul was obliterated and blasphemed to smithereens by what the Human Being had done, and was doing, to this beautiful planet as well as to the human inhabitants, if that's really what they were. Amongst my curses there were blessings also and I counted them over and over again, so very thankful to have been spared, before resettling embittered on my curses. I saw the grim, gaunt glare of despair in the wild-eyed miners as they emerged exhausted and disillusioned from the very bowels of the earth, their nightshift over for another night, or day, whatever it was, it didn't matter when all life was night. Sardines in a tin experienced luxury compared to these here of my own species, cramped together like black, tightly bundled sticks of charcoal in a wire cage which was pulled up and down, year in and year out through filthied black countless fathoms, by an ageing steel cable into which was interwoven the trust of every single miner. Strange to think of yellow canaries in cages whistling sweetly down there; why not subterranean allotments, floodlit lakes with lilies and carp; why not a sky all 'Sistine-Chappel-ed', with swallows and clouds, homing pigeons, rainbows and weathers painted on its ceiling ... why not?

Nature had no place here, even though hearts were beating and warm blood flowed in veins; cold water was blasting in the communal showers offering the miners an undignified splash in the most utility of ways to help them look presentable for a quick pint and a fag, a cheese sandwich and a shag before feeding the racing pigeons in their black and white striped loft down the garden, release them for a burst of freedom above the grim grey roofs, then retire to bed and sleep the pain of it all away. Then doing it all again and again and again until Captain Death, on a coal-black horse with a cart, came close on the heels of 'emphysema' and carted the corpse away; why them, not me? At this point, a foul-smelling breath steamed into my ear and a tired voice grunted, "Don't worry, Captain Death aint gonna forget you!"

I was born just a twitching, screaming skinful of questions, a whole debris of irritable curiosity which took an age for it to settle sufficiently for the vague, embryonic form of an artist to emerge. It was no different to the relative time it took for an oat to become flour to become bread to become toast to be eaten and then to become earth again. So unimaginably many things had been handed-down, passed on. Within my own body-vehicle, I was that major highway upon which 'Life', whatever it was, pressed relentlessly on with my own body-shell being expendable within the great encompassing eternity, just an old lorry going on driverless once it had delivered its one and only load.

I wouldn't be here at all had I not won a race; it was the only race I won in all my life. All I was, was just another 'hand-me-down' seed, more precisely, a 'sperm', a microscopic tadpole of pure energy, with a million facetted drawers marked 'Do not open until notified' written on them. There were countless others in the race, all plimsolled and in prettily numbered vests, all of them fit as fleas; geniuses there may have been, idiots too, who knows. When I won they all perished never to be known and never to know, just as swines ate aspiring acorns and denied oak trees their timbered expression, further murdering their dreams of forests. For this reason alone I knew in my deepest bones to respect my very being alive at all and to honour and treasure all learning upon this most wonderous planet, which time itself had somehow made my home or at least my lodging. To honour and bless also, all those others that were alongside me when the starting-gun fired and were the losers, the oats that fell by the wayside.

If Art had any meaning at all, it had to be fulfilling and worthwhile in a whole wealth of ways. It had to find resonance in all people in some way, just like everything in nature was complexly inter-related and resonating. If being an Artist was not a charmed existence, then it had to demonstrate this to those miners in particular and to make their enslaved lives richer and their minds wiser for it having touched. There had to be a reason, a 'functional' role for artists currently slap-happily doing their 'thing', while miners simply and ultimately gave their everything! Surely there had to be a 'levelling' component, an 'equalizer' of some sort, somehow, somewhere if we were not all to go fragmenting into meaningless oblivion. 'Balance' alone was not the answer because even I knew that a ton of gold weighed exactly the same as a ton of shit! Was it too much to wish for something that recognised the difference?

Something deep down told me that it was all to do with 'respect'; this triggered another thought in me; those unambiguously streetwise words in the Ten

Commandments, just two of them in particular; Love thy neighbour as thyself' and 'Do unto others as you would others do unto you'. That seemed to spell-out the word 'respect' to me, more fragmented and fragrant dust of a wise and gentle thinking, sadly lost of meaning and yet, still so compellingly rich as to be mouthed monotonously like a bad poem. Especially from these gold-encrusted palaces where bigoted clerics of the 'Holy Opulence' preach that which any fool can interpret as, 'Do as I say, not as I do!"

How sound and perfectly sensible were those Commandments, not just these two, but the other eight as well; I simply couldn't find fault with them, they were beautiful wherever they came from. I didn't think that it could have been here on Planet Earth, more likely to have been instructions given to a newly-arrived, technologically-inclined, intergalatical species, dumped here for some reason or other backalong; that very species 'Homo sapiens', orphans of a home unknown. 'Go forth and multiply' was another such particled fragment intended to preface the original 'Instruction Manual', parting words in fact, all of them, suggesting that Planet Earth was to be the 'New Home' and with 'God' being the astronaut who brought us all here. He promised he'd return one day just to make sure his instructions had been followed; suggesting that it'd be 'God-help-us' if we'd disobeyed; then he climbed back aboard his incredible 'Ark-of-the-heavens', and sped off.

## 9. 'Handel's Water Cistern and squandered Rainbows'

I meandered somewhat hauntedly amongst my friends, thinking plenty but finding it hard to even attempt to address my embryonic deeper thoughts, finding eventual comfort in the realisation that everyone had their private thoughts, and that they mostly kept them a secret, it saved the unpleasantness of being ridiculed and considered to be nuts. A greater comfort to emerge from the debris was that Art itself was possibly the only listening vehicle that could be entrusted with thoughts that'd turned feral and in need of a 'caring home'. I knew that 'Surrealist' Art was probably born of feral parentage and, in its apparent wildness, smashed fences, put cats amongst pigeons and generally waltzed wherever it so fancied. The very idea of what had been labeled 'Surrealism', really excited me because I knew that it could equally accommodate Writing and Music as well as the Visual Arts in all its forms; it could even combine them altogether, or just in part. The very concept, as well as the prospect, was thrilling.

As time went by, I struck up a friendship with another of my colleagues in the First Year group. I was rather taken by his most beautiful watercolour landscapes and I could tell that he had a similar 'countryman' dimension to that of my own. 'Dave Peel' was a most conservative and unassuming, steady sort of bloke, prematurely thinning on top and without sophistication of any sort. Just a very potato-ordinary, classical music sort of nobody-snob without a cause, that wouldn't say boo to a goose, a vegetarian from birth. He seemed to merge with anything that was browny, greeny, greyey, tweedy, ordinary; but he possessed a fine artist's eye and, in a John Constable sort of way, a depth of ease in his addressing of landscape. I really loved Constable, especially his oil sketches, which I considered to have more vitality than his more notable works, wonderful as they truly were. I could see 'ghosts' of the 'sketchy'

Constable in my mate's sketchbook work, apart from which, he could draw like an angel and wasn't afraid of hard work either. Artistically we were very good for each other and generated huge artistic appetites in excess of the College's Academic requirements. 'Functional' Illustrators we may have been but, deeper than that and in a most natural way, we were both Artists, with aspirations no different to those of the Impressionists that came before us.

I was duly invited to satisfy his parent's growing curiosity and to be introduced to them on a painting weekend over at their home in "Stone', a lyrically landscaped, semi-industrialised small town in a 'pottery-cum agricultural' sort of way. Classical music and vegetarianism were both strangers to me; I was afraid that I might die of a sudden introduction into the terrible duo. I never before knew that music had to be reverently listened to in total, no farting, no burping, silence; or that the food on the plate didn't, by necessity have to possess a bone sticking out of it in a 'Desperate Dan' sort of way. The sudden shock turned me grey! I had in fact come across the most wonderful little family of shopkeepers; they were God-like, pale-skinned, sweet and Christian in their small corner-shop beside the canal bridge. Mister Peel was crippled and wore special boots and used crutches to get about, while his wife was whiter than a sheet and none too well herself. Together they were the most divine, gentle and fun-loving couple imaginable; they took to me like as though I was their long lost son, and apart from the funereal silence when classical music was being played, we were all in stitches over the simplest of things. On one such occasion, on returning from the lavatory, for a bit of devilment I brought up the subject of 'Handel', stating that George Frederick himself was a bit on the 'avant-garde' side, even to the point of being 'obscure'. This sudden unexpected and totally out of character 'knowledgeable' statement brought about an immediate silence and a straightening of faces. "I thought that you were new to music, Jim," Mister Peel commented with aroused interest, going on to ask "... and what makes you think that about our beloved Mister Handel?" "Oh, just some of the titles that he gave to his 'Water' music." "Like what?" he hungrily asked, feeling a degree upstaged by this village ignoramous, and I stood up before him and beckoned for him to get to his crippled feet and to follow me, which he most readily did. "There! D'you see that there ... I bet you didn't know that he wrote 'Do Not Lift'". The handwritten sign above the cistern said, 'Do not lift by handle. "Somebody's spelt Handel wrong," I said and he looked at me, then burst forth into a huge fit of laughter, bringing the others eagerly rushing to share in the fun.

It was like this the whole time I was there and I even survived Beethoven's Sixth, Brahm's First and Fourth as well as a Bruckner, which I was insistently told I would find equally mouth-watering. This 'Classical' music thing was certainly a new experience, one which imposed disciplines upon me hitherto unknown, reckoning it similar to taking medicine rather than swigging the juice of 'scrumped' apples; no time had ever weighed or dragged so heavily. The sun broke through when Dave suggested that we played tennis, promising to teach me the rudiments, suffice for us to have a good knock-about. I seized on this, my chance to sneakily catch-up on Julie back in Lichfield. I liked the idea! I borrowed Dave's sister's racket and he took me to the town hospital, where he had permission to use their courts. We had the most action-packed learning session; playing it was so very different from watching it and we had a whale of a time, it was great!

Back at the meal table, pink sliced stuff, which I was told was 'Nuttoline', looked a bit like 'Spam' to me but was made of nuts, not 'spammy' things left over from where a pig had been; it looked alright though and it smelled pretty good, even though it wasn't pig. The family ate sparingly, as though food itself was pestilential produce and an enemy to the human body. Wow! That stuff tasted real good to me and I wanted a whole piled plate of it but, all I got was one thin slice, two small halves of potato, a discrete green excretion of cabbage and a spoonful of gravy. I could have eaten a bloody horse, a cartload of spuds, cabbages and swedes and still have made room for a hundredweight of apple tart and custard!

Why was it? I pondered over these most inexplicable of human bodily priorities, why was the comforting essential of food itself not higher on their list of things; nothing was more Godly than food; why, why was it? Beethoven's Pastoral Symphony was but a watercolour landscape and he, by the looks of him on the record sleeve; I'd say a man of about ten to fifteen miles of intestines and I bet he ate far more enthusiastically than a swine. His music was surprisingly impressive too, in fact it was this immersion in the marvellous Pastoral Symphony that changed my life forever. I never knew that I was yet so empty a vessel; my wild village ways were more like swallows in a shed, all excited about a simple browny grey shitted rafter or beam on which to pile mud and to plan transnavigation of the globe. "Just keep listening to it and you'll get to like it," Dave kept insisting upon my feral state, not so blind to have missed the fact that I was already hooked, not only that, but was ravenous about the possibility of actually writing music. I already had a mouth-organ, musical sketchbook-like thing in my pocket. I used to think that, 'Writers' were 'other' people, never knowing that I was a writer myself, so, so why not the same with music?

It was a Sunday, all bluebelled and decadent as we strode the heavily pollened grasses with our easels on our backs and the burning sun in our hearts. A jewel caught my eye, a Jay's feather in the grass. I stooped and picked it up and held it before my astounded eyes; what language was this that a Jay possessed, and to convey what? It was fine and delicate, dominated by close bars of electric blue; black into blue fading to white, fine bars so dominant upon the fragile feather. Such an extravagant outburst, so precise and so very beautiful; surely nothing of such intricacy could be a mere accident of nature, that's the way it was intended to be for some reason beyond my understanding and I just shook my head; what kind of thing was this that Jays had and which we hadn't a clue about?

Looking at myself, all I was, was a pink lump with dark brown hair on my head and greyish blue eyes, any other colours or patterns I may have shown had been purchased. A Crow was black as were Rooks and Ravens, the Chough was black too but had red beak and legs. Hooded Crows had dull pink about their shoulders and belly, the rest was black; Jackdaws were black but had pale grey heads and even paler cold grey eyes. Jolly Jack Magpie, with his iridescent quill of a tail, bright white belly and shoulders and with white also on the wing tips. All of them functional in some explicable way, but the Jay was so completely different to the rest of the Crows, boasting both black and white as well as pink, brown and blue. I scratched my head searching for a reason, without one, all I could do was to consider the idea that perhaps Nature was not all to do with 'function', but accommodated also a highly frivolous side with colour and pattern being there for the sheer hell of it! I wasn't entirely convinced.

We followed a brook and came to where there was a steeply wooded bank with mature trees towering over the bluest of Bluebells. Here we set up our easels and started painting quite some distance from each other, it was so unbelievable marvellous that it felt really Holy, a truly Golden moment! The sun-goldened meadow beneath the cool, dappled shade of the wood was divine; Jays squawked and tinier birds whimpered amongst the leaves. In silent interludes, the tinkle of the brook water could just be heard like frail glass bells and I could hear too, the happy babble of laughter as two girls in flowing frocks were playing, chasing each other through the tall meadow grass. I think they may have followed us and they settled beside the brook beneath us, tickling each other with plucked grasses and giggling in sweet, fluttering fits. They could see us and we could see them and that's the way it stayed. It was all so abundantly beautiful, so frivolous, yet functional too if our painting a landscape had any purpose beyond frivolity. I felt that it had without properly understanding the reason why; I was being driven as well as seduced by a strange forceful desire to be gorging on this apparently 'essential' activity in my life. Dave had similar forces pushing him against all other tides and I knew that, whatever it was, it most certainly wasn't frivolous.

The girls suddenly shrieked as a kingfisher flashed beneath their noses, I heard it faintly 'piping' as it vanished; all that remained of it in my mind was that 'impossible-to-create' blue. Dave stirred and gave me a gasping sort of look, signifying that he was just as speechless as I was myself. Why the heck should a thing that plunges into water to catch fish and then eats them head first on a branch, nests down on sludgy, smelly old black holes in a bank, why should such a bird require flamboyant colouration, so excessively gaudy? It went against any functional consideration within the precise rule of existence known to my own bewildered awareness. The reasons were there but, vital links were missing, hence the mystery. The garment of Life had holes at its elbows as well as moth-holes generously littered down through the ages. Strange to think that a marble-white egg down a fish-stinking blind hole in the dankest, gloomiest of sludgy banks, could hatch into being the most sparkling, dazzling rainbow. I looked across at Dave and could hardly see him at all, so carefully drab was his colouration; he could have been a Nightjar or a Woodcock, these being camouflaged, Dave being just drab. For all that, he wasn't afraid of using colour on a canvas, but he did most certainly avoid it where he, the gangling, pink-skinned 'stick-insect' of a person was concerned.

I loved colour but I had no money so as to indulge myself in it, just enough for two daily teas and a bun. What clothes I wore I had no choice in, so I most readily stuffed any flower that availed itself into my top pocket and I put feathers in my hair and in my hat somewhat rebelliously, although I rather liked the flamboyance and the vociferous provocation that it aroused. It was so very apparent how 'colour' was regarded; it could divide entire families and communities and, given a chance, could even trigger-off the next World War! Similarly in Art, colour was all threatening upon an ordinariness as was a glandular plague that induced garbled stuttering and fluorescent vomiting, even on a Sunday. Back in the war, the cry of the day was 'Walls Have Ears' now it was, 'Beware of Colour'! Painters who painted realistic landscapes, still-lifes and portraits, didn't provoke the kind of hostility that a freer user of colour was dragging out from the dark ages.

# 10 'If Sunflowers weren't so big, they'd be Dandelions!'

Dave and I hitch-hiked to London to a Van Gogh Exhibition and to saturate ourselves in whatever the London Galleries had to offer; it all simply blew my mind! Vincent Van Gogh was surely the very greatest artist of all time! Nothing contrived or pressured by the dictates of Religion as so much dreary old stuff had for far too long dominated what had somewhat piously and snobbishly termed as 'Art'. Van Gogh was, and I'm sure will always be, the very 'breath' of God; the very painter of God, 'God' being all things made beautiful and with colour being shown to hold a wealth of functions beyond the simple joy of its very self. His makings of colours beautiful before the eye and mind being function suffice in itself. To make things beautiful was surely what 'God' intended. For me, 'Nature' was 'God and vice versa; this made sense beyond all nonsense and demonstrated to me that it was 'Nature' that we needed, not 'Religion'; 'Art' being the description of heaven itself.

Dave and I were like resurrected corpses, just staggering there amongst throngs of the 'initiated'; we were both already exhausted, having not seen more than half. I looked at him, drained myself of energy suffice to cart me through the remaining day, unless we could find an island upon which to reflect, exchange ideas before plunging back in and to risk drowning. Eventually we found such a bench and concluded that what Van Gogh was doing, was speaking to us very nakedly, so cleanly and purely; no Artistic bull-shit as was so often the case, in fact we were drawn to conclude that there was nothing, absolutely nothing that spoke to us in this most passionately humble sort of way. It was hard to think of him as just being an ordinary person doing, what for him was a simple 'ordinary' thing which he felt overwhelmingly compelled to preach and paint, just like breathing. We were both well and truly overwhelmed, his Portraits and Self-Portraits for me being the most powerfully beautiful images I'd ever known, Samuel Palmer apart. For Dave, the magnificent wealth of Landscapes still had the heat of the sun and smell of the organic air and a myriad of flower-scents radiating from them. We just wallowed ourselves weak under this most humble of glorious celebrations, even though the one who had popped the cork was laying dead and buried.

We looked at a few 'Gauguins', mouthwatering and staggering as they were, they remained silent upon the canvas where they glowed. "Just another bloody genius!" I groaned, realising just how vast this Heaven of Art really was, and with Samuel Palmer's self-portrait in crayon still remaining for me the greatest individual work of art of them all; of this I was in no doubt whatsoever. I'd drawn myself a few times for some strange need beyond vanity; I learned all too soon what a demanding subject this was, seeing one's own face in a mirror and trying to draw it, any ideas of vanity went clean out of the window!

When Artists didn't have to wrestle with the living, writhing beast of Art, they made 'masks' of it, symbolism of one sort of another designed to pacify the viewer after its marginally compromised deliverance from the artist. Peaceful and spiritually presumptuous as Gauguin's beautiful images were, mesmerism was finite and 'masks' remained 'masks' in the screaming, forever screaming air that seemed to blast out from wherever Vincent Van Gogh had placed his hand. That for me, was the difference between the pair of them in purely artistic terms. Socially they were worlds apart, a country bumpkin on one side and a streetwise whore of a man on the other; bloody hell, there were hopes for the likes of me yet!

London Galleries were such a treasury in themselves, especially if one had a totally virgin year unhindered by other demands and to offer oneself all such splendours; a hitch-hiked couple of days was really no more than a meagre itch upon the surface of its vast potential. I just glowed and glowed, smiled and smiled on realising that I was part of it, miniscule as that was, I was still part of it! The question was, remembering the question, the answer was a beast who's temper could change at any given point, and to have me running away rather than opening my arms to embrace it; teaching me to be forever wary of Answers, and to trust only in Questions, perpetual questions.

From the quiet stillness of the village, faraway London seemed more like another country, a whole new noisy civilisation and not just another city like tiny Lichfield was, this was also a city with its own individual Jackdaws, two railway stations, a 'Woolworths' and a 'George Masons'. London was a complex, catastrophic collision of towns and villages that'd been crumpled up so tightly against each other that they had lost their sense of being individual islands in sensible indefinable isolation from each other. It was a most fascinating jumble all the same, being both abundantly palatial and squalidly slumlike; decadent opulence and pitiful poverty side by side, just like a Hogarth painting in fact, with a handsome Cathedral there to brand it a city. The very centre of commerce and expectations of a million sorts. Anarchists danced with Alchemists, one trying to change the world with confused wet dreams, the other, simply pregnant with greed and here trying to have its baby with all the world watching. 'Legally' plundered Gold was already here, deeply vaulted, billions of tons of the stuff, with memory by now finding it 'Christianly' forgiving to turn a blind eye to the gluttonous, murderous Colonisation that'd bullied this 'pecking-order' upon other humanities. Why, for goodness sake, this Gold was so blessedly, spotlessly clean by now that you could eat the stuff!

Pompous statues were everywhere, although I didn't see any in memory of the countless millions of slaves that Colonialism had displaced and murdered, or any of those that'd fallen trying to fight off this invading monster with shiny-buttoned uniforms and gunpowder to feed its despicable greed. It was a weird sort of 'Love thy Neighbour'; Caesar had done it, so had Hitler, but Colonialism was different, apparently ... 'Setting people Free', that's what they called it ... well, they would, wouldn't they!

The more I thought on the subject, the more I came to the conclusion that, this 'settler' here upon the planet, actually revelled in war, was excited by plundering and killing, a behavioural fact borne-out all through recorded history. He, 'Homo sapiens', had always been a total murderer, a plunderer throughout, right through to this very moment of time. 'Greed' being the original sin, the Mother of all sins, and the most likely reason for our having been sent here in the first place. Of course, as with all families of things, there were bound to be occasional contradictory throw-backs to the purer species. Hence the likes of Jesus Christ, Mahatma Gandhi and others who gave their lives in absolute, total dedication to teaching the ways of Love in a world where 'Order' always smelled suspiciously of corruption; any resultant anarchic disorder and revolution never coming anywhere near to providing the long-term, long lasting answer. Whatever the species did, it was bound by its very nature to be 'alien' upon the adopted new planet, just as virtually the entire of 'Man's' grossly ignorant activity upon it has so proven.

People were, in all promise and capability, the most miraculously wonderful species in existence, having the potential to learn and go on learning; to allow new questions to replace old answers that were born of habit and not of logic, prejudice and not enlightenment. 'Must try harder' is easily distracted and tends to be disruptive in 'class!' Where and why, I wonder, did I hear that before?

Dandelions knew only one word ... 'Yellow'! They spoke it firstly in a whisper and then broke into full rejoicing. They gave-off bitter milk when anyone snapped their tubular stems and girls gathered their leaves for pet rabbits. Some people roasted their roots to grind into 'coffee', others took their golden yellow petals and made wine that'd grace God's own table. They made no sound at all, even their glowing silence was less by light-years than a whisper. I loved watching the transition from flower to seed, the hushed quiet time when the golden petals became enshrouded in the mother-plant's green-speared embrace, followed by a mysterious suspension of time before the caressing green fingers broke slowly open to the light and the most intricate of heavenly clocks, softly and silently opened into a most wonderful, fluffy, cushioned globe which, from first-light, flirted with the breezes, tempting one to be so bold as to blow it off its feet and carry it away to somewhere wild and wicked. Nothing could be more romantic and yet still remain to most people, a bloody weed!

Just another worthless thing, along with the Skylarks. A wealth unknown, a treasure beyond measure ... and it was all free and making me feel, in a somewhat contradictory sort of way, that I was an equal, quite natural part of it. At least I was in these humbled transient moments before my own limbs were obliged to clamber back into the human suit of armour and join a billion, trillion others in pursuit of the alien nightmare dream of another kind of Gold. In all truth, I really couldn't see myself ever fitting into this, or any other suit of armour. I saw myself belonging more to the world of Larks and Dandelions, Butterflies and all those countless other 'nothings' which together constituted magnificence; any thought that lingered in me that I could somehow break free of the surging tide which I was so unavoidably caught-up in, were less realistic than my becoming a tramp. A tramp was really the only alternative to just remaining a number in this lemming-plague of aspiring alchemists.

In the meantime I had little choice. I was here, locked in Art while my whiskers gradually turned to wire and the 'man' in me ripened more rapidly now with all the fuel that Julie was stoking my furnace with, making me realise that it'd be rather more than a miracle if we were to remain safe from the threat of spontaneous combustion. God was all that we had protecting us from this cataclysmic transition from gold-flamed dandelion to feathery seeds flying under white umbrellas across the expansive sky, where the sun's own spontaneous combustion burned so brightly that it obliged even the stars to close their eyes and turn away.

Art students waited in hopeful anticipation at the estuary of their hands, anxious to see what the river that flowed down from their hungry minds might bring. Some like Grizzly Bears, others like teddy bears waiting for the silvery spawning Salmon but, most catching tiddlers, other times a cold. On very rare occasions a monster would wriggle out, too slippery and awkward by far to keep hold of but, eventually they managed a token something before the river dried up again, leaving them to dream about the one that got away and having to gnaw starvingly over their specimen tiddlers and make them last until the minds sparkling water accumulated and spilled down once more, heralding another time of spawning.

These college days were perplexing almost to the point of being surreal, but in a downright predictable sort of way. Although I wasn't surprised, I hadn't expected the roasting I got from Dad after he'd received a letter from the Principal informing him of my unscheduled trip to London to see the Van Gogh Exhibition. Lucky for me, a lot of other Dad's received similar threatening letters, not that that made any difference to Dad, who wasted no time in making me realise that my life was distinctly not my own. I needed the Army to hurry up and take me, give me a taste of discipline and make a 'man' of me, as it was all too soon going to do no matter how many times I broke the rules in addressing my own ripening priorities.

There was no turning back. What's done was done, what's gone was gone, what was going to be, would be and it would more than likely be what someone else dictated and not what I wanted or needed in any way, shape or form for myself. This realisation alone determined me even more ferociously to steal whatever precious moments I possibly could and to gorge myself full to bursting on their most fortuitous golden offerings, meagre crumbs as they may so be. Sometimes rebels were fools, other times heroes and I was on a perpetual collision course with something or other because I would not tolerate wasted, idle moments upon my mind, life was too short for that. Even a rebel could die and, from what I had gathered, that ultimate state lasted a bloody long time!

I cast my mind back over the years and recalled in mystified disbelief how laborious an age it took for childhood to pass. By contrast, what I'd noticed to be happening now was the alarming gathering of pace that'd got into life's lengthening legs, revealing new contradictions whereby the minutes, hours and occasional days, were leaden and hardly seemed to move at all, while at the same time, the months and years just kept coming on too fast and getting faster. There was never enough 'something' and increasingly too much 'everything'. As options dispersed outwards, life's previous little delectables became de-valued and scattered even further apart, making rarities of what once were common, everyday niceties. In fact such treasures were rapidly crumbling to dust with the danger being that dust particles were far too numerous to have any worth, thus becoming completely meaningless. I desperately fought to re-establish a new structure of priorities with Julie being pinnacled on top, just as she was fighting to keep me up there on top of her ever-dispersing list, but the 'system' was now possessing our minds and bodies and was in total disregard of this most crucial and essentially ideal period in our early growth towards approaching fruition. Filling our aching minds to bursting with a myriad of things tottering at the point of obsolescence as well as loads of other dreary stuff that was already extinct. Nobody in this heirachy of 'Chiefs' was ever going to place any value at all in two young 'Indians' wanting to be in each others arms, isolating 'Love' into becoming one of the treasures we'd have to steal, along with priceless exhibitions that Council Educational Grants had no way or intention of accommodating.

Cycling was another such weekend treasure to prioritise; there was something about the 'wheel' that was beyond fundamental beauty. Cycles ... circles; bicycles ... two circles; no-one could ever have invented the wheel because cycles and circles always went in cycles, no beginning, no end. The 'wheel' was forever and I treasured it and couldn't wait to be back on the saddle with the wind in my hair and flies in my eyes, listening to those singing, sighing tyres responding to my exuberant energy. It was far more than doubly good when 'Art' Tomkins was there alongside me, ours really was a 'brotherhood'; nothing like the pre-Raphaelite's 'Brotherhood', ours was genuine, not an elite 'club', ours glowed in our veins and was shared in our pains. Its beauty lay in the fact that it had absolutely nothing to do with intellect and was a totally separate expression of body-energy only, nothing else at all and was so essentially refreshing, relaxing and blissfully exhausting. Nothing was ever so miraculously, glowingly soothing than that inexplicable state of utter exhaustion that settled just after we had pedalled ourselves legless to the point of death; it was wonderful and gave the brain a well earned rest away from it all, its what weekends were for.

So many other priorities were being crammed into these inadequate two days, one of which belonged to God, that long established method of contraception which Julie and I had chosen, otherwise known as 'abstention'; it was foolproof. Proof against fools? That didn't sound right ... we were not fools ... were we? I pondered awhile. This was the time of fools, a time when worn-out, miserable old carcasses unzipped their leathered skin and became fools for the odd hour now that enslavement had turned its back in order to sneak off somewhere secret to count its miserable money. Such an hour-long fools paradise was the 'Common'; Granny, Grandad, Uncle Les and Uncle George; fools for an hour, all of them. I even saw Dad smile during this hour, in fact everyone smiled for an hour and the whole world became light, bright and shining. To lose this most precious priority was more than my life was worth and I would fit it in even if it killed me. As for my cycle racing, this was no problem because the time-trials were always early Sunday morning affairs and were over and done with by the time the rest of the world was up and smiling, with luck providing me with a fool's chance later of an amorous encounter somewhere amongst the dappled leaves with Julie ... and 'God' of course.

I could never imagine Vincent Van Gogh, head down, arse in air, doing ninety on a racing bike, leaving a trail of sweat on the road and having to keep button-sized priorities sewn about his garment to remind him of a thousand things not to forget. Come to think, I couldn't conceive of any great artist doing anything other than painting and it occurred to me that, when someone else was paying, one could let 'Art' be the only priority. Benefactors didn't grow on trees like mistletoe did, otherwise they'd be available on the National Health. For Van Gogh, it was his brother who did this out of love and belief, while the Church did it entirely for its bigoted self. Far more widespread was the notion that artists needed to starve in order for them to become, or remain, artists of any worth. I wasn't entirely convinced by this prognostication, just as I could not recognise any possible advantage to be gained by dying of starvation either. Being born rich may have been the answer, or probably better still for everyone to be born equally poor and for their flowering to be the main distinguishing measure of worth; yes, that sounded more like the answer I was looking for.

## 11. 'Alchemic Dreams in new-fangled Polythene'

I was amongst a plankton of dreams of wheels and fortunes, clocks flying as feathers and a world at-smile for a Sunday hour, while the colour yellow remained but a golden whispered word breathed long before astronaut Noah sailed the stars and made orphans of us all in a world of milk, honey and weapon-grade Plutonium. Amongst all this, the term 'Pre-Raphaelite' had become a hyphenated swear-word to be associated with the very worst in Art; a state of thinking that was hard to figure out, let alone agree with. Holman Hunt had always inspired me, so too had Maddox-Brown on more than the odd occasion; Millais simply blew my mind with his attention to detail while, William Morris I considered to be a very fine Botanical Illustrator-cum-designer. His paintings however were as those of Rossetti and Bryne-Jones, 'preciously' subjective and overly sentimental and dream-worldly. I think it was the 'Brotherhood' thing that got up the students' noses, this brand of elitism, so self-conscious, spiritually pretentious and incestuously opiumed with an 'Avalon' 'Hiawatha'-sentimentality. A bit like religion where recruited armies of prostitutes worked flat out in servicing Cardinals whose verbal diarrhoea on debauchery remained incurable; so foreign and so far removed from the teachings of Jesus Christ, which they swore to be their guiding light.

I found myself somewhat befuddled by this ages-old state of affairs; was 'Honesty' so necessary a thing or was I just being naive and wishful in my thinking? Any such doubts were abruptly short-lived and readily turned to anger in me as I felt shame for permitting the question to have entered in the first place. 'Honesty' was 'Integrity' no less, it was the most precious thing we possessed; 'Truth' was an entity, not multi-divisible, with each fragmented version of it pretending to be as wholesome as the next, depending on the nature of one's greed. I expected honesty in Art too, just as I expected it in everyday life; I'd already found it in abundance in the work of Van Gogh, Samuel Palmer too, in fact it existed fairly generously in Art. The exceptions being where

Religion and other forms of tyranny had kidnapped and made a prisoner of it, turning it into a weapon of Politics. In Creative Art, the multi-variable interpretation of ideas was so very different, so completely opposite to the deceitful laceration and distortion of truth as exemplified in the Commercial world where Politics and Big Business scratched each other's backs, with Religion being their cosy pet cat that killed tiny birds, smugly grinning in the background.

What I found so amusing over the way these fine-art students screwed their noses up at the mention of 'Pre-Raphaelite', was that they'd only just learned to ride their first bikes, especially where painting was concerned and were in the illusionary paradise-zone of exploring more ambiguously abstract possibilities of paint and colour in all its 'Dada-ist', 'anything-goes' attraction. It was a new toy which had elevated them way up into the stratosphere and was providing them with a clouded place to hide, a place from where they could peer down and slag-off the 'Pre-Raphaelites, largely because they could paint in the most enviable way which they couldn't. In a way which all parents and even grandparents absolutely loved and had taken their romantic, old sentimental hearts. For a fine-art student in particular, if there was one single thing that was as a red rag to a bull, it was to have parents actually approving of and, worse still, 'liking' all the outrageous new things that they were now doing. Where 'Art' was concerned, parents were not there to be pleased, far better for them to be induced into puking and driven cross-eyed and stiff with shock or disgust, preferably both; anything was better than having them actually like what they were now doing in the name of 'Art'.

There was so much in past art which had terrified me. It stood there like a statued army with its Gods and demons, and with gaggles of flabby little cherubs and half-swan angels, impossible winged anthropomorphous products of power-mad minds; even plucked geese were more capable of flight than these were. All this pie-in-the-sky pretend-anatomy spoke more of authority than it did art, a prescribed 'reality' which was beyond anything remotely real, largely because it had fallen into the hands of that pious order which gripped the reins of power and needed something so intimidatingly humbling, as to hypnotize all who stood in awe, making them believe that this could only be the work of the 'Almighty'.

To my vulnerably tender, yet rebellious mind, the Renaissance had been that very age of Power; more of a military campaign on behalf of a Religious War-Lord, one that stole the best Artists from their Art and made professional soldiers of them instead. So spectacular was it that it immediately captivated the Art world and continued to do so for centuries to come and with the same religious driving force there providing endless, albeit repetitious subject matter and hypnotic enslavement over a far, far wider canvas.

While the meek were inheriting the earth, dog shit an' all, and usually about a miserly measured egg-cupful each, the Roman Catholic Church were inheriting the entire wealth and the power which that represented. Nobody had told the people that they only ate ostrich eggs in the Vatican, where they were using their artists just as an Advertising Agency uses them ... to promote and sell Product; to glamourise it and exaggerate it out of all proportion, if that failed to whet the appetite, they'd frighten the living daylights out of you instead and they had the very 'big-guns' to do it. Having a Botticelli or a Michelangelo in your arsenal was the equivalent of having a Mediterranean half full of battleships all fully armed and bristling for a fight. Thrown into the arena, a highly gifted nature-boy by the name of Leonardo. An eccentric who found sanctuary in vegetarianism to avoid slipping into cannibalism on account of his passion, bordering on obsession, for carving human bodies into pieces and then drawing all the separate morbid bits in unbelievable detail and meticulous accuracy. Add this weapon to your list and you'd got an anatomical powerhouse that'd frighten the balls off even the devil!

Whilst this Leonardo-chap could draw equally well with both hands ... bloody showoff, most of the paintings he did either cracked and flaked to fragments, or they simply refused to dry and, after a few dreary months just dribbled from the walls. His arrogance being such that all such other 'mundane' expertise on the Painting 'Craft' and the science and nature of paint were of no importance and were beneath him. 'Creation' for him was the 'Germ', not the whole bloody 'catastrophe'! Thus, his tolerance levels were practically nil and he established a reputation for never having the discipline necessary to see a job through to its completion ... 'Leonardo produces good ideas but lets himself down by never finishing them. Must try harder!"

Nothing seemed to worry or hurry him, he was a fanciful, opinionated drifter of a man, totally intoxicated by the Science of Nature and in discovering its secrets. He was the sort of man that would rather invent an impossible machine that would fly him to 'Heaven' to prove its existence, rather than to have to take somebody else's word for it. He was incorrigible; a stimulating, outrageously crazy character about the place and he seemed to be a pretty alright sort of bloke to me. Especially his fascination with Nature and his insatiable appetite for questions rather than dreary, unproven stock answers. Having said all that, I can't say I'd have much liked being invited round to his place for a glass of red wine only to find him up beyond his elbows, enthusiastically dissecting his Granny on the dinner table!

These Vatican-owned artists were really foisting a glorified, over-perfect anatomy on a people in a 'super-race' kind of ideology, being driven by the gross aspirations of their theological 'advisors' within the Vatican, who were hell-bent on there being plenty of tits and willies and balls by the barrow-load. With Amazonian Madonnas whose unkissed lips wouldn't even melt butter and who, to avoid scandal, immaculately conceived. Powerful medicine ... need Indians, not Chiefs ... too many Chiefs, makes too many Bads! Added to this there were poncey male models, hairdressers on steroids, flashing their bits and rippling their muscles long before the first blood-red Ferrari came off the production line.

This wasn't the 'real' world here so lavishly being promoted; mere mortals down on the ground didn't look anything like that. They were limping with rickets, coughing phlegm, scratching unhealing scabs from rabid dog bites; had bloody bits missing through wars and were all twisted up with arthritis, as they migrated this way and that with their eggcup inheritance, trying to dodge all the bloodthirsty battles that continuously flared-up in power struggles.

Such emphasis on 'Perfect' anatomy had more to do with Privilege than it did with Holiness, it was Politics more than it was Art; it was Religion, the most powerful weapon of war, even to this day. With its mollycoddled, all-powerful Popes enthroned like severed pigs' heads in party hats on glittering heaps of bejewelled robes, never one, not even in the briefest unguarded moment resembling those muscly 'hairdressers' depicted in paint and marble. Not only that, neither Popes or Cardinals ever seemed to move at more than a snail's pace sort of shuffle, as though they'd had their muscles removed so's to make room for more golden bracelets and other glittery adornments!

The whole weighty lot of it frightened me and I was glad that it was history now; even the book on the subject that I was browsing through weighed a ton, but it did contain two most delightful exceptions by Botticelli, 'Primavera' and 'Birth of Venus'. Such fine, utterly Light, Airy and Joyful masterpieces, probably the very sperms that fertilized the Pre'Raphaelite egg; these, along with the untouchable genius of our very own Bill Blake. 'William' as he was more properly known, was a man of God and, to my mind, an artist of far greater creativity and imagination than anything to come out of the Renaissance, due entirely to him remaining true as an artist and never allowing himself to be owned and turned into a performing puppet by the Church.

The Renaissance was, in all honesty, the hardest of acts to follow, just as Julius Caesar's football team was, having earlier kicked the rest of civilisation clean off the pitch; another bloody show-off, a bit like Mussolini, dangerous midgets the pair of them, with aspirations of Gianthood. No matter what the Italians did, they did it with great gusto and style and they always made sure that their womenfolk never got in on the act; they kept them in bondage away out of the limelight, either in bed or in the kitchen. Everything they ever did was similarly pompous and dictatorial, narcissistic and prima donna; I blame those dodgy-looking mushrooms that they threw into their stews. I took comfort from knowing that there'd always be those who claimed to have succeeded in threading a fully grown camel through the eye of a needle, just as being an artist bore no resemblance whatsoever to 'knowing about Art'; normal life wouldn't be 'normal' otherwise.

My first Diploma year had slipped by and another high summer was tall about the sky and sprawled abroad through oceaned, ochre acres, whetting my appetite anew. I needed just one precious packet of it in which to hide and find some simple divinity away from art. Some priceless breathing space that I could really call my own, some moments where history had not yet trodden and left its ghosts to haunt and roam. Wishful thinking; history had not simply trodden everywhere, history WAS everywhere, everywhere and everything besides, there was no escaping it. The Bible had got it wrong when it said that the Meek would inherit the Earth; it should have said the Dead would, not the Meek! There wasn't a handkerchief-sized patch of it as far as the eye could see that wasn't already owned by some wealthy landowner or another and, for me to taste any craved-for morsel of it would require me to trespass or to steal, become a vagrant and a thief, so cluttered had the pathway to myself become. I couldn't rightly see how far I had travelled from myself since I last tried to discover who, what and where I was.

Like history, things just didn't go away because you thought of something else instead; there wasn't in fact, any hiding place from anything. For it to suddenly become night just by simply closing one's eyes would take a miracle no less, and miracles didn't exist. All that a 'miracle' was, was a name given to something beyond explanation or understanding, both were there somewhere, they just needed finding that's all. To be ignorant was to be surrounded by miracles, a sad fact which explained so much madness; to be kept in ignorance was to be held captive, appeased by the 'goody' lollipops of miracles and I guessed that most of us had been visited by the 'tooth-fairy' as a result of sucking on those lollipops.

I was three years on from being a boy and I was two years away from being a soldier; for me to change this sorry scene of things entire and to shatter it to bits, would take rather more than a miracle of my own. It was the only 'real' thing I had to believe in as I struggled to release myself from my straightjacketed garment of the illusionary thing called 'Art' and to finding a place where I could write my name somewhere out of sight of the wind and away from the squinting eye of history. I didn't want it greedily like something I could keep, I simply wanted to touch it and taste its briefest sweetness and ... I knew of such a place, all snugly buried away in a grassy glade back in the history of my decomposing childhood memory.

Julie and I had planned a cycling day in the country, to be crowned by a picnic which she had lovingly prepared. It was the ideal opportunity for me to introduce her to my family at long last, despite Mom's predictable response to the suggestion when I had earlier raised it. "You're not bringing any wenches here m'lord, so there!" It had always been the same with both Mom and Dad and neither my sister Fay or I, could ever bring our friends home because we weren't considered to be good enough. Nothing was ever going to change them, so deeply rooted were its origins, so I'd just have to go ahead and do it regardless, it was the only way.

On her bike, basket of food-treasure piled at the front, Julie looked wonderful, with the soft warm brush of air trailing out her golden hair behind her; I'd never cycled this slow before, it was all like a slow-motion dream. The wondrous lanes were ours, all shimmering in a secret paradise of jewelled, lavishly upholstered verges, galaxies of seeds crowned on towering pea-shooter stems in realms of twenty-two carat Goldfinches, Yellowhammers and Reedbuntings, ecstatic Sparrow-flocks from farms and a heaven with Larks embroidered to the sunbeams, singing their dear hearts out just for us. There were yawning pale cauliflower ghost clouds almost invisible and so very, very far away that they never seemed to move. I had found that most precious place whereupon to write my name, it was here all around us in the lanes, as we both turned giddy with love; seeing our slow wheels whirling in their aimless exuberance being taken along by our steadily pedalling legs, pausing for kisses and smiling with joy raging throughout our hearts.

Before pressing on to my remembered grassy glade, I took Julie into my village to give Mom her unexpected shock. I really wanted them to meet each other, knowing that it'd all work out fine and would stop Mom from worrying about who I was associating with. It all worked out just as I knew it would, with Mom going into her customary fluster of apologising for every imaginable thing, never once stopping smiling and blushing, never once taking her sparkling eyes off Julie; they absolutely loved each other on impact. Even Dad got into the act, blushing furiously as he gave Julie a flabby handshake which betrayed his lowly esteem of life's pecking-order as he suggested that he'd oil her chain and hubs and carry out any necessary adjustments to her brakes. Mom then rushed off into the 'front room', the 'best' room, to fetch the 'best' china cups and saucers from the always locked cabinet. They had been kept there for years in readiness for a visit from the Royal Family popping in to see how Dad might be fixed for painting the palace ... either that or something similar. With Mom now in the kitchen mashing a pot of tea and Dad outside tinkering with Julie's bike, I looked at Julie and shook my head in helpless resignation. There was absolutely nothing I could do to dissuade them from showing their welcome in the only way they knew how, and we both laughed and hugged each other; glad and happy the pair of us.

As we were drinking our tea, I suggested to Dad that he fetch some of his drawings and watercolours for Julie to see, but he shrugged off the idea and muttered ... "They aint no good ... it's Jim that's the artist in this house!" I shook my head in despair and left the room, returning a few moments later with my arms full of rolled-up pictures that were cobwebbed from long abandonment; Dad promptly left the room, unable to conceal his embarrassment. Very carefully I unrolled them one by one and Julie just gasped in shocked disbelief, totally lost for words. "There!" I said proudly, "now do you believe me ... I told you that my Dad was no ordinary painter and decorator!" Mom was blushing worse than ever now and Julie went over to her and was at last able to express her utter astonishment, suggesting that they all be properly hung up where they could be seen and appreciated. Never again to be locked away in the dark, emphasizing that they were the most beautiful pictures she'd ever seen.

With Mom still blushing and stuck for words, I took the opportunity to make our exit, apologising to her explaining that Julie and I hadn't intended staying and that we were on our way to going on a picnic up along by Fisherwick Woods. My words triggered off so many memories of the war years, making it seem like only yesterday. This was dangerous ground I was on and I knew by the way Mom's eyes suddenly lit up that she was ready to go ploughing through those precious memories; I had to be forceful and make for the door before it was too late. Dad was nowhere to be seen, he'd simply vanished into thin air, showing me that the gaping wound between art and him was still raw and painful, it wasn't ever going to heal. I knew also that once we'd waved our goodbyes and were back on our way, he'd suddenly reappear from wherever he'd been hiding, and he'd have Mom shouting at him for not saying goodbye to Julie.

In that short space of time, the mood of the day had changed; it felt hotter, airless and still. Those ghostly cauliflower clouds had grown hugely and had stolen silently and steeply over the village, causing a haze to dull the sun before swallowing it and for tiny black insects to stick to our perspiring skins. Regardless of which, the day was still ours to write our names upon, making history which was memory, in the time-old history that was still holding me now, as new memories were tenderly being made. We drifted on beside wild woods, where Hawks shrieked and Owls slumbered and we followed the winding lane along beside hedges and potato fields till we came to a sea of grasses. We settled there amongst the grasshoppers on a common where gypsies with clay pipes and cart-wheels back in history made hand-painted villages on wheels amongst the scattered pond, where the silvery willows grew, which they made pegs and baskets from. There were no gypsies here now, just memories, Julie and me in the high ripe grasses where the grasshoppers fidgeted. Whilst it wasn't the first picnic I'd had here, it was the first time I had lain down upon this spot with my Dad's demob-suit trousers on and my sweetheart trying to get them off. Whatever was on these tantalizing sandwiches didn't matter anymore, food had suddenly become the very last thing on our minds.

The grasshoppers watched and rasped their back legs with excitement as we thundered on, helpless in the containment of our raging desires, making grasshoppers, butterflies and even the ladybirds blush as we bared ourselves before the mercy of our inferno; enforcing an intervention divine to raise up and puncture the monstrous sky and drench us rudely back to our senses and onto our bikes, as all the wrath of heaven was thrown down in anger upon us. God didn't miss a trick!

We sped along the newly wetted lane like the lightning itself, beneath all the thunder-rumbling and crackling electricity of the suddenly merciless sky; anxious to be away from the overhanging trees, neither of us afraid so much as enraged by so untimely an intervention. It was then that I caught sight of what I was looking for, a little red-brick hovel at the end of the field where a night-flying Wellington bomber had come down during the war. "C'mon, follow me!" I yelled and we both tore along the edge of the field with our bikes and crashed into the sanctuary of the old hovel. A Barn Owl flapped out in panic, disregarding the storm that was raging and giving us both a fright, as we propped our bikes against a bale by the arched entrance. We looked like drowned rats the pair of us, as we feasted our eyes on our new surroundings and smelled the beautifully scented straw bales which were stored there, both of us smirking and thinking the same passionate thoughts. The whole world beyond roared in an even more fearful bedlam with testerone now gushing, even through a hole in the roof drenching us anew, accelerating me to my terminal condition in my trousers, and Julie to a rapidly collapsing resolve that was about to enter the annals of history.

In a despairing, do-or-die last minute attempt to regain composure and control, Julie insisted that we turn our minds instead to the picnic and the special sandwiches that she'd taken the trouble to prepare. It was our only chance and so, shaking somewhat nervously, she opened the bag, revealing two smaller bags of sandwiches which I could actually see through in their elastic-banded, strange new wrappings. "Hey ... that's a bit posh, aint it; wot, no greaseproof paper?" My astonished remark made her laugh and she waggled her finger at me and said ... "You've got to move with the times, darling. This is the very latest invention from America, I think ... it's called Polythene." "Trust the Yanks to come up with something flash to replace our good old greaseproof paper! Call me old-fashioned if you like but, greaseproof paper is still the best ... and a damned sight cheaper I shouldn't wonder!"

We small-talked over the pros and cons of greaseproof paper in our desperation to prolong the inevitable which was, by now elevating my trousers to the point of fracture and bringing Julie out in the most vivid geranium flush as her failing words blurred and lost commitment ..."It ... it keeps the food fresh .. f ..fresher than greaseproof ..and .. its waterproof. Oh Darling, darling I want you, I want you ... properly!" In one turgid agricultural eruption, the picnic went flying as we leapt upon each other, me with my trousers and pants around my ankles, she with her dress up over her shoulders. As I was pulling her pants down, she yelled ... "Darling ... No, No! We mustn't!" and she pulled them back up. "I want you to, darling, but we mustn't, it's not fair. If you had 'proper' protection I wouldn't be able to say 'no' ... I'd not be able to stop you!" This was the most miserable of ecstasies and the most painful of words to be hearing; there wasn't a lad that I knew of that had the nerve to stand in a queue in 'Boots' and ask for a packet of those things. In a sudden flash of inspiration-cum-invention, I snatched up one of the bags of sandwiches and unceremoniously shook the contents from it. "There! What d'you think?" "Oh, darling; it'll surely come off ... I daren't risk it! With necessity being the mother of invention, I grabbed the elastic band and made sure that my presentation was secure to the point of hurting. "Nothing's gonna shift that!" I crowed, determined that 'No' wasn't going to be an answer anymore. She stood trembling in excited anticipation when, out from the barking thunder, shouting voices were rapidly advancing and I barely had time to snatch my pants and trousers up before the hovel filled with a platoon of heavily camouflaged soldiers, out on manoeuvres and branding a variety of weapons. It was catastrophic as well as being yet another confounded bloody miracle. They showed no regard for us at all, as though we were not there, as they all muscled inside under the screaming orders of the ugly corporal in charge.

This ranked as probably the lousiest moment in my memory; a love-nest fit for doves, here turned instantly into a witches cauldron under instruction from a very spiteful God. This was most certainly no longer the place to be, thunder or no thunder, we had no option and instinctively forced our way back into the tumultuous storm and trusted our luck as we pedalled with all our might back to the village. We gave Mom and Dad their second major surprise of the day and finding the rest of the family there too and making more bedraggled introductions. Julie was absolutely drenched from top to toe, but she was right about the new polythene stuff being waterproof. On inspection my 'willy' was the only dry part of me, still being held firmly in position by the elastic band ... although sadly not having been put to its ultimate test. As I dabbed myself dry with a towel, I couldn't help noticing that Julie was staying unusually close to me and with a rather anxious look on her face. In an opportune moment she whispered down my ear that I mustn't dispose of the polythene bag, that she really must have it back because, so rare and precious were these new-fangled polythene bags, they were what her Dad took his sandwiches to work in and was unaware that she had borrowed them. Even the great Leonardo hadn't come up with an invention like this to change our lives, and with such apparent practical everyday uses.

## 12. 'No Free-wheelin' to an unforgettable Cup of Tea'

After the thunder came a worsening of the weather; what had started with roses and had arrived in full luxurious splendour amongst cream-dished elderflower celebrations, was now but a dismal broken dream in a very much compromised Summer vacation. Poor Dad, he couldn't get on with the 'outside work' which was his Summer lifeline; instead he was reluctantly forced to bring forward what bits of 'inside work' that he was saving for the Autumn. This was already the dilemma he faced when summer turned foul on him, rearranging his plans and then leaving him with time on his hands. It wasn't just Dad that was affected, the farmers were also similarly undermined, crops being delicate, temperamental things that needed everything to be just right before performing, unlike weeds. This year was proving to be particularly bad with the corn all flattened in the fields, promising a disastrous harvest. The flattened corn was even starting to sprout again and mice were moving in, just like raindrops on paint-work that wasn't properly dry; the kiss of death that reminded us all not to squander the good things and that, Summer, like Spring was but a fleeting moment to be cherished and never undervalued.

Dad didn't react well to this kind of situation and became like a fish out of water, all fidgety and irritable. I hoped and prayed that at long last he'd be able to get back into doing some drawing and painting, but no, instead he frantically set to work building a brick garage-cum-workshop. A place where he could work on rainy days tackling a whole host of unimaginably vital things that'd always been there lurking behind things, all ready and eager to prey on his newly acquired availability. His vacation of the dirty old coalshed meant that my bike had found a dirty new home, having being ousted from the passageway where Mom always somehow managed to scuff her ankles on the pedal on her way to and from the toilet. For me though, where cycling was concerned, it could rain as much as it liked; the way I saw it was simple. I couldn't get any wetter than wet, so I just got on with it, pure bliss, all cooling and soothing, with no mudguards to lessen the hose-like onslaught coming at me from both front and back wheels. 'Art' Tomkins and I with our 'knocking-bags' bulging with Mars bars and puncture outfits, were more like fishes in water and we very seriously traversed the puddled roads, covering up to a hundred miles a time; such was our determination as to be the ones to beat in our neck of the woods.

Our cycling-club secretary, a bloke called 'Laddie' Green, had for some time been observing our efforts with keen enthusiasm and was watching my own progress with particular interest. Especially so on account of the heavy-duty, fat-tyred bike that I was riding to such impressive effect, ironically letting the side down by it not quite looking the part. A bit like doing my painting at College with Dad's decorator's gloss paint. In his eagerness to help, he made me the offer of his own racing bike, a specially hand-built 'Raleigh Record Ace', Raleigh's own lightweight racer, one which he just replaced with a brand new one. When I told 'Art' about this, he fell about laughing, urging me not to rush into any decision at this stage. It was all too late though, I'd already told 'Laddie' that I'd take him up on his offer and I wasn't going to go back on my word, no matter how much the thought had tickled 'Art' down to his toes.

What 'Art' found so amusing was that, the bike in question, had been specially built for a physically deformed cyclist. 'Laddie', great pursuit-cyclist though he had been, was sadly somewhat crippled; the bike had in fact been built for a cripple. Each of his hands were absolutely fingerless, just a small stub for a thumb and another for a finger on each hand, and frighteningly muscly as his leg were, they were severely shortened to about half the normal size. His arms and torso were absolutely huge and powerful, almost twice their normal size, ape-like even. Nobody argued with 'Laddie', he was at least twice as strong as any normally proportioned man, and it was said of him that he could lift a car clean off the ground, I guessed that he could probably throw it a hundred yards as well! As a result of his unique shape, 'Laddie' had engineered his own saddle-extension, one that allowed the saddle to be extended backwards rather than forwards, positioning him, not over the pedals but over the back wheel. Similarly he'd engineered his own handle-bar extension, one that extended fully twelve inches, added to which his handlebars were so acutely bent forwards that the bike would defy anyone but 'Laddie' himself to ride it. As if that weren't enough, the bike had no gears, just a very low –geared fixed-wheel and just a solitary front brake, all that the law required it to have.

'Art' Tomkins found the idea hilarious to the point of my having lost my marbles, but I hastened to point out that, the only things that were wrong with it could easily be replaced by standard parts, making the bike look like a fairly normal racing machine. He thought on this for a few moments before seeing the potential which I could see, and we both started to enthuse over the prospect of creating something 'sporty', and didn't look any more like something that had been supplied by a clinic! He cycled over with me to the colliery town of Cannock to do my bike swap; he wasn't going to miss this for all the world, the sight of me attempting to ride this monstrosity back to Whittington and remaining in one piece. It was a daunting prospect; I'd never ridden a fixed-wheel bike before, let alone the additional complication of having to stand on the pedals, a tortuous position at the mercy of a hitherto unknown solitary front brake. My only positive thought was that the bike was very much lighter than the one that I was sadly about to say goodbye to. Secretly I was full of regrets, not entirely believing that what I was doing was sensible. I cursed the misfortune of being a pauper, wishing that there was money in the family that was available to get me a decent second-hand proper racer. One with 'Campag' gears and fitted my body properly, but beggars couldn't be choosers and I'd just have to make the best of what I'd got. Among the seemingly endless miners' terraces it seemed like a poor man's circus had come to the street as this half dwarf, half giant of a man, with 'Art' Tomkins showing off his recently shaven and oiled bandy legs, both men trying to keep me on this deviously mysterious machine, which kept bucking me up over its handlebars, and into a twitching heap on the hard, dirty road. The process being repeated over and over before I eventually found a way of staying at one with it; the secret being that I had to remember that free-wheeling was impossible, failure to do so almost certainly meant being thrown over the handlebars.

It was 'Shank's pony' for me until I could get together all the second-hand bits and pieces that I needed in getting my machine into racing order. 'Laddie' had assured me that he'd spread the word around the club of the few bits and pieces that I needed and there was plenty of stuff available too, especially amongst the well-off prima-donnas who had more flash racing-bikes than sense. They were forever replacing perfectly good bits of this and that in the misguided belief that, by throwing money at it, the minutes would simply melt away from their previous best times.

Julie was going to have to bear with me; walking was alright but it took up too much of what little time was available and, the sooner I had my bike in racing order, the sooner we'd be back together in whatever order that availed itself.

'Art' Tomkins was temporarily on 'Shank's pony' too, all immaculate in his charcoal-grey drainpipes, black patent leather shoes with a buckle, starched white cutaway collar shirt, black bootlace tie and a military-precise tight-fitting charcoal jacket. He was dating a Carnival Queen, both of them in a dreamworld under the lurid intoxication of an outrageous scent that'd apparently been extracted from the bollocks of bullocks in Outer Mongolia, cunningly blended with ferret-piss and vanilla essence. A sure winner, even without a new-fangled polythene bag!

The Art-world was on hold, at Sabbatical rest, its most vociferous exponents being 'away', most probably in Italy getting reversed vertigo and spinal dislocations from paying homage to Michelangello's Cistine Chapel ceilings; how I envied them ... lucky, well-off so and so's! This life wasn't big enough for me to do all that I most dearly wanted to do, to see all the things that I most wanted to see. The only thing that I was able to pay homage to was the overflowing energy fountain that was showing me my shape and the explosive burning capability that was there like a sea of sunflowers about to detonate into colour. I couldn't ignore this and simply become one of life's feeble, timidly submissive observers, not when God in his wisdom had made me such a virulent, ever eager participant!

Cycling was of no purposeful use whatsoever; it was just something I had to both tolerate and accommodate in the absence of something better. Much as my heart spoke, so too did my muscles and the ravenous appetites of my heart and lungs, and how they all operated independently of each other; pulling in various directions leaving my brain like an egg sitting on the wall ... and the wall wobbling. It was all too easy to see elderly people all lame and lacking in energised aspirations; it was all too easy to see bodies that'd never physically celebrated and, through lack of sparkle and light, had grown grossly too fat. It was all to easy to see minds that had lock-jawed into pig-iron and would snap far more easily than they would bend. Bullshit made of rubber, bull-shitters mouthed chewing-gum words yet, when Humpty Dumpty fell from the wall, there was no bullshitty rubber to break his fall, and all the King's horses and all the King's men couldn't put Humpty together again!

If there was one thing that was causing this seemingly fruitless cycling preoccupation, I very quietly recognised this as being the even more futile invisible gun-barrel that was pressed, all cold and heavy, against my temple, that of, on successful completion of my diploma course, being rounded-up like a sheep and thrown into the Army for the next two useless years. Added to this the likelihood of being sent to fight in one or more of the stupid wars which our country was still involved in having learned absolutely nothing from the last epic monstrosity that'd had taken so many fathers, as well as countless millions of other precious lives besides. It were as though I needed something stupid in my own life so's to prepare for an even bigger dose of stupidity, the nature of which I hadn't the slightest idea as to how I would cope. The reality of being expected to kill a fellow human being was like a plague upon my sensibilities, especially so when it would be classed as being a 'Christian' act. With this miserable lunatic hypocrisy hanging over me, I found it impossible to just switch off and sit back and wallow in inactivity, both physically and mentally. After all, we were the young people that were supposedly going to change the world, the aspiring alchemists who were now gradually coming to realise that we were not going to change anything and that, old nightmares were no different from new nightmares, same ones in fact, just older that's all. If they wanted to make soldiers of us all, why not minimise the damage by taking us straight from school, when we might benefit from a bit of discipline, allowing us then to do our various degrees and diplomas when we had got our confounded National Service commitment out of the way. At least there'd be the common-sense factor of some continuity between studying and starting in a profession while the iron was still hot; or the Gold yet in its molten state, having not yet turned to iron.

It was another wet Sunday and my bike wasn't looking so much like the torture device which it did when I took charge of it. I'd got new second-hand handlebars with a short alloy extension, I'd also got rid of the previous saddle extension and had a replacement which positioned me properly over the pedals. Added to this I had an alloy pump and tiniest of alloy bells, which I was told was obligatory, so with new Dunlop Road Race tyres on my 26-inch 'Weinmann' alloy rims and hubs, I had a pretty mean-looking machine. It was gleaming ... and the weather was filthy, ideal for our Club-run to Alton Towers, a particularly good ride for the bike and I to get to know one another. It was a striking sight, close-on a hundred cyclists, all in bright yellow capes and on multi-coloured bikes, all of them gabbling away oblivious to the inclement weather; each in his or hers private ecstasy over this, the highlight of their dreary week. Few things could compare with the Cycling Club for setting the world to rights in so many private ways, turning fool's base metal into dreamers Gold.

The outward journey was always a fun-thing, undertaken at great leisure and always with too many cooks to spoil the broth of repairing the odd puncture that resulted from where farmers had recently slashed the hedges. My exceptional low gear hadn't gone without notice and I provided great amusement as I pedalled as frantically as a hamster on a treadmill going nowhere really fast, while the others could simply pedal a bit, then free-wheel a bit, change-up a gear or two then drop down a couple. They could even sit back no-handed and swig stuff out of bottles, exchanging cakes and biscuits, whilst leisurely free-wheeling; I half expected to see someone knitting! It puzzled me why 'Laddie' had chosen such a low gear for this bike I was riding, but it made no difference to me right now because I was its slave every inch of the way. Bodily at one with it whether I liked it or not, soon learning that I could use my fixed-wheel to slow me down as well as to give me the most amazing acceleration. I was still afraid of applying the front brake, fearing that it might snatch and toss me over the handlebars as it had so done on my first acquaintance with it; there was still a lot to learn but I really was getting to enjoy the experience, despite being laughed at.

There was a wicked hill going up to Alton Towers and it had a very severe 'S'-bend halfway, few cyclists attempted to cycle up it because, not only was it exceptionally steep, but it was very long also and had the effect of spoiling an otherwise leisurely long ride. It didn't however deter the 'fast boys' who had a whole stack of gears which they could throw at it, together with an attitude of never wanting to be seen to be beaten by a mere hill in the road. It didn't therefore take long for someone to throw down the gauntlet and for what had been a tightly packed bunch of riders to suddenly become a drawn-out two-mile straggle; all puffing and panting with the majority of them sooner or later dismounting and struggling the much too steep remainder on foot. For the very first time, on this new 'old' bike of mine

I was in my element and, as the road steepened, I got my head down and fair flew up the hill, leaving the rest behind. So ferociously was I attacking it that there were two loud snapping bangs coming from my front wheel, immediately followed by scraping sounds; I'd busted some spokes and the wheel had suddenly become a figure eight, which caused my rims to scrape on the side of the inside of the front forks, rendering my front brake ineffective and highly dangerous. Such were the stresses that I was bringing to bear on those untested 26-inch alloys, they simply couldn't take it and my elation of being first up the hill quickly took a nose-dive. I was wishing that I was back in Lichfield with Julie, indulging in another polythene bag of her delicious sandwiches.

It seemed to take an age for the stragglers to eventually reach the top, the last quarter of an hour providing them with far more strenuous exercise than the long ride from Lichfield had done. Looking around me, the gardens here were most picturesque, even in the rain and under leaden skies. There were pools with lilies and a beautiful Chinese pagoda, like something off a willow-pattern plate; rustic wooden shelters were scattered amongst the trees beside the winding pathways. It was these that we were all aiming for like fertilizer-bags in a squall, a bedraggled sight, all this yellow plastic pushing coloured bikes and stacking them several deep against tree trunks in the clamour for a sheltered place to eat packed lunches, and to really let-off steam. This was a most idyllic, peaceful Country estate, charming in every way, a National Treasure, no less. Deep emotional feelings were welling inside me, thoughts of Dad as a young man having himself cycled up here on a fixed-wheel bike, but with a heavy easel and large drawing board tied across his back; he seated himself here and produced the most hauntingly beautiful pencil drawing of the Hall with its reflections in the water. The drawing was four feet long and two feet deep; it really was a most masterful work of art, goodness only knows how he managed ... I don't think I could have.

With half of my mind caught-up on this and the other half mithering over my buckled front wheel and busted spokes, I wasn't really feeling part of this day-out any more. I had really been looking forward to the 'burn-up' back to Carol's Cafe, but it all seemed like a nightmare now, especially with having this cursed hill to go down with a badly buckled wheel, a very low-geared fixed wheel and no brakes. The rest of them could go free-wheeling down it with their brake-blocks on fire and still doing ninety and they could remain in this freewheeling mode for several luxurious miles, such was the terrain. 'Art' Tomkins didn't say much, he knew how I felt and was not dwelling on the subject having earlier expressed his doubts over the suitability of the bike. Apart from which, he was really fired-up for the 'burn-up' back to the Cafe and was in no mood for taking prisoners, let alone caring for the wounded.

I watched them all go excitedly rolling away before ironically testing my crippled, ex-cripple's machine, attaching the broken spokes to ones that were not broken, then testing it and getting myself familiar with its new peculiarities, in particular my ability to control it with no brakes. As satisfied as I could possibly be in the circumstances, I concluded 'Sod it!' and set off on my suicidal descent. This wasn't the right moment to discover that I most desperately needed a front brake. It really was like a suicide-attempt and I had learned too late that, strong as my legs were, they were no match for this murderous downhill as they flew round in an ever-increasing blur, helplessly unable to perform the function of being my brakes. In a terrifying worsening of things it was too late for me to recognise that I was totally out of control, my feet firmly strapped to the pedals as the road fell even more steeply away to the dreaded 'S'-bend. I saw the bend and I saw the bank, it was my only chance, I had to contrive a kind of falling-off-sideways, glancing-type collision with that steep, lumpy bank, an action which almost certainly saved me from a worse fate.

It was a miracle no less, and I lay there trembling in disbelief only yards from the lethal bend. I could feel my heart pounding as I gathered my senses, too afraid to think of what might have been. There was no way that I could repeat the collision manoeuvre even if I tried; even more of a miracle, I'd escaped unhurt, apart from a grazed elbow. It was of no comfort to know that, by now, the others would be blissfully free-wheeling two miles or more further down the valley, their brake-blocks having left the rancid smell of burning rubber in their wake for me to breathe. I extricated myself from my temperamental contraption and did a quick check to make sure that nothing else was damaged before attempting to proceed with caution on foot, discovering too late that my cycle-racing shoes, with their metal-plated soles, were never intended for walking down acutely steep tarmac roads. I was thus skidding and sliding all over the place, unable to keep my footing, causing my frustration to boil over.

I now knew the real reason why 'Art' hadn't stayed with me, he was doing what I had set my heart on doing, having a burn-up with the 'fast boys' back to Carol's Cafe. The very though of which got my blood boiling anew and I skated recklessly down the hill using my bike as a kind of Zimmer-frame, and as soon as I possibly could, re-mounted the crippled thing ... I wasn't finished yet! I knew that the boisterous, heavy wet headwind was going to be a good leveller, one which possibly appealed to my masochism rather more that it did to that of those several miles down the road. So, once I had tested the bike and come to terms with its scraping front wheel wobble, I threw caution to the wind and decided to chance my luck where my ineffective front brake was concerned, at least my bell would provide warning of my approach. I didn't care how many more spokes might break, I was determined to ride total commitment, flat-out, uphill and down dale and not slacken off, until I could see Carol's Cafe there looming up before me and without a single racing bike propped against the wall outside!

The race was on and it wasn't very long before I caught sight of the main bunch who were not finding it so easy on the level now and with their capes acting like air-brakes in the heavy, wind-driven rain. My own cape was rolled-up in my knocking-bag and I was going so hard that I needed the wind and the rain to keep me from boiling. I tinkled my bell as I jerkily wobbled past them and I could hear them all cheering as I left them behind. It took rather longer for me to get my first glimpse of those that were making a race of it and who had already started to feel the pace and were unable to respond. This was as manna from heaven, it was the boost that I'd been hoping for and I had the comfort of knowing that there were no more impossible downhill gradients to come to terms with. Barring getting punctured, or my wheel collapsing, I was in with a chance now of getting amongst the 'fast boys' and really giving them a fright.

One by one I ticked them off, getting shouts of encouragement as I did so, they could see that I meant business and wasn't in the mood for taking prisoners. Then after a long gap and the clearing of a long, steady hill, I could see a cluster of riders, all heads down, arses up, sweeping away round a bend less than a mile ahead. I grinned even broader, I had them in my sights at last. 'Art' was in for a bit of a shock and I knew from past experience that I needed the element of surprise and to strike a decisive killer blow out here on the windswept open road, preferably on one of the remaining up-hill stretches. I couldn't afford a self-congratulatory breather and leaving it until the outskirts of Lichfield before making my final effort. I wasn't one for showing off by going recklessly flat-out through crowded streets, as was 'Art' and a few of the others, to resort to those tactics I considered to be unsporting, as well as stupid. With my brake problem, my race had to be won before I'd passed the Cathedral Close, the very place where the rest of them would explode into a reckless sprint, overtaking cars and alarming the pedestrians and probably worse besides.

Calculating just how quickly I was gaining on them wasn't made easy by the up and down banks and hedges with twisting corners, but that really didn't bother me because it meant that they couldn't see me either. A situation that worked out just fine when, on rounding another bend at the end of another hill, they were suddenly there, just a hundred yards in front of me, all playing cat-and-mouse as I kept up my still undetected murderous pace, causing gasps and groans of disbelief as I decisively clattered past, determined not to ease off for several more miles; not until I had those three Cathedral spires on my left and then easing off down past the Art Gallery and Minster Pool, switching off the power so's to be able to stop at the traffic lights if necessary, hoping, just hoping that Julie would be there to give me a wave.

It felt absolutely, unspeakably fantastic to be sitting glowing there in the Cafe with a large cup of tea, waiting for the mindless sprints of the others to come crashing to a halt outside and to see their dejected faces when they came inside and saw me sitting there. I waited almost five minutes, I'd even started on my second cup of tea before hearing those congratulatory words ... "You bastard!" followed, rather begrudgingly by ..."Where the bloody hell did you suddenly pop-up from?" I just laughed; I was sweating like a pig and divinely exhausted even though, as so often was the case my 'willy' had gone completely numb and had shrivelled from being strangled and suffocated in the saddle for so long, with the added discomfort of having to suffer a penetrating wind and cold, driving rain. Right now I was more concerned with this, I'd experienced it before, especially in winter, desperately wanting to pee but with apparently nothing to do it with!

Other cyclists had arrived and were noisily circulating, all eager to know who had been first back to the Cafe, and giving a loud cheer when they were told. Two of the girls cyclists came and made a fuss of me, ruffling my hair and hugging me, all wet and flattening their bosoms in my face, making me pray to God, not to bless me with an erection now of all times for fear of it blowing my backside off in the absence of my own struggling circulation. 'Art' Tomkins came over and joined me, grinning like a Cheshire cat, immensely chuffed over the fact that I'd annihilated the most obnoxious, self-proclaimed 'number one', a 'prima-prima-donna' with the most sophisticated and expensive, hand-built Belgian superbike. Then 'Laddie' himself came over, his deformity hidden by an inordinately long sweater; his delight was there for all to see. "Well done, Jimmy, that was a damn good ride ... first up to the 'Towers' as well, I believe; I told you it was a good bike!" I couldn't let him get away with giving the impression that I'd had a bargain put on my plate when, in fact, it had proven more of a headache than a bargain. I pointed out the various issues and he expressed surprise, asking me to show him. 'Art' came with us and, to my surprise, another spoke had broken in the front wheel. "There!" I complained ... "that's what I mean; that's what I've just come back from Alton bloody Towers on!" He raised the bike's front end and spun the wheel, allowing it to speak for itself as it refused to spin more than once before its figure-eight shape stopped it. "It never did that with me," he muttered and shook his head ... "Some ride!"

Heels were normally at the back but, this bike's Achilles heel was at the front and I snapped spoke after spoke whenever I made an attack on a hill or in just piling-on a sprint. I was thoroughly sick of it and despairingly tried 27-inch wheels, only to find that the front one wouldn't fit, its rims being beyond the adjustment of the front brake to line-up with; I gave up, I wasn't going to be a racing cyclist anyway.

## 13. 'Winds of Change'

It had all been so necessarily different to the deeper stillness and the quietness that I had kept locked-away inside me; it was fixed there like the wind was to the air. This 'art-thing' was worse than a toothache and appendicitis put together; it was far worse than a headache simply because there was even less to show, not until, like the wind, you'd actually 'blown' and had made something move into a state of 'being' of sorts. Achievement was one thing; being driven and expected to achieve demonstrated an abstraction in expectation. Rather like waiting for the invisible wind to blow down a branch with which to make a fire to boil a kettle to make a drink to warm a soul; no part of which ever gave a clue to the shape, size, colour, weight or whatever of the wind which made it possible. Bureaucracy was the ultimate badly bungled Alchemy, which believed, through a zillion dictatorial bits of paper, that it had succeeded and could water-down Gold into insipid, piss-like stuff that could be force-fed into anyone showing even the slightest resistance to it. It had other grades of 'Gold' in varying forms of sludge, which it administered according to status. What was 'Achievement', anyway? Were 'Expectations' not simply proof of earlier, previous failures in others ... or were they dreams? This world was so much bigger, broader, deeper, richer than any bureaucracy ever recognised and the gap was widening in utter futility ... learning from What, as it gathered pace?

I was now eighteen years old; no-one had even recognised the fact that I was old enough to be both husband and a father, as well as a dead soldier. I was old enough to stand up and argue against the 'dead soldier' bit, but a fat lot of good it would have done me, no Government Department had those kind of ears. I could understand why coalminers were exempted military service, but I couldn't see why a bloke driving a tractor in a field was considered equal to the miner when girls could grow cabbages, milk cows and gather eggs. Someone said that if I became a 'Plymouth Brethren', I'd not be called-up. The thought puzzled me ... I'd always thought that 'Plymouth Brethren' was a rare breed of chicken! I was a 'Wolves' supporter but this wasn't enough, not even if I called it a 'Wolverhamptomotumus Wandererangelicus Supporterous Sect'. The listening Government had a rubber stamp marked 'BOLLOCKS'! and they used it most effectively!

Julie and I had survived our first year and were still miraculously virginally intact ... or thereabout given the odd skirmish here and there with that confounded Yanky Polythene stuff. National Diploma was another of my first year survivals and one which was clattering back into motion. Some old faces had gone and new ones had arrived to swell the gaps with me finding myself sandwiched between hopeful, tender new First Years' and last year's Second Years now hardened into Third Years. Over this break in my metamorphosis, I had matured several notches and was now having to shave regularly if my lower face wasn't to resemble a 'Venus Love-triangle' ... or, as in the case of a few straggly specimens about the place ... possibly an arse. New beards were being attempted here and there, they tended to be out of place, a bit of a joke on such young people; rather poser-ish in a 'look at me, I'm an artist' sort of way. Something to match their busted sandals and general unkemptness and betraying illusions of Alchemic aspirations, together with a smugness that boasted of success in this most wizardly, phoney of Nirvanas. There was an orderly form of pandemonium at large everywhere. Some new Third Years had abandoned 'Woodbines', 'Players Weights' and 'Park Drive', and had taken to smoking pipes or foul-smelling foreign fags in long holders. They were cultivating frowns of concentration and appreciation across their brows, whilst reciting obscurely poetic gems from the pen of their most recent idol, Dylan Thomas, just to show the new 'Kultured' depth to which art had plunged them.

The college was undergoing a process of change and was in a state of rabbled confusion. New staff had been appointed, old ones had left, among them my old heart-throb from back in my Commercial days, 'Spud' Murphy. The pain of realising this took me by total surprise and hit me like a kick from a mule. I was in grief and could feel the emptiness that she had left, it was haunting, showing me that I really had been in love with her all that time without fully realising it.

Life was moving on at an alarming rate; once Christmas was over I'd be halfway to becoming that most dreaded of things, a Soldier, and it was making me more serious by the minute and putting concentration-lines onto my own forehead. Rumours were rife that we Second Year Illustrators were to be re-housed in a recently acquired annexe which, according to the caretaker, had some time previously been a brothel. It wasn't very far from where 'Burto' lived and probably helped explain why he had so often been late to arrive in the past! We were assured that this infamous new-old Victorian annex would accommodate our ' out-of-the-ark' 'Cropper' printing press, as well as our ancient litho-printing gear and the newer screen-printing equipment. This would provide us with more of a graphic workshop environment, as opposed to that of a purely academic college one. We'd still be required to go back to the main college for stuff like Life Drawing, pottery, bookbinding and calligraphy and to generally keep in touch with old friends. It was all getting a bit scattered, unsettling with none of us ever properly knowing where we were supposed to be, or what we needed to take with us, in fact it was nothing short of chaos.

The whole disruptive muddle set me off questioning things that I had for so long taken for granted. After a World War, young people studying should, above all be forward-looking and with emphasis on experimentation, in a search for new ways of addressing old methods that'd either failed or had outlived their usefulness. I had chosen 'Illustration' as being the most exciting amalgamation of artistic variety, functional as well as frivolous, humorous, hard-hitting, witty, political, poetic and abundantly creative, but I was damned if I could figure out the continuing relevance of Calligraphy. Something uncomfortably similar to 'Standard English' in the way it destroyed 'personality'; everyone ending up with writing the same and speaking the same and to be doing it with a goose-quill on vellum was really like florally embroidering a tarpaulin to cover a tractor. Similarly, 'Bookbinding' was questionable in the brave new paperback world that was forging ahead. Creatively satisfying and interestingly therapeutic as they both undoubtedly were, I could think of better forms of therapy if that was what we needed; I'd settle for a therapeutical polythene bag and an elastic band in preference any day!

Earlier rumours came to fruition and, what had once smelled rank with bodies and cheap perfume from the Orient, now smelled of council paint, turps, linseed oil, putty and newly sanded floorboards. No longer a Newport Road brothel, we'd got our new Annex and a tall gaunt man in heavy-framed glasses to run it. 'Ralph Nolan' came over immediately as a down-to-earth, no-nonsense, straight-talking, smashing bloke; funny, even-handed and highly learned in the Art of Print and all allied graphics. He was a believer in there being no substitute for hard work and had no time for shirkers or arty-farty pretenders; he knew a gimmick when he saw one and didn't mince words. His nervous energy was electric and he was on the go the whole time, frequently stepping back from himself to roll-up a very thin cigarette, and then to speak with it in his mouth as though this was his fuel supply. These first impressions of the man were to prove accurate, but even then I hadn't expected him to be such a fine watercolourist. He was the very breath of fresh air that the Art College needed, and the sense of confidence that he gave us was the very best thing that we could ever have hoped for.

While the division between the 'Painters' and the 'Illustrators' remained, I found myself becoming more deeply engrossed in painting, aloof to Her as sometimes I pretended to be, her persistent seductions were irresistible to me as they had also been to others down the centuries. Looking at the illustrations of Rowlandson, Cruikshank, Gillray, Hogarth and the more recent Arthur Rackham, it was no different to the drawings of Leonardo, Durer, Michelangelo, Millet or whosoever; they were all simply bloody wonderful artists, all of them similarly involved in the expressing of a common language, that of visual expression. It was somewhat sad that, until 'Peter Rabbit' popped up, women's names never figured in what had been an exclusively male-dominated region: it wasn't just the Italians that kept their womenfolk enslaved in kitchens and bedrooms!

People everywhere were different from one another; 'personality' wasn't a 'diversionary' thing so much as a 'uniting' thing. Personality was colour, ideas and perceptions were exciting elements of entertainment, which made the sharing of things so very stimulating. Greed was what divided people; greed shared nothing, it had nothing to share. The great splendour of art in all its manifestations, was the greatest of thrills to behold, so generous, so giving and never taking; Life was never going to be big enough to come to terms with everything that 'Art' was.

In 'Art' you could like things just as readily as you could hate things; there was nothing that was everybody's cup of tea, not in Music, Literature, Design, or dare I say it ... even a cup of tea! 'Art' was there being all of this, being everything to everyone and always something to someone. It embraced dilemma and made an extravagance of miserliness while itself remaining intangible, mysterious, tantalising, sexy.

Whilst there was nothing that wasn't 'Art', 'Anything' most certainly wasn't; the differences were there to be seen, as clear as night was from day ... or possibly, morning was from afternoon ... or one o'clock was from two o'clock', the differences were there ... somewhere. When the Will was Willing, the Thrill was Thrilling!

Our latter-day Brothel looked more comfortable than the priciest whore with its big bulging bay windows, wide-bosomed on either side of the curved stone steps leading up to the gaping open double front doors. It was even more interesting when approached from the rear, where a long, boarded-up shed-like building stood and which we were led to believe was ours, just awaiting the Council to come and clear it of its years of junk which was barely visible through the filthy, cobwebbed windows. It was anybody's guess what this pile of junk was going to be transformed into but, the general opinion was that it was to become our desperately needed Design Studio, spacious, workshop-like and a bit 'different'. However, such speculation was guesswork, made more frustrating by the blatant realisation that there was no urgency being shown over whatever it was going to be. We felt ourselves to be nothing more than un-regarded 'egg-timers' and it was our precious sand that was running to waste on someone else's boiled egg. To us, this was as a red rag to a bull, aggravating it into making a charge, futile or otherwise, but a statement nonetheless, obliging us to take the law into our own hands. Taking advantage of a bureaucratic 'meeting of minds', more commonly known as a 'Staff-meeting' up in the main College, we smashed our way into this puzzle of a place and were met by the most obnoxious stink of time that hadn't changed its pants since before Hitler died. "Bloody hell, there must be bodies in here!" We all covered our noses and mouths as we laughed and our adrenaline surged in the realisation that what we were doing was unlawful. “There’s a decomposing whore in here,” ‘Burto’ surmised. “Or a decrepit old client that sprang a heart-attack while he was on the job!” I interrupted, and we all stifled our laughter on realising that we had come this far and couldn’t back-out now.

We stood there gawping in morbid fascination, afraid to venture any further for fear of our wildest, most bizarre speculations proving true. The place had probably been an Alchemist’s den and, more than likely had a cauldron of abandoned ‘manufactured’ Gold buried here amongst the filth somewhere, proof that the secret had been discovered, then immediately lost again as the discoverer probably celebrated with a whore that was too fit, too fat and too heavy by a mile for him to cope with; his smiling, cross-eyed body being part of the stench which we were so bravely enduring. Tentative probings suddenly exploded into shrieks of astonishment as the stinking old filth revealed its buried treasure, namely a virtual historic library of ancient books going back to the very roots of Printing. Illustrated with Woodcuts, Wood Engravings and Metal Engravings; some were hand-coloured, largely bound in leather and printed mostly in Latin and in a Romanesque kind of typeface and upon what looked like a hand-made parchment-like paper, the most unlikely stuff to find in a shed at the backdoor of a brothel.

Our guess was that the stuff had at some time way back, been stolen prior to unexpected events causing it all to be forgotten. Fascination very soon turned to avarice despite the inescapable knowledge that this stuff rightly belonged to the College and we had no right to be here at all, but as I had discovered over the past year or so, greed had never been more than a scratch deep in a lot of those around me and their attitude suddenly became like a rat-plague bordering on Civil War. Hands were like dredgers and the whites of eyes were glowing like candles as 'Jack', our good old caretaker stood grinning in the doorway, amused by this astonishing transformation in those he'd always thought that butter wouldn't melt in the mouths of. He slowly shook his head, farting quite obliviously, a thing which he perpetually did almost to the point of it becoming a notifiable condition as he muttered; "I aint seen a thing ... not a thing!" He really was a good old stick and we knew that we could trust him not to breath a word of the incident as the students greedily bundled past him with their arms full to the limit before vanishing away to unscheduled earlier homecomings than usual.

I went over and stood by Jack in the doorway where he was silhouetted and enrobed in shafts of dusty sunbeams, making him look biblically dramatic as he tried not to breathe in the newly aroused stinking dust which the others had stirred up in their crazed exodus. Stink as it did, it was no sweeter standing there next to him; Jack's virtuosity was the result of a lifelong dedication to Brussels sprouts, dried peas and brown ale, so accomplished was he that he could fart at will, long or short, high or low; he'd missed his vocation by a century or two and could have had letters after his name, or even a statue. On hearing a bit of a scuffle behind me in the shed, I turned and stepped inside once more where I distinctly heard squeaking sounds ... there were three rats. I gasped, "Bloody hell, Jack; we've got rats!" Jack's first reaction was predictable and trombone-like and he promptly vanished. As I moved closer to the beady-eyed cretins, I stumbled over a partially hidden box, quickly dispersing the rats with my clatter; then my eyes caught sight of a protruding book-end that'd been overlooked by the others in their haste. I took hold of it and blew the dust away, surprised by its weight. It wasn't very big but about five, almost six inches thick and bound in insect-eaten leather and with part of the spine missing. It was printed in Latin, a most lovely Roman-ish print upon a fairly thick uneven edged, very much hand-made sort of paper which was yellowed and blotched with time. It really was a treasure, a graphic time-capsule which I simply had to get into the light before I could see it properly. In my haste, I stumbled yet again over the box-like object and, as I did so, in almost slow-motion its lid fell open and a silver wind-instrument softly fell out and lay there before me ... a 'Euphonium'. I couldn't believe my eyes, this was the best find of all.

I saw Jack's shadow come slanting across; he was back with his trouser bottoms firmly tucked into his socks, the thought of a rat going up his trouser-leg had really put the wind up him. "Hey, Jack; what d'you reckon to this then, hey?" I exclaimed smugly, holding the silver instrument up for him to see. "Just you be careful when you blows it, that's all ... there's probably a family of rats in it!" His retort was crowned with another virtuoso fanfare, forcing me to take despairing evasive action, he really was beyond a joke. "Bloody hell, Jack!" I gasped ... "You with your arse and me with this 'ere Euphonium, we could form a band ... a 'wind ensemble' sort of thing; what d'you reckon?" He broke into a semi-serious snigger and waggled his forefinger; "You aint 'eard nowt! If you want to hear a real farter, you should hear my missus ... I couldn't hold a candle to her, no messing!" "Blow it out, would she, Jack?" I laughed, and he boomed ... "Blow it out my arse ... set the bloody house on fire more like!"

The vulgarity gradually subsided; I was growing restless standing there clutching my treasures; Jack could sense this and stole a peep at his pocket watch and groaned ... "Bloody hell, is that the time; my missus'll have got the peas out off soak and the sprouts on." He gave me a shove ... "Goo on with you; get going while the coast's clear ... I shallna breathe a word to anybody ... silly sods, its all rubbish anyway, just waitin' for the Council to come an' teck it to the tip, so I wouldna worry no more about it. Goo on with you, it'll all look like 'new' when I've nailed this plank back across the door!"

## 14. 'Rebellious Passage from Holbein to HighJazz'

There was no turning back on any single thing, every precious separate moment had to count from now on in. Gallant young men of my age had, only a sparse handful of years earlier been forcibly turned into cannon-fodder and into mass-murderers prior to becoming bullet-holed corpses themselves. It was all the luck of the draw, be it good luck or bad luck and they had been sent by luckier, more privilege cretinous monsters of power, who could sit safely back in offices somewhere and never be required to take another's life for real, all bloody and horrid, or to have to risk their own lives in the process. They did it all on paper instead, all neat and disinfected, thousands upon thousands at the stroke of a poisonous pen. There was no turning back for any single thing, not even the good things; it was just a question of treasuring the best and forgetting the rest, keeping finger crossed that the good luck would outweigh the bad.

There was still a lot of the 'Boy' and boyish innocence caught up in my sprawling youthfulness and, relentless as the hardening process of growing was, some bits hardened quicker than others; some bits were very hard to part with, their lingering nature making me hope against hope that they'd never go and could eternally sparkle no matter what. It was a dream of keeping something alive which was forever young, preserving a little precious plot of innocence somewhere inside that was safely out of the reach of those plundering, wicked fingers. Three score years and ten sounded like a long time for keeping a secret of this sort but, it really wasn't long at all, judging by the way time was already blowing my hair straight back by the speed it was travelling. Seventy years was never going to be even remotely enough for holding on to a treasure of this magnitude and by the luck of the draw, it had got to survive in a thousand horrid places, a bit like having to carry a wren's egg in your mouth without so much as cracking it during the murderous campaigns of a lifetime's carnivorising. To sweetly and lovingly carry this precious egg and then, before dying, see it hatch and then to whistle its own song along such honoured moments, forever. I would make this pledge before the very light of all time touching, no matter how straight it blew my hair behind me; I would carry this priceless gem with honour throughout my given 'moment' of life. Nothing, absolutely nothing, would ever cause me to endanger the existence of this dearest of songs cradled inside an egg cradled inside my heart, my soul, and it'd still be heard singing long, long after I'd gone.

College had become a very big place to be, not size-wise but in so many vital and diverse, sparkling other ways. The blossoms that had earlier buzzed loud with bees in the incestuously crowded Mother-tree, were formed fruits now being graded into separate, smaller 'annexed' boxes further afield. Mystery was sneaking, snaking along with intrigue; we were in danger of losing track of one another and that was akin to killing the goose that laid the golden egg. We had grown to be creatively vibrant and buzzing as a family, learning so much more from each other than we ever did from solitary Lecturer figures alone, no matter how brilliant they may have been. It had become a marvellous, really 'Big' place to be; wild and anarchic as it gloriously sometimes was, but it was undeniably a hive producing very fine honey. Bureaucracy had decided that the swarm needed splitting-up; elements of a 'divide-and-rule' philosophy coming into effect, although it had to be said in all honesty that the College really did need more space, having always been perched on the top floor of a five-floor 'Ism' and 'Ology' factory full of alien, hostile ant-like creatures. It was so comforting and stimulating in our cocoon that, even if 'Art' Tomkins managed to contrive a way of staying on for yet another year, early symptoms of a creeping instititutionalisation, I guessed. Whatever it was I was glad, even though we hardly ever saw each other after disembarking from that old red double-decker, annexation saw to that.

The only thing that put some perspective into my envying our Painters was, quite simply the job at the end of it. Unless one went into teaching, making a living from selling paintings would be about as dependable as finding and selling four-leafed clovers for a living; furthermore, the kind of paintings which one would very likely be compromised into churning-out in coming to terms with the responsibilities of domestic life, didn't bear thinking about. No, I reckoned I'd got it right in my choosing to be an Illustrator; this way, my painting could maintain integrity without compromise, unhindered in the exploration of ideas and themes. I'd find another way of paying my rent when that day came, without having to resort to Teaching. There was a saying which I'd heard pertaining to this, which said:-

'Those than can, do; those that can't, teach!' I wasn't sure that I'd understood its intended meaning because without exception, all the teachers that I knew really could dazzle with their ability to 'do'; sour grapes I guess. My own reticence over 'Teaching' as a profession was its high-profile; not a thing that I'd been brought-up to handle.

Envy apart, we had some staggeringly good Painters at College, the whole department seemed to buzz; other times it squeaked, then shrieked! They had a secret pet white rat called 'Holbein' which they discreetly let loose when the nude model had settled into her pose. This verminous 'pet' was as much owned by the third-year Illustrators as it was by the Painters and they employed it to the greatest effect, understanding of the creature's inquisitive nature, knowing that it would go off on an exploration and, sooner or later suddenly pop-up and cause the poor model to explode into hysterics and go tearing off in her nakedness, shrieking about the corridors. It was stuff like this that gave mirth to deathly academia and helped bond the broader College into a unified body, serving to remind everyone that they were 'students' and not simply young people growing old.

Being one of the Illustrators invariably involved having to do deathly boring things like 'typesetting', to which end we were sent by train one afternoon a week to Wolverhampton College of Art where they had modern Printing Presses and held Typography in high esteem. If any one single thing made me wish that I could switch over onto the Fine Art Course, this was it. It wasn't just me, the whole second year group of us hated this 'cosy' arrangement between our Principal, 'Bong' and his 'fingers-in-pies' Masonic chums down the line. It was all a waste of our time and our parents' hard-earned money and, judging by the hostility and gross irritability shown to us by the pallid

Church-slave Lecturer, miserable in his white overall, the arrangement had been on a 'you scratch my back, and I'll scratch yours' basis ... and at 'Grand Lodge' level; it wasn't for our benefit that we had been sent here. There simply wasn't time to achieve anything, it was a joke and I ended up having a flaming row with this white-overalled 'cleric' in charge of us when he belligerently refused to allow me to print my Christmas card design with my own poem inside it, on the grounds that it contained an illustration of a cockerel, insisting upon me that this couldn't be allowed on religious grounds. "You can't have a cockerel on a Christmas card; surely you know that!" "You can have one in your bloody oven on Christmas Day, so why can't I have an etching of one on my card!" I yelled with rage. He sneered at me as though I was dirt and dismissively muttered something about a 'cock-crow' being of religious significance, branding me a heathen in effect. It didn't take long for the rest of the gang to gather around me in support and I distinctly heard the white-coated man say to a rallying assistant, "Blooming Stafford lot! I wonder whose idea it was to saddle us with these!" We could all see that we weren't wanted and I furiously dismantled all my meticulously set type and scattered it all on the table under his nose. "Thank you for your help, I don't think! You can shove your type you know where; we don't come here for Bible Study, in case you haven't noticed!" We all gathered our bits and pieces together and stormed out rebelliously into the congested Wolverhampton street where the air was grey and stank disgustingly; someone said that it was coming from a brewery but I had already formed my ideas as to what it was.

On the train back to Stafford, our bravado started to wilt and our pockets started to strain under the weight of type which we'd just grabbed for spite in a spontaneous 'getting-our-own-back' act of wickedness, all of us suddenly of the same opinion that we had to get rid of it before the train pulled-in to Stafford Station, where we had a sneaking suspicion that some form of 'reception committee' would be waiting for us. We stood in a line at the open windows, trying to be discreet as we scattered handfuls of type out onto the track, and not a moment too soon. The train clanked, clattered and wobbled as it slowed-off and other passengers busied themselves in readiness to leave the train. We were in no hurry and neither were we anxious to be seen by anyone waiting for us. "BONG!" I shouted ... "He's there, look, pressed against those railings!" Sure enough the speed of the telephone had beaten the train and we scurried along the corridor as far as we could to the front of the train, desperately trying to choose our moment to slip out into the crowd, out of sight of our purple-jowelled, triple-chinned enraged Principal who was so really steamed-up, he could have been coupled to the carriages and to then tow the train to Crewe. Instead he just hissed outside the gates, waiting to pounce. We stayed-put in a cubby-hole and reviewed the situation until he'd given up and gone.

My idea was for us to seize the initiative and to get in first and for all of us to march into the Principal's office and register a complaint over the way we'd been treated. The idea was well received and given a much needed boost when we all found agreement over what a waste of our precious time this was. The more we thought, the more we felt justified in standing our ground, remembering to quote the sarcastic references to our College, hoping that this alone might just win the day for us. "Are we in agreement?" I asked and was met by a bedraggled chorus of yesses. 'Burto' was convinced and turned to the others and said ... "Look, you lot, we don't want any last minute backing-out; we've got a good case ... and we've got to stick together, one voice. Okay, we're going to get bawled at, that's to be expected; you all saw 'Bong' at the gates and Jim's right, he won't be expecting Us to confront Him!" I was really so glad that 'Burto' had intervened in this way because I had already sensed wimps amongst us, even my mate Dave was looking a bit wobbly.

We arrived back at College where 'Millie' the secretary, on seeing us, gasped and whispered behind her hand, "You're in trouble, you lot are!" Two-and-a-bit voices simultaneously said, "We wish to see the Principal, we need to see him now, please!" "Oh, God help me!" she sighed and picked up the phone; "Go through," she cringed, knowing what was coming. It was like entering a dragon's den ... it simply wasn't real; this ruptured boiler of a man that'd never known being nice or even remotely friendly, funny or of any artistic sympathy whatsoever. Not even the great Dickens had discovered a character to match, despite him being stereotypical of the monstrous figure that he hid behind. His technique was to intimidate with what he obviously considered to be the 'Power of Office', but not in a subtle way, oh no; 'Bong' was determined to let us stew while he went redder and redder dredging for breath while his poor skull strained under the heavy drapes of his miserable frowns. "And what have 'we' got to say for 'ourselves'? Blaggards, that's what you are; you've let the college down, the lot of you!" "Excuse me, Sir;" I managed to somehow squeak, only to be drowned under another thunderous outburst. "I'll do the talking; who the hell do you think you are ..." he couldn't even think of my name as, to my relief, 'Burto' spoke; "That's what we've come to speak to you about, Sir." I then quickly leaped back in and interrupted again, "We feel that it's the College that has let 'US' down by sending us where we're not wanted!" His eyes suddenly looked like turkey eggs as a fiery flush came over his swollen jowls; "WHAT? WHAT? How dare you, you impertinent scoundrel! You've got too much to say for yourself ...!" He was once more stuck for remembering my name and I felt that I had no option now other than to continue, our grievances had to be heard. "They don't want us there, Sir," I persevered, ".. they think we're a nuisance and we heard them say that we came from a rubbish College!" At this point, Dave found his voice, saying, "They won't allow us to print the work which we have designed here and have taken there to be printed." Then 'Burto' chipped-in again ... "It's all a waste of our time going there, we could be more usefully employed back here in College," then, turning to face the couple at the back who were conspicuous by their silence, added "couldn't we!" There was a sudden scuffle of voices coming to life ... "Oh, yes; yes, that's right!" An irritated momentary silence hit the air as the enraged man's bright red face glared the headlights of his eyes down upon me as he ponderously plodded back and forth, returning and then stomping off again, hissing and seething. He then spun about and pointed to me; ... "You? ... You?" "Jim Bridgen, Sir!" I helped him out as he yelled "You, Bridgen! It was reported to me that you behaved in a 'heathenish' and violent manner, threw your type at your Lecturer's feet and mouthed obscenities ... what have you got to say for yourself?" I looked about me in disbelief and muttered ... "That's a gross distortion of the truth if ever I heard it; the man refused to allow me to print my Christmas Card, an etching and a poem, on 'Religious grounds'. So I gave him his type back and told him what he could do with it, wasting my time like that, not to mention my Dad's hard-earned money!" He glared across to the others ... "Is that right?" "Yes, sir; that's exactly how we all saw it; they're lying, Jim didn't use any bad language." 'Burto' was there again when I needed him and, to my surprise the others leapt to my support and were on the warpath at last. The Principal pinked-down several notches, leaving the tiniest vulnerable underbelly of opportunity, prompting a rabbled chorus of stuff about our Dads who'd take us away from College if they knew how our precious time and their scarce money was getting thrown away on fiascoes like this. "That's enough of that sort of talk!" the Principal bellowed, calming quite noticeably ... "You've not heard the last of this, so I 'd suggest you spend the weekend reflecting on your behaviour!" He showed us the door and we all sheepishly walked where he was pointing. "Thank you for your time, Sir," I muttered as I squeezed past, giving 'Burto' a sharp pinch on the arse, causing him to suddenly skip and stagger into the back of Dave; our ordeal was over.

It seemed quite likely that he'd given the matter some thought too, because nothing more was said on the subject and the previous 'cosy' arrangement was discontinued. A bloody good job too because we had our Art Ball coming up to focus our minds, our annual 'Renaissance-fragment' and with this year's theme being, 'La Boutique Fantasque'. There wasn't a college or University in the land that could compare with ours when it came to Art Balls. Genius shone both in terms of Design and Theatre; from seemingly nowhere sprang the most outrageously Poetic, most marvellous invention, inspirationally choreographic, beautifully humorous and with Costume all dreamed-up out of a non-existent budget. If ever there was an 'English Renaissance', this few-year flowering span was it, never to flower again quite like this small flowerbed of priceless years, and not a Pope or a Vatican in sight to nail us all upside down to Chapel ceilings and employ and implore us to do it for God and Italy!

Even the mighty 'Bong' showed signs of pride at these highly artistic occasions, mercifully, or perhaps 'conveniently' overlooking the occasion when we attended an 'away fixture' having been invited to attend the Burslem Arts Ball. Typically we upstaged the Burslem crowd, going there as 'St. Trinians', holey black stockings, suspenders, gym-slips, pig-tails, the lot, announcing our arrival by tossing a terrifyingly loud firework into the crowded hall, instantly silencing the band and scattering the crowd. We all noisily rushed in and staged a hockey match with proper hockey sticks and a tennis ball... nobody did it like Stafford did! One of my own favourites was our own 'Silent Films' one; Chaplin, Keaton, Keystone Cops sort of thing, hilariously choreographed in speeded-up jerky movements and with the hugest cane and paper bi-plane suspended from the very high Borough Hall ceiling. It was a masterpiece of craftwork, constructed in three large sections and somehow carted through the crowded winter-weathered streets of Stafford and re-assembled and hung; a most dominating and terrifying marvel of artistic invention, no doubt violating every conceivable safety regulation!

Amongst our Third Year Dress Designers was a bearded, lanky bloke, Edward Hislop, known as 'Teddy'. It seemed a bit strange to see this whiskery chap amongst all those fabulously beautiful, nymphlike young women, all of them sewing away, lovingly stroking textures, embroidering intricate design, fashioning dresses for dreamlike bodies and in odorous perfumed air and seemingly always flowers about the place. 'Art' Tomkins was suddenly, compellingly in love with one of these beauties, A Uttoxeter girl by the name of Jean and, it was through this liaison that I got to know 'Teddy' Hislop who, at around six o'clock each evening metamorphosed back into a black chrysalis before kick-starting an old 'Ariel' motorbike and went back-firing and crackling all the way back to the tiny village of Yoxall where he lived with his widower Dad in a remote cottage with a tank of tropical fishes on a smallholding where wandering sheep left their wool on the barbed-wire for 'Teddy' to collect and use in his Art. He and I became really good mates, the kind of culture-shock that my system needed and lacked.

'Teddy' loved 'Arts and Crafts' in the most fertile sort of way and was, to quite a large extent, one of the reasons for our Arts Balls being such magnificent artistic achievements. I accompanied him on the pillion to stately homes where we could study various collections and most splendid artifacts of an England which we treasured. 'Teddy' was the most even-tempered, easy-going person; in a strange way more like a woman than a man in behavioural attitudes. I just put it down to his being 'very sensitive'. Mom and Dad thought he was great, which astonished me; his 'posh' talk and refined, precise mannerisms made them think that I was associating with aristocracy.

My Euphonium was now getting to be a feature of my life and I'd taught myself to play it in a fairly 'basic' sort of way and I was getting better at it all the time, carting it around everywhere with me, oblivious to the ridicule that this aroused on my numerous impromptu practice sessions. I obviously had, like my sister Fay, an inclination towards the musical art, myself having been able to make a harmonica 'talk' since an infant and without anyone considering it to be any more than a bloomin' nuisance, a bad habit that I needed to be broken of. Music, being highly conspicuous by its inescapable audible nature, essentially required there to be encouragement if it were to ever flower; a self-confidence bordering on conceit was a vital necessity in preventing the canker of shyness from killing the precious gift in its infancy. One could always draw and paint in total seclusion, unheard and almost unseen as well, shyness didn't really matter one way or another. It was only because the

Euphonium was something of a joke that wasn't to be taken seriously, that I was able to hold my own with the monster of shyness, which had already closed the doors on music having any meaningful, fertile growing place in my life, sad to say.

In a recent stolen free-period, I constructed a 'percussion-device' in my old 'Commercial's' studio, my way of relaxing spiritually after a self-induced study of Stanley Spencer, an Artist who had suddenly dazzled me and whom I was about to compile a thesis on. 'Art' Tomkins helped me gather all the bits and pieces that I needed, basically anything that produced a sound when struck, arranging then re-arranging them into what I felt made a musical logic which I could access when I put it to the test. I'd never played a drum in my life before but, when this rather 'Heath Robinson' contraption had been strung-up, balanced to my liking and then struck with a piece of dowel-rod and a long brush, I ventured forth into the most textual sound-picture; the music of ordinary things at long last having a voice of their own. 'Art' just stood there beaming, he couldn't believe his ears; bits of wood, glass, tin, cardboard, pottery, copper-piping, steel ... you name it, it all came to life in this, the only single solitary occasion in time. My problem now that I'd got started, was knowing how to stop this continuum of crazy, beautiful sound. I'd attracted an audience by now and could readily see smiles of approval rather than condemnation and I was nevertheless more than 'relieved' when 'Art' joined them, explaining; "Jim and I are trying to discover what sounds there are locked away in ordinary things; we're not trying to disturb anyone, seriously!" Too late; Lecturers had now come to see what this 'jangly' perpetual-motion thing was that'd disrupted their classes and an old family shyness-blight came over me and killed it all dead. There were smiles everywhere as I blushed, fearing that I'd be reported, even expelled, having already tipped the scales over the wretched Wolverhampton episode.

It was days later when I was getting back to grips with Stanley Spencer's 'Resurrection' that I heard a clarinet expertly being played together with the first bars of 'When the Saints go Marching In' on trumpet. I dropped what I was doing and rushed into the corridor where two rebellious Third Years were 'testing the air'; a College Jazz Band had just been hatched! Colin Peters was the clarinet wizard, Walter Heron was the white 'Louis Armstrong' on trumpet. I knew and loved them both well; I even rated 'Wal' as probably being the most brilliant student in the whole college. He was creatively energetic through and through, a genius no less ... and very funny with it! Meanwhile band-members gathered like wasps on jam; this was serious business. 'Bong' went 'Bang' when he heard the uproarious din coming from the 'Life-room' where a white rat was already causing mayhem. He did his predictable ritualistic charging about the place ... before on seeing the rat, immediately fled and phoned the Council!

'Teddy' had provided me with a small camp-bed at their farm cottage and so, with him really enjoying this new 'Jazz' dimension, I experienced rare new freedom to explore the hours beyond College. Our brand new Band, with myself as a member of sorts, had actually got our first booking, a bit of an opening 'blow-out' at a pub called 'The Crown Inn'. Everyone was a hive and a half of activity; people were working furiously on the coming Arts Ball and the Band were battling against all sorts of odds in trying to get meaningful practice sessions, somewhere ... anywhere.

A frustrated group of us were racking our brains over the problem when Tom Crossley, a third year Illustrator, casually came up with a stroke of genius by suggesting that we explored what space there was beyond the trap-door on the ceiling of the 'Intermediate' Life Drawing room next to the metalwork room. In hardly any time at all, Tom, being supported on 'Wal's' shoulders managed to reach up and unfasten it and pulled down an attached loft-ladder. Like rats up a drainpipe, Tom and I went up to investigate leaving the others below keeping a lookout. It was the most thrilling and scary thing I'd ever done at College; a window opened out onto the roof, taking my breath away in one heart-stopping instance. There was a two-foot walkway with a short protective parapet wall running all along the edge, one which would just about provide the Jazz Band the 'leaning-back' elbow room which it so desperately needed to practice, without sliding off into oblivion. It didn't bear thinking about; we were terrifyingly high up looking out across and down onto miles and miles of Stafford, a gaping match-box world with match-stick people. "Bloody hell, Tom!" I gasped, trying not to foul my pants, and he grinned falsely and muttered "I hope they've got a head for heights!" We then made our way back down with the good news.

Over the space of the last few hectic days the Band had expanded; Ivor Brown, another third year Illustrator had come in on Alto Sax; Ken Turpin, 'Turps', a rather extravagant third year Painter, had entered the arena on percussion, this currently being one cymbal plus anything else that just happened to be handy. Victor Todd, another superb Illustrator of our third year, had also joined on Piano; alas, right now we couldn't get a piano up onto the roof. In addition to these, two 'outsiders' had joined, both being musical mates of Colin, now 'Pee-Wee' Peters; one a Guitarist, the other on Trombone while, down here in the real world, Tom Crossley was our Bass-player, on a tea-chest, broom-stick and length of string. There was no way that his particular 'Stradivarius' could be accommodated on the roof either so, while the Band were gingerly settling themselves on the roof, Tom nipped away and very swiftly returned with Fred, our human skeleton, causing an absolute riot up on the roof when he strung Fred up and dangled him from the guttering, high over the street below. For the sake of discretion, the loft-ladder was pulled back up and the trap door fastened, only then could the musicians ignore their vertigo and get the session underway.

People going about their business like ants far below, stopped in their tracks in disbelief and looked up to Heaven as our opening 'standard', 'When the Saints' rasped with venomous gusto out across Stafford ... and with just a rattling white skeleton hanging 'dancingly' from the guttering. Fear of heights was keeping the rest of us lain back on the slates letting rip at forty-five degrees, with Tom tossing out leaflets advertising our next 'gig'; we were now 'The Crownin' Glory Jazz Band'! "There's getting quite a crowd down there all lookin' up an tappin' their feet!" Tom enthused carefully as a rendition of 'Stevedore Stomp' rearranged the last clouds. In what seemed like an Ice-age below, 'Bong' was in torment, hearing the Devil's music in his head as he marched this way and that, not knowing where it was coming from. He knew that they'd take him for mad if he mentioned this at the 'Lodge' and he'd accordingly be disregarded. This was, beyond any trace of doubt, the most sensational experience that I'd been part of, and on a very high roof of all places; even a Police car stopped to listen while the crowd were dancing on the road. As a farewell gesture, we all gingerly disregarded our fears, leaned over the rampart and waved; they all cheered, no doubt muttering stuff like ... "Bloody Art Students!" Few things in my life could ever equal this!

In all truth, the Band was very much 'hit-and-miss' at first, due mostly to there not having been time to work-out numbers; improvising alone, exciting as it was, tended at times to be more confusing than it was constructive. What we needed was a solid bed of recognisable 'standards'. People, for some strange reason needed something they didn't have to think about, something they recognised. We all knew this and, those of us with record-players listened our ears dry and exhausted to the music of Ken Colyer, Chris Barber, Muggsy Spanier and, more importantly, the golden original stuff from the Deep South. We soon got our repertoire together, and with 'Old Vic' proving to be worth his weight in gold on the piano and 'PeeWee' working out jazz duets with Ivor Brown on sax, 'Wal' on trumpet, raspingly bare and effective, something raw and fine was emerging.

## 15. 'Wizards, Blizzards and Science Surreal'

The small insignificant town of Rugeley was providing the College with an unusually fine vintage of students. An unrepeatable phenomenon which I put down to the soil there being migratory and enriched by a close-by mining activity, which had resulted in freakishly high-iron cabbage crops and unusually enriched rabbit and pigeon meat. In addition to our Jazz Piano-man, 'Old Vic' Todd and Ken Turpin, single cymbal minus drums, we had Claire Archer, painter and Goddess of the 'Social Dimension', other-worldly and lavishly beaded, achingly desirable and laid-back ... at least she was whenever I thought of her; a rich girl who could have taken me far if only our confounded paths would have crossed! Then, there was the most extrovert, flowery breeze of a young man, a real 'Oscar Wilde' if ever there was, Nigel Wilkes was his name ... a proper 'Nigel'. I referred to him privately as 'Chicory Essence' because of his being more 'Camp' then coffee in a bottle; others called him 'Sponge' for some strange reason ... all soft and cakey, I suppose. Whatever the reason, he made my mate 'Teddy' seem like an all-in-wrestler by comparison and was a seriously gifted Artist who brought so much to the Arts Ball effort, never once stopping smiling.

These two things, the 'Jazz Band and the Arts Ball' were the most priceless of experiences; no other things came so breathlessly close to producing pure Gold from Chicken-shit. Between them they were the very essence of what being an Art Student was capable of revealing. It was simply a wizardly alchemy of uncertain origin or purpose, a vapour of pure gilded holy breath that just appeared, was breathed, then vanished. The Band got so good, that I felt out of place sitting there pretending that I was capable of contributing something of value when I still hadn't mastered the Euphonium to a standard which I was happy with. Besides, our new trombone player was so deafeningly brilliant that I could no longer hear what I was playing; so I graciously threw-in the towel and just enjoyed listening to the others instead.

Destiny worked a bit like God was supposed to ... mysteriously. Whatever ambiguities there may have existed between the Euphonium and myself, God came to shed light on, sending in his wisdom, a morning of treacherously icy roads, upon which Teddy, the motorbike with me on the back, and me with the Euphonium on my back, in the perilous process of trying to avoid coming to grief ... we failed! Everything suddenly parted company with everything else; it was a long bending downhill skating rink and we travelled from top to bottom like a crude, accelerating plankton dispersing even more as we descended. The world kept coming and going, each time giving me lightning glimpses of the various particles which had previously been an inter-related working organism consisting of motorcyclist, a pillion-passenger and a Euphonium. I just caught sight of my wind instrument as it shot over a bank and vanished down a ditch ... immediately followed by a big, black, heavy motorbike, then Teddy, then myself in that order. "Oh, Bagger!" Teddy cursed poshly, comforted by recognising that the body in the process of unravelling itself from him was actually alive. "Are you okay, James?" he breathed. "I think so," I spluttered, still a bit too shocked to properly understand what was going on. By degrees we clambered out of the ditch, making the silly mistake of jumping back down onto the road, failing to have calculated that the road surface was a sheet of glass, upending us onto our behinds once more. Those were far and away the worst conditions that we'd encountered and were left in something of a dilemma; firstly we had to get the motorbike out of the ditch, check it to see that nothing was broken then, wait until the ice melted. By degrees we got the big, hot thing out, it was okay, but my Euphonium, sadly, was totally flattened! I thanked God in all his thoughtfulness and tact for his endorsement of my leaving the Band in this most subtle of ways; any feelings of guilt that had lingered were 'miracled' away at a stroke. I looked at Teddy and he looked at me forlornly standing there with my crumpled tubular silver thing in my hand. "Oh dear, I think it's poorly!" he smirked ruefully and we both burst out laughing. "It's got a headache," I concurred in a daft voice and returned it to the ditch, adding "you were getting a bit too big for your boots anyway!"

Dark nights that clung like wet bandages and, abrupt, fleeting smears of the palest of greys which dimly illuminated the tightening tunnel of daytime, was where we once more had found ourselves. Winter was nevertheless a two-ended nocturne of extreme hard work; hibernation provided precarious solutions for some creatures; others more sensibly migrated, travel broadening the mind while sleeping only fattened it. We 'people'-things just bashed on regardless, stalwart and stupid in procreative copulation with the nymphomaniac Goddess of Commerce and with an incurable disease-like habit of forever associating rigidity with strength and flexibility with weakness.

Our 'Fantastic Toyshop' Arts Ball happened like a dream, I even had a speaking part, playing a pre-Victorian child; every bit as nerve-wracking as playing a Euphonium on the Art College roof! The audience all gathered tightly around our stage, enthralled, surprised that this one was not as other Balls had been ... 'Surrealist Wild Theatre', but poetic instead. We all received a most enthusiastic applause, after which we could relax and let off steam. I was just happy to become anonymous amongst the beautiful young women who, only hours before had been scruffy, grubby-fingered students. My sweetheart, Julie, had been invited but her parents thought it safer and wiser to deny her request; they'd heard a lot of strange things about Art Balls and the 'things' that Art Students got up to. So, I was free ... that is to say I wasn't free at all. She was worrying over nothing, I couldn't be unfaithful to her no matter what, even though eyes were flashing alluringly like fireflies in a featherbedded night, colliding with mine quite intentionally before flickering away into the exciting darkness.

One such collision which was putting me to the test, one which I had secretly battled with for some time, was with that of a most beautiful, shy, sweet blonde from Bloxwich; neither of us had the nerve to break the silence that ached between us and, here we both were, fireflies colliding for hungry precious seconds before the enveloping dark. I was in a prison of my own making where, flirting in this manner was illegal. 'Art' Tomkins had by now become a praying mantis and was lathering at the mouth, devouring his new dress-designer in a 'snogging-until-death' ritual in a corner. It was really quite embarrassing, always deadly serious and never romantic. As I turned away, I caught sight of Gavin, a very likeable, trendy whiz-kid about the College, he was searching for someone. "Ahh ... there you are, Mister Van Gogh!" he exclaimed on spotting me trying to be invisible and still with both ears. He snaked his way over to me, took hold of my wrists and said "Jim, you've got to trust me ... will you?" Somewhat perplexed, I nodded that I would. This didn't satisfy him and he asked me again, "Jim, there's somebody in this hall that loves you and really wants you and I want you to do exactly what I do ... but to her; do I have your word?" "Yes," I sighed more in exasperation than anything else and, before I knew what was going on, he came up and kissed me on the mouth. Urgh! I wanted to throw-up; he was pulling me across the hall and pushed me face-to-face with the blonde from Bloxwich who was there all shy and blushing waiting for me. "Go on ... you promised me; go on ... kiss her!" I just collapsed into a jibbering, squirming worm-bag of writhing shyness at this revelation which my upbringing hadn't prepared me for, even though I wanted to kiss her. I really wanted to, more than anything else on earth but ... I couldn't. I let her down unforgivingly and hated myself as I watched her blush and lower her golden head in embarrassment; I just couldn't cope with such a life-altering revelation in public, I really loved her far too much for that, something which she was not to know ... something which I would never, ever forget.

Life was full of revelations, another one of which was the Snooker-room which Teddy and his Dad had at the back of their farm cottage; one which resulted in his Dad's dream of solitude being shattered when Teddy invited the Band and a like-minded gang of us second and third years over for a 'snooker party'. A baked spud and home-cured bacon, sleep on the floor afterwards sort of thing and, with there being a few of the girls invited, it promised to make a bedtime rather intriguing, especially with 'Burto' and Alison there.. It was indeed a solitude-shattering evening, the Band were on form, helped by there being an old upright piano which, up until now had only ever played hymns and carols. Poor Mister Hislop, I felt so sorry for him as he kept appearing and re-appearing with more and more logs for the ever ravenous open fire, looking increasingly weary as the night wore on. "You go to bed, Daddy!" Teddy instructed him, "I'll sort out some blankets and cushions for our guests, so just you go and get some sleepy-byes, there's a good Daddy!" It seemed so strange hearing him call his dad, 'Daddy'; a bit sort of 'baby-talkish'. Whatever, it worked and a very tired Mister Hislop graciously bowed-out under a spontaneous and depleted rendition of 'When the Saints go Marching in', 'Wal's' way of saying 'goodnight and thanks for having us.'

Eventually yawns were gaping darkly and the snooker balls, as well as the Band had idled to a thankful grave, as chrysalis-like bandaged lumps started to fidget and twitch around the floor. "Nighty night, everybody ... come, come now ... hands on the outside!" I heard him titter before turning out the light and leaving only the death-throe flicker of a flame in the hearth. There followed a cacophony of farts, snores, snorts and sniggers which lingered for quite a while and I suddenly winced as 'Burto' leaned over me to whisper something to Tom who was sprawled on my other side. "If you touch Alison's breasts, she'll sing for you!" was the whispered message, followed by stifled laughter on both sides of me and I could hear heavy sighing breathing coming from somewhere over by the piano, together with the squeaked puncture of a kiss that'd shed its rubber; two pigs at the same trough. Then, the trough emptied, a mothly silence dusted over the place and Alison started to sing, very whisperingly, sweet and soft as a dove two hedges away while the last dull cinders fell in almost silence to their bed of ashes, leaving the dove-croodling snooker room in darkness, all the balls asleep in their pockets and the hardwood cues dreaming on the dark viridian cush.

Dispersal was swift once half a pig and an entire county of rudely boisterous brown eggs had vanished into the ether. I'd seated myself next to Tom on the sofa, the pair of us mesmerized by the inch-long electric-blue fishes, the way they moved ... so balletic in their pint-sized Universe safe from faecal bombardment of whales, sharks, seals and ocean liners lengthening the lives of the already-dead, (an old Alchemist trick.) 'Burto' looked like death, bravely managing to lean over Tom without collapsing head-first into the fish tank; "I told you she'd sing for you!" he chuckled and wryly, Tom smiled and added, "Not only that, she's got rather nice vocal chords as well!" We both watched 'Burto' melt clumsily away into an ineptitude of post-nocturnal lethargy a million miles from the nearest Catholic. I'd somehow managed to sleep without, to my knowledge, being tampered with, even though I had hoped maybe that Claire might have dragged me feet first and awarded me with my first 'O' level. The winter world was empty again, apart from the flock of Fieldfares and Redwings stripping the vermilion haws, while symphonies of weeping Peewits grieved all plumed and miraculously blotting out the briefest of suns in the briefest of moments in the briefest of existences. I had read all the signs, winter was sleeping beyond our stubbornness and it would catch us out ... of course it would!

Stafford's town roads had been salted when Teddy and I left for the 'Crown Inn' on that dependable old 'Ariel', supposedly built for comfort rather than speed; 'truth was, it was just 'built', full stop. We left Stafford's last streetlight before realising we were entering a blizzard which was worsening by the minute. Using our legs as stabilizers, we precariously inched our way into the swirling white choreography, struggling on with snow clogging Teddy's goggles and making it impossible to see either with or without them. We had reached 'Milford' and could go no further because here the snow lay deep, not crisp, but even; upwards of six level inches of it. The old bike was willing but the world wasn't; it'd been itching for this for some time and nothing was going to stop it now, so there! All we had to see by was 'snow-light' and a sad, small torch with two little bodies in it rather than batteries; neglect came too late. We could just about make out a garden frontage and, with some difficulty, Teddy wheeled the motorbike through a gateway, cursing the torch for its untimely choice of moments for having a blackout. He wanted to scribble an explanatory note on something, anything. "Oh, I know what I can use;" he whispered with an inspired chuckle, and he passed me his gloves then firked about down inside his inner jacket and came out with a letter. "This came this morning, haven't had time to read it yet." Shielding it as best he could from the driving snow, he removed letter from envelope and returned the letter to his pocket. "This is as good as a note!" he murmured and fumbled about for the letterbox to deliver the hastily torn envelope with his name and address on it; and that's where we left the old bike.

It was way past midnight, Teddy in leggings, crash-helmet, oilskin top and leather boots; me in demob-suit, college scarf, dufflecoat and flimsy slip-on shoes. The world was dead, no anything, just the relentless goose-plucked snow stinging into our bare eyes, encrusting our entirety as we persevered on our do-or-die march, rolling a snowball which just grew and grew before making a gigantic snowman at someone's front door, giggling ourselves stupid at the prospect of them opening the door and being confronted by this giant. Then we trudged on over Milford Hills where the snow lay inches deeper and the wind wilder, burying our smiles before the handful of miles to where Rugeley lay hidden; then the bleak blizzarded, even more formidable lanes which had become featureless in the white darkness, where only higgledy-piggledly signposts offered the ghostliest of lifelines. We'd long since passed the point of no return and I placed my faith and trust in Teddy and his impeccable knowledge of this well-wearied rabbit-run, all its twists, ups and downs, beast-moaning byres and ghost-hollowed stumps left by time, leering like gargoiled tombs without names. We had turned into creatures of the night, dimly able now to pick our way amongst these ghosts, new found brothers the pair of us.

My feet no longer had blood circulating through them, the suction of snow repeatedly causing me to walk out of my shoes; it was an agony which I fought with all my might to contain; this was the reason that snowmen had no legs, the icy cold had frozen them away! The problem got so bad that I even tried walking in just my socks, frustrated that so much time had been lost by having to dig my shoes out from under the snow. Teddy meanwhile, on his mincey little strides, was dry-footed, warm-toed in his leather boots, insulated throughout while I, like a sad blob of blotting paper grew heavier and heavier and even heavier. Making things better and worse in the same perplexing, failing nightmare, the temperature took a dive and the last flakes fell, hastened by a dull red smear dimly crayoning an awakening haemorrhage, raw and sore, diving the two brutes that'd brawled and battled throughout the night. One the sky, the other the frozen earth, where, even in this ghostly dimness, a robin was glittering a silver thread, crystalline and intricately sweet; it was unbelievable to be reminded that we were still alive in this way.

Heartened by this spirit rising and the reddening of the blood now flowing from the wound where night had been, the first far cockerels re-staked their claims to harems and further still, in crying choirs the sheep complained, unable to comprehend such an overwhelming casualty of white weather which the night had slain, burying their breakfast and gone again. Cocoons of snorers were slowly midwifed into life by the strange new light that gave shape to curtains full two hours earlier than expected as, one by one, like jewels the rectangles shone golden far and further yet in this eternal rebirth of yawning, dawning, morning. Parishes were butterflies, no longer cardboard cocoons; all now awakening with wings anew and the new-dawn scent of smoke from fires lingered where the last heels of a blizzard's wind had raced away. I could smell the apple logs and I could smell the coal as more and more rectangles of gold enriched the grave of yesterday; bouquets of cottage Windows, no longer wreaths but a million button-holes instead.

We had made it back to Yoxall where Teddy's Dad hadn't slept a wink for fear that something horrid must have happened. Hot coffee appeared out of nowhere and I was relieved of my dead-weight wet clothing and re-bandaged in garments which were strangers to my shivering body. My feet throbbed agonisingly as the blood ventured back down to my toes; a pain that made me laugh and cry at the same time. We sprawled in the dawning firelight and began to glow in thoughtful silence knowing that God had been on our side for sure. I looked at Teddy and his Christianly smile just said it all, we simply couldn't speak and I watched him slowly sink into the cushions and slip away to sleep. His Dad had been watching and he turned slowly away muttering, "I don't know!" I could see hot tears stealing down his cheeks, then I must have fallen asleep.

So much was temporary; in fact, if I wanted to really nit-pick, everything under the sun was temporary, even life itself. More realistically, snow was more temporary than the winter that contained it and, winter was more temporary than the year that contained it. Being at College was temporary and it contained a host of tinier temporary things, transient, transitional and making it hard sometimes to fuel the enthusiasm to remain focused over the duration of the temporariness of being an 'Art Student', knowing all too well that another more dastardly temporary phase awaited, that of becoming a Soldier. This, its wretched self being temporary, did little to dispel the trepidation that the mere thought of it aroused. For temporariness to have any worth, it needed to be large enough in breadth and depth in which one could actually achieve something substantial and worthwhile, and not for it to be too piddling small to be able to do anything with.

The process of Art was temporary; the writhing, animated energy of the idea in process only lived for a precious amount of time before it lost its animation and became permanent, lifeless ... but strangely, never quite ever dead. Looking at Paintings, permanent as they may have been, was never the same as visiting the cemetery. Artists, in fact, were very strange things; they could behold the germ of a concept and wrestle with it as it wriggled either eager to be born or, fighting against the very thought of it. Then, for it to be left to dry into a state of permanence, still miraculously possessing the energy and the vitality to ignite fires in minds eternal; sweet feelings, those of anger, sadness or whatever; giving always giving. It was always the poor old Artist that lay dead ... unless of course he or she was still caught-up in the temporary state ... like waiting for the snows to thaw so that Teddy could get his motorbike back.

Time was an insatiable wind that raged and roared, whispered and breathed throughout the 'Universe', itself a timeless, shapeless, topless, bottomless impossibility for it being 'Forever', without end and therefore to my blessed, temporary learned nature, without beginning either. Eternity was precisely that; having no beginning or end, yet existing as we, 'temporary arrangements' were proof particles of the ultimate existence. The Universe was an endless suburbia with solar systems strewn like housing estates all with allotments and sheds, dinosaurs in paper aeroplanes, crocodiles with skipping ropes, people swimming in goldfish bowls on windowsills, spilled sugar everywhere; parasites parasiting on parasites ad infinitum proving that the moment 'Now' where I sat playing see-saws, was the pivotal balancing point between an Eternity in two complementary halves, one of them vast and ever vaster, the other miniscule and ever more miniscule; inner space and outer space. Planets revealing themselves to be birds eggs with elves on the back of grasshoppers racing amongst stars of icing sugar, white umbrellas from long-broken clocks; bubbles with rainbows painted on them, each one containing a seed of a flower and the song of a bird, billions upon billions upon billions of them. The airless air was deafening with all the imaginations that Religion had evicted to become electric-dust and to go on playing as children, becoming lightning; gipsies of dark. The very concept of Eternity once it had stopped being just a word, was, quite literally, maddening; 'Eternity' was this moment forever 'Now'!

Science was a bit like Art, aspired alchemy down another route; a gazelle with more brains than sense, never satisfied with simply exploring and discovering. While Art was there to delight the mind, Science was there to dictate to the brain, leaping gazelle-like, often in the wrong direction in its haste to prove itself greater than anything else. Alas, with Eternity being timeless, endless in every conceivable direction, it was impossible to match egotistical appetites with answers. The most frustrating obstacle barring the way to calculating a 'Beginning' of Time, Matter and Species, was that of there being no point by which to start measuring. It was driving them mad, they needed a starting point. They'd grown weary of the, 'And God said, Let there be Light, and there was Light' routine, countless others had done it throughout the scienceless Planet; Gods were like second-hand clothes, so common that they were brawling all throughout the inhospitable, intolerant, ill-fitting and ragged-arsed Heavens, some of them mouthing this and others of them mouthing that, all of them 'Blessedly' guessing, permitting blood-letting on tsunami-scale. Disembowelment and beheading under 'Sacrificial' licence, with stoning to death as an okay hors d'oeuvre ... or optional pudding. Theological, anarchic mayhem ... the usual thing, while ordinary people watched radishes grown and climbed trees in search of nuts, berries and doves eggs; not a single one of them wearing a wristwatch or even bothering to crawl into a cave or a shallow black-hole and inventing one. They were just 'happy', pure and simple; unburdened with all that 'Divine' speculative stuff that had appetites for endless river of blood to flow and to go flowing for 'God' or whatever they called this 'Master' of all things sparkling beyond the sun and the imperfect moon.

Out of utter desperation, Science invented itself a wand-like measuring-stick at last, one that could be used as a weapon against paganism, whatever the label! An unassuming sort of bloke from Shrewsbury, fond of pressing wildflowers and stroking cats, a typical 'dabbler' at bird-watching and could name every member of the Crow family in alphabetical order without forgetting the Chough. Well, this bloke really put the cat amongst the pigeons when he went off on an all-expenses paid sailing expedition to observe little-known, and to hopefully discover unknown species upon the planet. Rainforests had zillions of such species yet to be recorded but, this sailing ship named after a breed of dog, set sail for the Galapagos, a group of volcanic islands off the coast of Ecuador, site of gargantuan earth-movement and transformation, remnant no doubt of a vast continent, a lost civilization which the Planet had swallowed up in one of its 'no-holds-barred', age-consuming gluttonous orgies. The whole experience fascinated him and set him off thinking; surely there was a link between the humble 'Morris Minor' and these frighteningly large Tortoises; it was too much of a coincidence for them to look exactly the same, and with roughly the same performance. But, that was nothing, he almost thought he was back in Shropshire when he saw Finches, just like those back there in his garden. Being only the 'average' birdwatcher, as most were, he took all Finches as being ... 'Finches', these being 'slightly' different, carnivorous in fact, real nasty little bastards. His imagination did seven somersaults, luring him into chancing his Ornithological luck and daring to stab at a guess and even into suggesting that, Finches were Finches, full stop;

but for some reason known only to themselves, these nasty little sods had actually selected the option of being different!

Surrealism had found a friend in Darwin, Art was way ahead of all those Scientific boffins; Hieronymous Bosch, William Blake, Max Ernst, Joan Miro, Salvador Dali and so many others had gone off on their own sailing ships of discovery, creating vivid worlds believable by the very dissection of reality, an association of impossible ideas prescribed upon a dumbness. Science seized on Darwin's latest work of 'Surrealism', that of showing things actually 'Naturally Selecting' and changing into slowly becoming 'other' things, like fishes leaving the sea and choosing instead to be land animals; lizardy things, like the Fishes turning scales into feathers and becoming Birds. Worse still, for Monkeys and Apes to elect to become 'Humans' ... 'hairy parents' not, 'heirs apparent'. There were far finer surrealists around than Darwin who, to my mind, was the only Surrealist Scientist ever, and it's sad for me that he hasn't ever received due acclaim, for this.

## 16. 'Mutiny with Chips and a Strange Game of Football'

By way of surprise, Teddy said that he'd like to introduce me to someone; he wouldn't say who it was at this stage, he wanted it to be a pleasant surprise. My mind boggled and we arranged for us all to meet up at the 'Swan Inn', the pub in my village where, as a boy, my pale blue-eyed, golden-haired childhood sweetheart Pauline lived. I felt nervous; it was going to seem quite strange to be brushing against those most treasured memories again after all this time; a whole lot stranger and sadder than I had expected once I had achingly revisited the memory, finding it still strong and so very lovely.

I made sure to be early on that particular evening, considering it my advantage to be able to hear the motorbike approaching, giving me a sneak preview of the 'surprise' and allowing me the benefit of whatever initiative there was to be gained by doing so. It was obvious that Teddy had had similar thoughts, motorbikes tended to prevent one from looking at their best and so, five minutes tidying-up would have been helpful. Too bad, I was already there, but only just; no sooner had I arrived when I heard the unmistakable rattle of the old 'Ariel' coming briskly up the road. Trying my best to look casual, I leaned back against the outdoor porch in an attempt to conceal my nerves, which were jangling somewhat and I could see the look of surprise on Teddy's face as he drew up to a halt beside me. To my utter astonishment, a beautiful young woman wearing a pretty silken headscarf and a tweedy trouser-suit, dismounted graciously. "Bloody hell!" I gasped to myself ... "he never told me he'd got such a stunning sister!" He struggled to unfasten his weatherproofs, plainly delighted by the look of shock on my face; my sham casualness was well and truly blown; I couldn't take my eyes off her. He grinned and turned to the woman proudly, "Jim-Jim, I'd like you to meet Avril. Avril, I'd like you to meet my fellow Diploma student, Jim-Jim." She and I shook hands and I felt a complete prat far having been called 'Jim-Jim' of all things, I sounded more like a pet rabbit or something. Niceties were blushing and tripping over each other, I was desperate to know 'who' she really was, apart from being 'Avril'; was she his sister, cousin ... who? Then, quite smugly he decided to put me out of my misery and announced; "Avril is my girlfriend," and I felt the braces of my heart's trousers snap, leaving me all gaping and exposed inside.

We smoked 'Senior Service' and drank lemonade in the 'Outdoor', laughing as Teddy and I recalled our walk in the blizzard and the giant snowman we had left on some unsuspecting person's front doorstep. I told him that he was a bit of a dark horse by keeping Avril a secret for so long and I was rather surprised to learn that she was a nurse; I'd rather more expected her to be a breeder of thoroughbred race-horses or, maybe an heiress to a family Fabric Design Company. I didn't feel quite so much out of my depth now and I could relax at last, how nice ... a nurse; I simply couldn't believe it. Teddy 'Dark Horse' was a friend whom I simply couldn't fault; he was level-headed, sensible, kind and delightfully funny. Everyone at College loved and respected him; he was a superb Dress-designer and had obviously inherited the most impeccable of tastes. I never ventured into asking him about his Mother, but I knew that she must have been no ordinary person, just as his Dad was no ordinary dad.

'Art' Tomkins meanwhile, was still fighting against being a square peg in a round hole, frustratedly searching for a 'calling' in life, very much aware that, once he had finally and decisively left College, he'd be on his own in a way which he couldn't bear thinking about. There had always been a military tradition in his family, a long and proud association with the Scots Guards and, deep down he could see himself standing there outside Buckingham Palace in an immaculate red-jacketed uniform with gleaming buttons and wearing a huge 'Bearskin' headdress. More than that, he wanted to be an artist but, with this, you either were one or you weren't; for 'Art' sadly, wanting wasn't enough. All that 'Artist' was, was a state of mind, that's all, and he didn't possess this, I could see it all too clearly. He and Teddy were light-years apart and it therefore shocked me rigid when 'Art' took me to one side and wickedly whispered to me that he had made a date with Avril and was going to take her to the cinema in Stafford, behind Teddy's back. I gasped with horror and disgust ... was nothing sacred anymore!

I was on my way to see Julie when I inadvertently bumped into 'Art', standing all anaesthetically immaculate, guardsman-like and intimidatingly well-groomed, looking stern and concerned over something; he really was a man with the world on his shoulders. "Good film, was it?" I asked in a fusion of flippancy and disgust, still unable to come to terms with the burden of knowledge of his treachery which he had left me with. He gritted his teeth and muttered; "We didn't even make it as far as Stafford!" "Serves you bloody well right!" I snapped ... "she's Teddy's girlfriend, she is!" "Was!" he smirked "not after what WE did, she aint!" "You don't mean to say that you ..." "Exactly that ... and not just once either!" he interrupted in a dribbling-at-the-mouth sort of way, clicking his heels and making sure that his bootlace-tie was to perfection. "We snogged all the way past Rugeley and we got off the bus on Milford Hills and headed for the heather and bracken ... and we just got down and did it!" "You lousy sod I just wish you hadn't, that's all. He's a good friend of mine; how can I face him now?" I sighed and shook my head disconsolately. "Look, Jim, Teddy was no good for Avril, she needed a proper man, not a fairy." "And if you've made her pregnant, what then?" "I'll marry her!" he snapped with a seriousness that was more starched than his collar. I just shook my head and he, rather irritated by my response, stepped up close and said ... "Takes two to tango!" Sadly I said "Can't argue with that... sorry mate!"

This single incident more or less marked the end of our substantial friendship and, for whatever reason, Avril didn't ever want to see 'Art' again, she just vanished into thin air, leaving poor old Teddy well and truly in the dark. I wanted to tell him what had happened but I couldn't bring myself to; it made me feel like I'd been poisoned and left me with the feeling that I was betraying Teddy myself, effectively ending our friendship. 'Art' was triggered into making a decision and he left College and joined the Scots Guards as a regular soldier; it could have all been so different.

Another year had turned its dog-eared page but, the new page wasn't pristine like a sketchbook page and instead was one that'd already been written on, with gaps set like mousetraps baited with questions. Growing up was like that, blank spaces had to increasingly be earned; life as a sketchbook wasn't going to come free anymore, the dream had awakened into a nightmare which itself had awakened and been blown away. Realisation was an intolerably long, albeit brief period which revealed that permanence was just another temporary arrangement along with all the contrary rest.

The mystery of our pre-war-whore-house became clear; it had been an antiques warehouse, hence the obscure type of treasures we'd discovered in it. Sadly, this desperately needed space was no longer meant for our use, as a result of wheeler-dealings higher up and behind the scenes; the 'Isms' and 'Ology' factory had now been granted use of it as a 'day-release' painting and decorating unit under their jurisdiction. Our world was shrinking, not expanding; it would have been far better had they left it to operate as a brothel ... with an arrangement for us to go there and draw. To make things even worse, a new noisy batch of 'Commercials' had been located in what was now a large, two rooms knocked into one studio on the ground floor, leaving we 'National Diploma Illustrators' with just two rooms at the top of the building. Having been ousted from the main College because of supposed 'lack of space'. It no longer seemed to me that we were much of a priority anymore. I discerned a steady downhill spiral and distinct 'wheels-within-wheels' game of Monopoly being played in hierarchical places. Rebellion wasn't an option with our final year fast approaching; to protest now would be a distraction too far, only we could be the losers.

'Burto' wasn't bothered in the slightest; not only was the place in question just a stroll away from home for him but, of far more importance, it was the cricket season again. He was once more showing his magic, upstaging even the 'Kremlin' when, two of the world's most powerful and feared figures came on a state visit to Britain, calling-in at Stafford where highly technical and electronically advanced technologies were based ... right next door to the pub where 'The Crownin' Glory Jazz Band' were also based. Bulganin and Kruschev, known everywhere as 'B and K', were providing the nation's headlines just as 'Burto' and his 'other-end' bowler, a lad by the name of Kendrick, ripped ragged a highly rated side and, there it was, plastered in large print over the Sports page ... " 'B and K' Declare War!" What a celebrity; no-one would have believed that this ordinary looking nobody could have stolen the headlines from the World's most powerful statesmen, and still remain humble 'Joe Ordinary'! The annoying thing for me was that, where Art was concerned, he played a dead-bat forward defensive stroke at everything, unwilling to put into Art that which he so passionately put into cricket; he really frustrated me with this 'playing-safe' with drawing and painting ... even romance! His charisma was all wasted; it was all so insular and measurably smug; I wanted to shake him. Then he broke his silence from a totally different direction; "It's alright for girls, ...they don't have to do National Service like us blokes have to. They can leave College and just get on with their lives ... their careers, without interruption." I could see now how a disincentive like this had affected him and I thought about it. Just what WAS the point of us going without and busting a gut in achieving something when, National Service was going to come and smash it all to bits and make target-practice of us all? "It's not the fault of the women," I said, ... "they have babies whether they want them or not and then become full-time mothers; it's just the same as National Service!" "No, it aint," he replied in a hushed voice, ... "women having babies is natural ... men being forced into becoming murderers aint!"

Insecurity and frustration were rife, dreams were getting baked brittle and sheltering under so-many false dawning suns, prompting the mutinous reaction of a planned mass-escape via hitch-hiked vans and lorries heading south to London where the great galleries were calling. We even took the bold, if not brazen step of notifying the College of our intentions, listing Exhibitions currently showing and which we considered were essential to our development as Artists. Rather surprisingly, no objections were raised; it was impossible to know whether this be due to negligence or approval of our enthusiasm. It wouldn't have made any difference either way because we were not asking favours, just stating our intentions, a kind of constructive 'compromise' rebellion. For me, the 'National' and the 'Tate' would more than take up my time; Dave felt the same but was trying to work out which sections of the Galleries to leave out in trying to give us a chance of fitting-in the 'Redfern' and the 'Whitechapel', exciting smaller Galleries which we'd had to miss out in the past. A group of six of us had managed to book-up at a dormitory-type

Guesthouse which our College had for some time had an arrangement with. We simply knew this as 'Missus Turnbull's', a cheap and cheerful, spit-and-sawdust' type of place with an image of Battersea Power Station dominating the London skyline.

Getting there was pure pot-luck; there was a whole straggling trail of us lining the gutters like starving fishermen standing there in the murky drizzle with out thumbs cocked, waiting for a bite in the miserable, whirlpooled river of shoaling tiddlers and whoppers. One of our more senior of senior Lecturers went by in the opposite direction at breakneck speed on a beast of a bike which had the distinct demeanour of having an attitude problem; I never knew before that the skinny Mister Wakeman cycled to work ... and in all weathers too; now I knew why I liked him so much. By degrees, our straggle grew less, some long-distance drivers were glad of company and had grown to be a bit choosy, scrutinising thoroughly, as though we were produce at market, before committing themselves. Others considered that we were doing nothing more than begging and turned away in disgust; the more polite ones of their kind just gave the thumbs-down or some other obscure signal that defied definition. Fortunately, there were those without complications who just slammed their anchors on and skidded to a halt in the gutter a hundred yards further on. Quite by coincidence, I was hitching with Karen, one of our Fine Art students, and we watched such a wagon screech to a halt ahead of Dave and 'Burto', then after the briefest of babbled utterances, we watched them clamber up into the cab and were away. Karen was new to this form of travel, it wasn't the way she'd been brought-up, but she was nevertheless quite excited at the way 'we', the 'other half' lived and was shouting, "Goody, goody" and waving furiously as they vanished; oh, such fun!

It was a further twenty minutes before we got our first bite and I felt the line tighten and my rod bending; we'd struck a big one and jumped gleefully as this great clattering wagon shuddered to a standstill ahead of us and its driver drop down from his cab like a suicide attempt. "Where to?" he shouted. "London, London!" we yelled back and he just casually gave the 'thumbs-up' and strolled round to the passenger side and unfastened the trailer-side, chuckling; "Hope yer don't mind roughin'-it, 'taint the Ritz exactly. There aint no room in my cab ... it's full of my stuff, but yer should be alright up there at the front, the cab'll shelter you from the weather. If it gets too bad yer'll have to snuggle-up under the tarpaulin!" He gave me a wicked grin and a discreet wink as we scrambled aboard his five-star wagonload of potatoes and crawled our way over the knobbly sacks to the front where the relatively luxurious tarpaulin was partially spread, cushioned by a layer of empty sacks. "Are yer okay?" we heard him shout, and we yelled back, "Yes!" then a great cloud of diesel-smoke billowed up and the great noisy creature began to set the world asail on either side of us; we were on our way.

My travelling companion was one of the better-off ones amongst us, self-assured and extremely confident, a stranger to poverty, that's for sure. She wasn't normally of a rebellious nature, yet her work demonstrated such an authority that I expected her to have a bit of a wild streak lurking somewhere. There was a certain indefinable unease between us, it felt like a superiority complex had come face to face with an inferiority complex, rather reminiscent of a rabbit with a weasel, letting me know that five hours was going to be a damned long time to be lying on sacks of spuds so very close to this rather uncomfortable person while getting drenched, frozen and forever at the mercy of cramp-attacks. Physically I found her attractive in a very 'Gauguin' sort of way; she wasn't fat but firm, splendidly muscular and tanned, especially her calves and shoulders ... I could only guess the rest. I'd never been this close to her before and I found myself unable to stop just stealing glimpses of her and, rather surprisingly, liking the bits I'd stolen, able to sense and to feel her sparkling aliveness, her special separateness that distinguished her from others. I wondered if maybe God might have had something to do with our being alone together on a lorry-load of spuds. The more I thought, the more I wanted it to be the Devil that'd organised it without God knowing; just to be able to share each other's warmth would have helped bridge the mysterious gap that separated us, even to the point of saving us from freezing to death.

Being of my 'village' stock, I was more concerned over her warmth than I was for my own and, at the very first sign of her teeth chattering, I gave her my coat, just as Mom and Dad would have done. Then I gave her my jacket to cover her breasts and I watched her tormentingly curl-up into the foetal position and fall asleep, remaining that way while I soaked-up the drizzle and froze to death's door all the way to London. My miserable mind throughout being plagued by fantasies of snuggling up to her and rubbing noses as she sweetly snored; why, under that coat of mine I could even have got her to sing.

Like farm dogs, gypsied and full of dreams, we livened ourselves and stretched as our heavy wagon twisted and groaned onto a pot-hole cratered lorry-park where the air was full of the deliciously disgusting smell of burning pig-fat; we were all ready for a tea and a pee and for a chat with the driver over where it might be best to be off-loaded. So long as this could possibly be within reasonable range of an Underground, this would suit us just fine, we could then aim for our rendezvous point, on the steps outside the National Gallery; failing that, and it had gone four o'clock, to just head straight for our digs and finalise our plans from there. Our driver was a really smashing bloke, rough and ready and accommodating to the last degree.

"Yer may as well stick it out on the back as far as Covent Garden; yer can jump on a 'tube' to anywhere from there!", which was what we did. As we were detaching ourselves from Staffordshire Produce, he gave me a saucy dig in the ribs and, with eyes only, asked me the question. I discreetly shook my head and gave a clownish-sad look as we parted company, Karen close beside me as we waved him out of sight. I was still stiff and frozen while Karen, by contrast, was suddenly all bright and bouncy after her long warm snooze at my expense. I still couldn't clear my mind of the grievance of our not having got to know each other a touch better; such 'ruralist' romantic opportunities were not commonplace and didn't merit being disregarded in this way. She gave me a sort of apologetic smirk as though able to read my thoughts, with the added guilt of having faked being asleep over the whole agonising journey. I couldn't tell for sure what she was thinking, so I manhandled myself off the subject before we got ourselves lost in a pointless eye-game.

It was at Missus Turnbull's Guest House where we all eventually met up, starving and dishevelled, food not being one of the services provided, so there was really only one solution to the problem ... good old fish and chips! With my mates about me, spirits were high; after all, we'd stolen this time and so every single minute of it had to count doubly. There was only one 'London' and this was it; the very best of everything on the planet was here, as well as quite a lot that wasn't and we were not going to waste a single squirt of any of it. I could feel that vital tingling sensation all around me, it even put mine and everyone else's hunger into a lower priority as that very hunger itself shifted to our eyes and ears; 'London' was the best meal that was on the menu right now. Having already sorted out our sleeping arrangements we were ready to set sail, minus Karen who, for some 'womanly' reason or other, insisted on staying behind where she could have the bathroom to herself, she'd had enough spuds for one day, thank you very much! We didn't waste our time in trying to persuade her, and so we set off on our boisterous expedition to eventually track down the 'chippie' of our belly's dreams.

Another small group of mostly third year Painters had made separate arrangements and were all out there somewhere, no doubt doing what we were doing. It was only here, this safe distance from College that they dared to admit that 'FN Chips' put Joshua Reynolds in the shade, although on reflection, richer students didn't need to resort to thumbing lifts and they didn't resort to F ... ing Chips either! The great 'leveller' lay out there in miraculous silence awaiting our eyes and minds tomorrow. Anticipation of those painted visions created from places within minds and from nowhere else; this was the treasure that'd brought us all here and we just buzzed and bubbled like six-year-olds on Christmas Eve.

My own hunger was for a clearer identification of what it was that made 'English Art' so recognisably 'English', without that reason being merely of 'landscape', 'dress', 'architecture' or whatever. I wanted to explore what being an 'Official War Artist' had possibly done to affect this Englishness and to further establish any natural links with Surrealism. Others had their own hungry agendas, each of us feeling very privileged indeed to be about to stand just inches from the paint, barely an arm's length from where the Great Painters had originally stood, or sat; to be within that confined intimacy of the Master's consideration.

After a lengthy and repeatedly distracted search for the 'FN Chip Gallery', we eventually found what we were looking for, masterpieces in oil! Predictably, gluttony got the better of me and I almost sprang a rupture as we all headed back laden down with our greasy hot parcels; our dormitory was going to stink to high heaven and we were going to need to sleep with the windows thrown open, regardless of weather, fruit-bats or vampires. We arrived back at our digs, thanks mainly to Dave's navigational skills, and we sped noisily up the stairs in a mad race not to be the last, bursting ravenously into our room where we were totally gob-smacked by what confronted us; Karen was in bed with the late-arriving sixth member of our party, Victor Todd, 'Old Vic' to his mates, a third year illustrator.

Something pretty substantial must have distracted them because they hadn't heard our commotion coming up the stairs and there was an almighty kerfuffle as they clumsily disengaged from their stacking-position and lay precariously side by side, both red-faced and sweating profusely and trying to give the impression that it was all a misunderstanding. "Hi!" our coitusly-interupted colleague nodded, trying to look cool; ... "I've only just this minute come!" We all roared with laughter. "I bet you bloody well have!" 'Burto' laughed ... "you don't have to stop what you're doing because of us; we're all starving, we, we'll look the other way ... won't we lads!" "Sure thing ... don't mind us," we uproariously agreed and sat around on our beds and proceed to gorge ourselves stupid, being lavishly entertained by our hopelessly compromised friends in the bed who just lay there, both of them on the very edge and having to cling onto each other to avoid falling out, neither of them able to reach out to retrieve their hastily discarded clothes and none of us offering to help them ... if anything, kicking them further away. "I always said that going to the 'Old Vic' was better than going to the 'flicks'", I spluttered through an over ambitious mouthful of outrageously delicious 'rock-salmon' and delightfully vinegary chips. "Fancy a chip ... keep your strength up!" I went on rubbing it in, making sure that Karen got the message and knew where I was coming from; everyone showered their beds with chips amidst a whole crude cacophony of tormenting laughter.

Our devilment satisfied and with tears rolling down our cheeks, we all went onto the landing, leaving the embarrassed pair to either finish what they were doing, or to get themselves looking respectable, whichever they felt to be the most pressing of their dodgy options, while we viewed the colossal panorama all lit-up and alive there spread out before us. When we opened the window to let out the stink of our banquet, a great wave of sound swept over us; it wasn't just one thing but the roar of thousands of things all jumbled up. A magical montage of every conceivable thing was going on out there; babies being born, people dying; rapes, murders, robberies, house-fires, cars crashing; people working, people playing, people singing, people praying. Ships on the river moaning, aeroplane engines droning, flashing lights all over the sky, lonesome trains rumbling in tunnels; police sirens, ambulances, fire-engines, silly car horns playing tunes; drunkards serenading in the key of 'P'-minor, whores and gangsters transacting dirty money while, in the room behind us, sounds of stirring as fresh grunts and groans of unfinished business broke wind, just as we were tossing out our fish skins into the night, way down onto some gloomy waste-ground left over from the war where feral cats would quickly clean-up after us. We didn't want the old fish skins or my large fish bones stinking in the litter bin or blocking the toilet.

What a thrill and a half these stolen days were; so many paintings were better than I had remembered them to have been and there were other marvellous pictures that I'd not seen before. Two days, two weeks, not even two years would be enough to satisfy my hunger for this Golden treasury; none of it had been mined using slaves, all of it dreamed-up in solitude priceless beyond measure. Whatever I had earlier contrived to set myself to do was largely swept aside in the most overwhelming energy-surge; plans just melted as image after dazzling image dwarfed me to my knees, showing me that my aspirations were to always, always and forever be wedded to this miraculous Alchemy.

What constantly amazed me was the enormous breadth and depth of variety that'd revealed itself once Art was moved forward from the Renaissance with all its obligatory Religious subject matter. The colossal liberty which I was experiencing here spanning the last hundred years or so of Painting, was a tribute to mankind, a Celebration of Freedom more Holy than anything resulting from big sticks wielded by Popes or Tyrants, religious or otherwise, that'd lost the plan of what 'Life' was really meant to be.

I gazed upon the power so deep and radiant in Stanley Spencer's larger-than-life self-portrait, comparing it with my most favourite self-portrait of all, the much smaller work in chalk by Samuel Palmer; two completely different kinds of strength, one of power, the other of frailty. It required a far crueller, more penetrating honesty and freedom to undertake a self-portrait than it did a portrait, as I felt that these two clearly demonstrated. On another broader front, I was most refreshingly struck by how it was possible to feel a sense of 'France' in the French paintings, 'Holland' in those of the Dutch, 'Italy' in the Italian and so on. All of these identifiable abstractions being colouration of a different kind, all of them vital and necessary in the expressing of a deeper beauty through these self-same things that made a Chaffinch different from a Bluetit, a Poppy from a Dandelion, a Peacock Butterfly from a Tortoiseshell, ad infinitum. It was so utterly essential for all things to retain their differences, to recognise and respect them, especially in others around us, failure to do so resulting in foreboding greyness and loss of identity bordering on Dark Age, regardless of the glaring headlights that blinded rather than illuminated from time to time.

I felt tingles of excitement when I stood before new Sutherlands; his powerful, tortured organic forms under a new regime of hope and exuberance of wild, biting colour within a poetic choreography of abstractions which was so romantically 'English'. I felt both proud and lucky to be here, it was pure magic. Then it were as though someone had opened the windows and let the gentle air in when I came across the sheer majesty of Paul Nash, his symbolic statements of peace and spatial stillnesses; a surrealist without making a fuss about it. Great breathing landscapes all mysterious and still, like as though possessing the power of being able to grasp the 'eternal'. What was so refreshing was the staggering variety; not one of those Artists being a contrived 'pack-animal' cloned into existence by 'Isms'. Diversity was nothing more than Integrity and could sustain without resort to hunting, or as I felt was more the case, 'scavenging' in packs, where the identification of an alpha-male was always debatable.

Taking-in and absorbing so many diverse images, together with the conscious thoughts associated with them was exhausting, bringing about a gradual blurring of clarity as in the preludes of sleep. There was a limit to my ability to think straight or to know really what I believed in anymore. I'd reached the point when I just needed to close my eyes and sit and think. I was already feeling a certain confusion as to whether it was natural when, something that'd struck home to one and had thrilled and excited, should influence one to the point of wanting to copy it ... as it seemed to me was the case with Pablo Picasso. He had been credited with inventing Cubism, a kind of chicken and egg situation with Braque, who I personally believe was the true originator. Forming packs gave a new respectability to plagiarism, as I'm sure Piet Mondrian would concur were he still around.

In my blurring farewell to conscious thought, I tried dreaming up a pack of my own who I could have around me as a stimulus; restricting it to a 'pack' instead of an army was the main problem; where could I start. Everyone had retired for the day, worn out like I was; I couldn't speak for Karen, she had been accommodated elsewhere. 'Old Vic' was dead to the world, exhausted for more various reasons; 'Burto' was already snoring, Cyril was fidgeting and picking his nose and Dave was elbows-out, head in hands, deep in thought. What I thought was going to be easy was proving me wrong; there were many fabulous Artists to choose from with the sad part being that most of the ones I wanted in my team were dead ones, so I was going to have to cheat-up a bit of magic and bring them back. After all, 'Art' itself was 'magic' and most 'things' in it had been invented. As I lay there, a sudden daft idea flashed across my mind, that of picking a football team, eleven players and two substitutes. I probed the idea still further, I was going to have to match their artistic skills with those required by the positions I put them in on the field of play. It still wasn't easy but I was helped by the fact that my mind was now getting squirts of adrenaline coming from somewhere and so I grabbed my sketchbook and a pencil and started to scribble myself a squad of players. With these rudiments in position, I started to chuckle, having freed myself from the deathly seriousness of Art, and now able to come at it from a more light-hearted angle. "What's amusing you?" Dave asked, his own thoughts having shown a vulnerability to the tickling worm of invading humour. "Nothing much ... just football, that's all," I answered, still tickled deep pink by my choice of centre-forward. The more I thought, the more the image amused me and I just lay there unable to stop laughing. Nothing was ever more infectious than laughter was and Dave, because of tiredness, readily succumbed to the disease. "What's going on over there?" Cyril's voice creaked out from his fidgetiness, then he was infected also and was laughing without knowing the reason why. It rapidly became like a plaque, penetrating Burto's padlocked dreams, and he rubbed his eyes and stretched himself back to wakefulness. "What's wrong with you lot ... somebody messed the bed or something?" A loud fart rasped out from over in Cyril's direction and laughter became uncontrollable, rapidly whipping-up 'Burto' into the pandemonium. 'Old Vic' stirred from his entombed state, sat up, got up blearily, asked if it was morning already and staggered clumsily out through the door shaking his head in disbelief.

My mind by now was pure 'Circus', an animated tableau choreographed in a treatmental fusion of Hieronymus Bosch and Rene Magritte, even though greedy money in America had denied mine and a billion other eyes the miracle of seeing Magritte's actual live paintings, leaving only the miniaturised reproductions in books for us to see; despite which, he was still the greatest Modern Painter in my reckoning. I could see this crazy balletic football match raging behind my eyes, my centre-forward, 'Vinny' Van Gogh there charging around like a lunatic, pipe in mouth and a blood-stained bandaged ear. I had no idea of what most of the players looked like, so I felt it reasonable in such cases to permit characters from their painting to represent them, hence my choice of 'Ghost of a Flea' for William Blake, Likewise, 'The Son of Man', the bowler-hatted businessman in an overcoat and with an apple in front of his face, for Magritte. I had scribbled out my team in spite of the problem of identifying each one, and had also chosen the positions in which I wanted them to play. I'd selected my opposition too and now I had to try explaining to the others what I was finding so funny; so I took a deep breath and threw caution to the wind. "I've picked a football team out of my favourite Painters, the one's I'd like most of all to have playing for Me. I've set them against a team that I am calling the 'Dillusionary Pretentionists', they're the so-call Artists that I don't like in other words. The tricky part is that of playing them in the position which you consider best suits their style and skill. You can't cheat and you've got to think 'Football' as well as 'Art', or it wont work." It all suddenly went deathly quiet and I sensed a state of bemusement about the faces; I feared that I might have killed them, or at least sent them back to sleep.

I was just about to give it up and die myself, when Burto showed signs of life and suggested that it'd be helpful in clarifying the idea, if I told them who I had picked, where I had positioned them and why, and to give an idea of the 'opposition' I had chosen. I was by now, more than glad to do this but thought it only helpful to explain that, when a chosen Painter has left no readily identifiable image of themselves, it was permissible to use any appropriate figure from their work, helping to explain in the process what I'd been finding so amusing. "Righto, here goes!" I chuckled, clearing my throat ready for action. " For my captain and centre-half, I wanted someone strong in stature, a visionary, so I've picked William Blake. I've gone for a good dependable half-back line, one with some flair besides; I've got little 'Sammy' Palmer on the left and 'Grey' Sutherland on the right." At this point the interruptions started. Cyril was first, "I'd say that Palmer was nowhere near physical enough for a half-back; you need someone bigger and stronger than him." "Who do you suggest?" I asked, putting him on the spot. He pondered for a long moment during which time, Burto jumped-in and interrupted Cyril's thoughts. "I hope you haven't got 'Nebuchadnezzar' representing Blake ... he'd be too slow crawling about on all fours!" In the midst of our explosion of laughter, Cyril shouted out, "Stanley Spencer; he was a bit religious ... he'd do for left-half next to Blake!" He'd been so wrapped-up in thought that he'd remained oblivious to Burto's remark and its effect. The game was definitely catching on and there were big daft smiles now sprawling across the faces and brightening the bed-smelling dormitory. I agreed with Cyril; "I think you may have a point there; Palmer can be our 'man-with-the-sponge' on the touchline ... I can just see him now, sponging Van Gogh's ear!" Everyone laughed and Burto was showing an eagerness for us to get on with it before it all subsided into a rabble of anarchic twitterings. "What about your forward-line?" he asked impatiently. "I'm just coming to that," I answered trying to be serious, pointing out that, with my '5,3,2' system, the forwards had to be creatively compatible with the half-backs. "I needed a strong centre-forward, one that's a grafter, never knowing when to stop and wasn't afraid of heading the ball, so I've gone for 'Vinny' Van Gogh ... he'll run his legs off for the whole ninety minutes, he will!" "You're not afraid that he might go and cut one of their ears off?" 'Burto' laughed, prompting Dave into playing his part in the game. "You're going to need a good dribbler in the wing ... Jackson Pollock's the biggest load of dribble that I know of!" "I've got him playing for the opposition," I hastily pointed out, "along with Rothko, Newman and a few other pretentious Painters and Decorators!"

It was all getting pleasantly and rather provocatively lively now as I hastened to complete my forward-line. "I've gone for a sense of 'Poetry' and 'Invention' in my inside-forwards; I've got Rousseau on the left of Van Gogh and Magritte on his right, with Marc Chagall on the left-wing and on the right-wing I've got a player that can juggle and perform magic ... so I've plugged for Miro. That's my forward-line, any comments?" Burto was first; "Rousseau will fall asleep on the job!" he suggested, considering Rousseau to be somewhat a dreamer and a touch obsessed with sleep. I didn't readily agree ... "I think he'll be effective, especially with Chagall on his left." This prompted Burto into staunch disagreement, pointing out that 'pace' was needed down the flanks, someone who worked tirelessly and fast, someone like Lautrec ... or one of the Surrealists even. This triggered Cyril back into the action. "Lautrec sleeps all day and only works at night ... even then it's only in brothels. Anyway, his legs are too short, so you'll get no mesmerizing pace out of him!" Amidst the laugher, Dave blurted out; "Seurat's your man, he'll knock spots off them!" his thinking more to do with textures than football, which was foreign to him anyway. I conceded to Burto that I thought he'd made a fair point and began searching my brain for an appropriate speed-merchant. "What about John Bratby?" Cyril burst forth ..."He'd give 'em the lot ... kitchen sink an' all!" No-one enjoyed this more than Cyril himself who just threw himself back wallowing in his own humour. "Never mind about that, Burto snapped ... "what about the defence ... have you thought about that?" "Sure have, boyo; I've got two players who can create space and can provide structure to the game two 'Pauls', Paul Nash, left-back; Paul Gauguin, right-back ... and in goal I've gone for Picasso 'cos I couldn't really think of anyone else that was so expert at watching what everyone else around him was doing before committing himself into making some spectacular leap of his own. "What d'you reckon?"

There was a brief silence, then 'Burto' looked rather owlishly at me and said; "I'll tell you what, Bridgen old chap ... I think your bloody mad, that's what I think!" I took this as a compliment, knowing that cricket would have been more to his liking. Dave sprang to my defence and commented rather authoritatively; "All the best Artists are a bit mad ... they wouldn't be Artists if they weren't; look at Bosch, Dali, Van Gogh, Blake, Magritte ... to name but one!" Burto gave a begrudging grin and I knew what was coming and braced myself in readiness. "I take it all back, James; you're not mad!" Readily I retorted; "And you, my dear friend Burto, you're the most sane person I've ever come across, and I really mean that!" The other two started laughing, prompting 'Burto' into hurrying off his new 'cat-and-mouse' thing he'd started and I detected a slight blush showing-up on his cheeks as he hastened to ask; "And who are your reserves then, we may as well hear having come this far!" "Kandinsky and Georgio de Chirico," I concluded; ... "If anyone's gonna freak-out the opposition, these two will!"

At this point, Cyril got up clutching his bladder and went staggering out to the bathroom, setting off a chain reaction of yawning and stretching which suggested to me that the match had suddenly been called off ... floodlights not working or something like that. Suddenly, Cyril came rushing back on tip-toes, finger over his lips as he whispered, "Come and listen to this!" We all shot out of our beds and followed him across the landing, down three steps to the bathroom door, which was bolted from the inside, where 'Old Vic'; and Karen had accidentally bumped into each other ... in the bath of all places, sending their bubbly water oozing under the door in their vigorous steamy breast-strokes, grunting away like a seal sanctuary in rutt, the pair of them.

We were all in desperation for a pee now and, with there being no wash-basin in our room which we could have used for this purpose, we were left with no alternative other than to get up onto the landing window-sill and then risk life and limb and doing it through the wide open window as we had similarly done earlier with our fish-skins. Through the gaping window, the night wind was wet and black as we balanced precariously there letting it all go blindly flying out everywhere, our perilous position made more life-threatening when Cyril, who was first to finish, switched on the light, leaving us not so much 'high-and-dry', as 'high-and-drenched' in pissing pandemonium!

## 17. 'Lost Horizons in an Ocean of Gold'

It had all flown by so terribly quickly and, having to rely on hitch-hiking for transport, one full day in London had equalled being absent from college for three days, a headache yet to come. Whatever the outcome, the experience had been invaluable, the very breath of air that our hearts and minds needed prior to our four-year honeymoon period coming to an end. Spring was already turning to Summer, and with it, the coming to an end of the greatest possible renaissance of friendships when, these brave young artistic clowns and miraculous jazzmen, prepared themselves to metemorphosize into becoming khaki-cocooned grub-soldiers. Some of them would be opting for exemption by going on to do a further year of Art Teacher training, ATD, more confounded letters to be stuck onto the end of a name. Right reasons or wrong reasons didn't come into the reckoning; it was a hard choice, particularly so if you didn't want to teach or be a bloody soldier either!

Much to our surprise, there were no repercussions concerning our 'London rebellion', instead, even more surprisingly, the College tossed-in a couple of 'Kulture-goodies' of its own. One of them a coach-trip to Blenheim Palace, the other a week long Summer School at Barlaston Hall in the Potteries, being under the artistic mentorship of the celebrated Watercolourist, Reginald Haggar, unknown to every single one of us. I signed up for both of these 'jump-lead' 'Kulture-shocks', I needed something with vitamins to build me up and prepare me for my final year, which was proving to be a far more daunting prospect than I had imagined it was going to be. The sadness I was feeling in advance of all the good-byes was affecting me deep down where I was already quietly crying.

On another front, Julie and I had been rather neglectful of each other of late and were in need of an adrenaline-burst of some sort to re-charge our batteries and somehow darn over the threadbare patches that were beginning to pinken our elbows. A cloudlessly sunny day, that's all we needed, away from all interferences, somewhere hidden, just the two of us. I'd had my eye on this lovely field for some achingly long time from the bus window; it was one of those small fields that my romantic young heart responded to in the most poetic of ways. I'd watched it ploughed from ochre whiskers down to deep madder-brown soil; seen it sown, then buried beneath winter snows; I'd seen little green spears in lines grow steadily into waving green and that green turn gradually to Gold, golden corn. We both went 'sick' for a day; it was end-of-term for us both and we felt that we wouldn't be missed. Inside my old painting knapsack I'd greaseproofed a few macho sandwiches and my rolled-up cycle cape to use as a groundsheet, grabbed an additional bottle of pop and some crisps on my way to meeting her at a bus-stop up the hill beyond the Art Gallery where we were less likely to be spotted. It wasn't spontaneous, much as we would have preferred it to have been, but I pretended that it was, Julie wasn't to know otherwise.

This was that very day that we had hoped for, beautifully warm and not a cloud in the sky. She looked a dream standing there in the dappled shade in her red and grey high school uniform. We'd timed it to perfection, the bus appearing within seconds and the saucy, lipsticky conductress who had by now become quite a pal, gave me a kind of, 'I-know-what-you-pair-are-up-to' smirk and discreetly pinched my bum as we went to our seats. Julie showed some surprise when I only paid for a two-mile bus ride when she had expected Cannock Chase at the very least. I assured her that I could find an idyllic picnic spot without having to go wandering off into the outback. She looked at me in astonished disbelief when I gave her the nudge for us to get up and for me to ring the bell for us to get off at the next stop. "Don't worry, my darling, I feel passionately inspired today, just you wait and see."

The bus stopped and we got off and stood in the gutter; the conductress nailed me with her slinky feline eyes and eased open her bright geranium lips and sensually slithered her tongue across the underside of the top one and gave a dark mascara-wink, this made me cruelly aware that I knew absolutely nothing of this particular world in which she'd become an expert. She waved as the huge red beast rolled away. "You two know each other?" Julie asked, with a trace of jealously and a hint of suspicion, hastening me to put her in the picture. "When you've travelled this route as many times as I have, you soon get to know all the conductors. That one's in love with one of the drivers and they always seem to mange it that they're on the same shift, same bus; they've got it made!" I could feel her fingers tighten their grip on mine and I knew that our love was intact as we gazed over the spired city browsing away in the valley beyond, and strolled but a few yards before coming to a five-barred gate set some way back from the road. Beyond it was a sea of gently swaying Gold, all shimmering alluringly. Wild flowers were in rapturous, rampant abundance; the hedgerow was dense and lush with its flanks crammed with Parsley, Mustard-garlic and Convolvulus on the rampage. There were still some Dog-roses on the dome and still some fledglings deep within, choristers in a green Cathedral. It was like our own wild wedding as we climbed the gate and entered the field, distancing ourselves decisively from our last lingering concern. "Well, what d'you think of this then, darling?" I said in a hushed whisper, as though this Golden field of corn was mine to give, my very own personal gift to her; "Today, the whole world is ours; every leaf, every flower, every buzzing bee in its scented bower, every lark rejoicing in Heaven's tower; my darling, I give you the world!" I stood there with my arms outstretched, pretending to be God for just one wicked moment. Julie turned, threw her arms around my neck and kissed me like as though she'd not eaten or drunk for a month.

Breast high, we strolled hand-in-hand along the perimeter of the field; Poppies, Daisies, Columbines, Corn-marigolds, Hawkweeds and wild Pansies everywhere as we left the sounds of traffic on the road behind and proceeded at bliss up the sighingly rising slope until we reached the furthermost point where we entered the corn and became lost of all horizons. We were entirely alone, distanced from everything and I lay with Julie on top of me in the most turgid embrace with tosterone lifting the lid of my saucepan and boiling over, prompting the corn to grow extra inches in furthering our concealment from the world. At the same pace as the conductress's tongue sliding across her slippery lips, we undressed each other, sensually and slowly, and I laid out my cape and we just lay there beneath the lark-screeching sky, touching, feeling, holding, tasting, exploring. We knew that the only thing now holding us back from completing the course completely, insatiably to its obvious conclusion, was our respect for each other together with the promises we made. I looked into her eyes and I saw the whole world there in that fish-bowl; the entire of life was there, so fragile, so terribly vulnerable before inevitable changes came marching in uncaring boots to make moments like this, but a lost dream. We could make babies as well as anyone could; the process we knew would be the most ecstatic, most beautiful of all life's offerings, a torment which I somehow resisted, and I saw her look of fear change meltingly to trust, giving me the strength I needed.

Young life, first proper love: without our being shackled with career-aspirations, we'd most certainly have been parents by now. History had changed that much since not so very long ago when things were so very different. The trap had nevertheless been set all the same, and we resisted the cheese so finely baited; we were working against Nature now, contriving a behaviour and a discipline to deny Nature its function. I felt so much blissful harmony just lying there nakedly body to body with my sweetheart but, things could have been rather different had she prepared the sandwiches ... greaseproofed paper wasn't the same as polythene! All that it would take now would be for her to whisper ... "I want your baby," and I wouldn't have seen the sky for the rest of the day. It would have set us properly free in one sense, the 'Natural' sense, but career-wise it would have proven restrictive, even disastrous by denying her a place at University, whereas for me alas, not finding it sufficient to exempt me from military service where I could so easily find myself and lose myself in the same blinding instance at the wrong end of a bullet. Babies right now were not a good idea ... bullets, for some weird reason, made far more sense!

No matter what cloud I happened to have been joy-riding on, be it cloud nine or cloud ten, being back in our ex-brothel annex was dependably sobering to return to. Like an old soldier, I was proudly wearing the medal of a life-threatening love-bite the size of a plum, just below my left ear, an adornment which hadn't escaped being spotted. Our head of department 'Rizla', as Burto referred to him, was his usual, refreshingly abrupt, earthy breath of air, able with consummate ease to bring airy-fairy dreams back down to earth with the most eye-opening jolt imaginable; no malice whatsoever, just plain, straight-to-the-point, well-intended, blunt talk. He'd already given me a few friendly glancing grins, making me a touch apprehensive over what I sensed was brewing; I didn't have long to wait. "Jim!" he said, ritualistically crafting himself a thin cigarette, keeping me waiting while he licked the paper, tapped it, fondled it, then took it between his lips, struck a match, lit it and sucked the first smoke deep into his lungs and a second later, blew it out for us all to share. "Jim, I'll tell you something that I think might be helpful for you to know. Having sex is like having a crap ... once you've had it, you don't want it!" Jack Dale, our caretaker standing in the hallway with his nose protruding round the door, had overheard the remark and burst out laughing, spitting his false-teeth out and triggering an unscheduled gas-attack. "There!" Rizla laughed ... "take a look at that, Jim ... that's what sex does to you; it shrivels you down to a wizened, wrinkled old turd like Jack there, and ... would you believe it, he's still only twenty-seven! So, James, let it be a warning to you my boy; you've got a Diploma to focus your mind on before you go getting yourself all messed-up with that 'woman-stuff'. A word of advice ... you're better off going down the road of masturbation; not only will it keep you out of trouble but, you'll meet a far higher class of person that way!" The whole place fell about in a uproar; old Jack was grovelling about on the floor on his hands and knees, still involuntarily farting, while trying to find his dentures and also the cigarette which he'd ejected along with his teeth. With tears rolling down his cheeks, he fumbled his cobwebbed teeth back onto their gums and said, "It's right what yer Gaffer says ... yer gets them times when yer want to eat it, then, a few minutes later yer wishes that yer bloody-well had've done!"

This entire sordid episode had started when Burto decided, in his subtle, provocative style, to ridicule and sow speculation as to how I'd come by so striking a disfigurement, never mind himself having had a love-bite requiring concealment or explanation. Short of wearing a polo-neck with its collar unrolled up under my nostrils, there wasn't much chance of my hiding this bruise where a hippopotamus of a kiss had come to grief. I also knew that, if Julie's parents had seen it, they'd have had rather more than something to say to her, no doubt jumping to the same way-off-the-mark conclusions that these here at College had done, and would have probably whisked her away for a pregnancy test to complete the humiliation. I felt invasively soiled and embarrassed, unable to conceal my blushes, especially with all the rest of my group here wallowing at my expense. Inside, I had the honour of a sweetheart to protect from such crude, intrusive disregard and I felt helpless to do anything to protect that honour. My painting-mate, Dave, was more sensitive than the rest and he came across and muttered quietly; "Take no notice, Jim, they're just insensitive twats ... a milk bottle's all they need, they don't need a woman to be in love with!"

I realised then that, with our final year about to engulf us, he and I would become as brothers once more. There was no-one else in the group that felt so passionately about Painting and Drawing like I did, Dave being the one exception. We hadn't properly assimilated or gorged the artistic feast that London's Galleries had provided us with, although it had to be said that fervour was disease-like amongst our painters in College; inspiration, in one case at least, was indistinguishable from plagiarism and, the English painter, Alan Reynolds had suddenly found a twin brother ... nowhere near as good, mind! There was far more to Reynolds than just a straight-from-the-tube deep ultramarine sky and a flat landscape of similarly raw cadmium yellow and chrome lemon, over which in the lower foreground, Teazels and Buckthorns could be preciously contrived in daubed black. No, there was far more to an Alan Reynolds than that! Whether or not the 'Minimalist-Constructivists' were being plagiarised was difficult to tell; accidents always looked like accidents ... spilled paint and the like, and, blank canvases never looked like anything other than that. Part of a busted bike, just the front wheel and forks, bodged into a hole drilled into the wooden seat of a busted chair, may for some have passed as 'Art', making Council rubbish-tips the Art Galleries of the future, just as two metal colanders welded together had done. Who by? Why ... Picasso! And yes, sold for millions to some American so-called 'Fine Art' Museum, this, despite the two colanders falling apart as a result of Mister Picasso's disregard for the apparent skills required in welding! Art was becoming a joke, and I was becoming angry, a very angry young man!

Our coach outing to Blenheim Palace was very much in our minds. This single event would more or less mark the end of the road, the parting of the ways for those notorious, if not marvellous Third Years whose considerable achievements were going to be a hard act to follow. Suddenly finding oneself at the top looking down, wasn't the same as being next down from the top, looking up. Having others above had been an inspiration never to be repeated. It went without saying that the bedraggled remains of the Jazz Band would be using this mobile venue as a kind of glorious farewell cavalcade, the only ones not to know of this being the few lecturers that'd signed-up for the Kulture-boost prior to their annual pilgrimage to Italy in plastic sandals and Bermuda shorts, vulturing for 'Art' when it was right here under their noses.

We'd already had it drummed into us about this being our final summer, the one that really counted, the one which would require us to fill our sketchbooks from cover to cover with things to impress, because they would form a vital part of our National Diploma assessment, all very scary. Telling that to a Dad that wanted me to stand at the bottom of a ladder for six weeks wasn't the easiest of things to successfully pull off, especially after he'd given consent to the Summer-School thing, which he considered was a holiday anyway. Something that he'd never heard of for himself.

I had an impending feeling of being adrift on an ever-widening ocean of fading things which I'd once been part of and had touched, while other paler ghosts of things which I didn't recognise, were appearing on other horizons. Lamenting over those last-remembered places and things was energy going to waste in the wrong direction. It was that which I didn't know and where I was going that was occupying my mind now and it was plain to see that, being at Art College, beautiful and entertaining as it had largely been, it hadn't even in the slightest way prepared me for the rude awakening of what was too fast approaching. To go into teaching Art was like a mirror in a mirror, a hamster on a wheel to never, with only one ultimate destination. Only unreal dreams could turn nowheres into a million somewheres; there'd inevitably come an awakening bump in the night somewhere along the way to break the incestuous cycle.

A strange, vaguely logical and ages-old thought came galloping across my mind like a ghost-train of gipsy caravans, leaving me with the words ... 'If it's painful and hurts, it's worth doing. If it's easy as pissing and feels nice ... it's no good, forget it!" Obscure as this may have been, I saw a parallel between what I considered to be 'Art' and that which I thought of as pretending to be. Furthermore, judging by the way things were going in the new pretend-art world, that was spreading from America like a pox, painkillers didn't seem to have much of a future! I simply couldn't see the point or the purpose of Art if it ceased to require integrity and show a majesty associated with the human condition, in all its glories all its moods. 'Art' should be a servant of mankind, not a parasite of it; it should be a shining light, not bullshitting a darkening confusion through pretentious intellectuality: wasn't that what 'Anarchy' was supposed to be?

I wondered what Blenheim Palace had in store to shed light and more, to dazzle; surely it was something to conjure up a vital beam of magic to set things right. Stately Homes, however, were not to be confused with Council Houses and

Dukes were nothing like plumbers nor Duchesses in any way resembling shop assistants. I'd had it on reliable authority that the Duke of Marlborough had never been on a Council house waiting-list, not had he ever kept racing pigeons in a black and white striped shed on an allotment; or had never sat barefoot on a canal bank with a cane and a bent knob-pin at the end of a length of cotton, fishing for gudgeon. Opulence was just a word that's all it was; it could never in a billion years become an experience for me; it couldn't ever be earned as neither could it be expected.

What we were all about to experience was nothing less than Alchemic Surrealism, a bizarre, historical pageant-like fusion of an eloquently gormless Landed Gentry and a magnificent palatial opulence penned and painted by the Gods; all Earth's generosity turned to a landscape designer's vast canvas, money-no-object. While John Sell Cotman was struggling to perform his magic on a half-imperial size sheet of paper, the likes of Capability Brown and others of his much sought-after kind were performing theirs on thousands of acres of virgin earth, disembowelling it, ripping out woods, commons, heaths marshes and, contriving in their place, lakes with waterfalls and fountains, parkland with 'designer' trees neatly arranged. Undulations unnatural with fake rocky outcrops and frivolous follies to look like ancient ruins, grand statues, both pious and pompous; geometric gardens with intricate terraces and patterned perspectives and with complex mazes for idling away the hours getting lost in. It was like painting a picture just for the delight of some unspeakably wealthy idiot who coughed-up caviar instead of phlegm and urinated Chablis, sometimes Port; kept deer for hunting and had starving village poachers hanged for taking the odd pheasant from its roost. There was always something deeply vulgar about opulence despite its magnificent, alluring titillation upon the eye.

Such gold-crusted boasting to something or other, or to nothing or other, seemed to me like some strange, mysterious colossal three-and- more dimensional Art-form, being both tomb and temple, anthropological and intellectual, hysterical and historical, extrovert and anti-social, pompous, miserly, splendidly unnatural and contrived to the skin-thin frontier of it almost having a place in logic. Nearly perfectly natural, but not quite ... even Angels had to defecate!

The plain, rude truth was that, because of the nature of 'time', nothing could indefinitely maintain itself, re-emphasised by the other even ruder truth that the 'blessedly' rich only spent other people's money anyway; that's how their kind came about in the first place! It took the inevitable escalating of cost of upkeep to bring about the more down-to-earth confrontation of issues that were suddenly, manifestly real. Self-made Gods were mythical monsters, mermaids were more believable and, when came the threat of them having to spend money of their own, the crafty buggers, distasteful as it was for them, turned to the common, ever-nosey 'riffraffery' to come to their rescue and be permitted to do the unthinkable ... to be granted access to pollute the palacial air with their wretched breathing, their grubby, smelly bodies that sneezed and broke wind; their ravenous inquisitive eyes that trespassed and burgled, driven by curiosity like plagues of clothes-moths. This really was the ultimate of horrid stuff to have to swallow but, money spoke loudest of all and they weren't too daft to ignore the fact that, if enough paying-through-the-nose peasants could be herded into infinite battalions and driven through the turnstiles on a business-like basis, the upkeep headache would have found its magic aspirin and would be cured at a stroke. Peasants had their uses in Peace as well as War!

Someone who'd been there before, casually mentioned that there was a magnificent lake and I immediately thought, "big-lake trout!" No self-respecting Duke would have piddling little roach, that's for sure. This genetic flaw in my upbringing had forced a hole to suddenly appear in my protective layer, I had no escape from its cursed persistence and I was afraid that there would always be a threadbare vulnerability in this area of my nature as now, my mind was already racing downhill away from me with this exciting new challenge. I figured that a discreetly hand-held spool of six pound breaking strain line, a size ten hook and a couple of lead shots would be just about right. For bait, a couple of red worms from our garden would be ideal, they'd keep fresh in my small maggot tin and none of it would take any room at all, no-one would ever know it was in my pocket.

For an occasion such as this, Mom insisted on preparing my sandwiches; Blenheim Palace was to her no different to Buckingham Palace, and she couldn't have any son of hers going there with untidy sandwiches. I could imagine the picture in her mind; an immaculately uniformed 'sandwich inspector', smothered in medals and armed to the teeth, walkie-talkie in hand, ferocious Alsatian at his side; everyone having to have their sandwiches inspected before being permitted to enter this Palace to the Gods of good fortune. A bad sandwich resulting in a discrete gun in the night that would put paid to the sandwich maker; either that or shipment to Botany Bay where the white man had already been sent by God to turn a verdant paradise previously inhabited by black poets, into a barren desert, for some inexplicable reason. The fuss that Mom made would have one mistakenly believe that I was going for tea with the Royal Family. Dad's old demob-suit had never looked cleaner, not only had Mom boiled it, but Fay had expertly ironed it and it was neatly folded in readiness to turn a sow's ear into a silk purse. To my further surprise, Mom had also boiled my knapsack and darned my socks, nothing had been left to chance.

I had to be up extra early on that morning as I needed to catch the earlier bus to Stafford and to make sure that I got a good seat on the coach, one down at the back with the Jazz Band. As was always the case with my family, there was Bedlam as the seemingly obligatory panic clumsied itself into life all about me as it gobbled up the moments. When I put my beautifully boiled trousers on I couldn't believe my eyes; not only had they shrunk but, Fay had never pressed trousers before and the creases weren't at the front and back, but on both sides making each leg look a foot wide and extremely flat! "You look really nice, our Jim," Mom lied, going on to lie even more in an attempt to appease Fay by adding; "This is the way people have them pressed nowadays!" This managed to halt Fay's tears from spilling and she very quickly joined in with Mom by insisting that ... "this style of trouser-pressing is 'all-the-rage-' now." It was far too late for me to have anything done about it now; my sandwiches were packed and I'd sorted out my maggot-tin the night before and had safely stowed it away together with the rest of my 'poacher's-tackle'. As for the trousers, I just took a deep breath and philosophically muttered the word 'bollocks!' a score or more times to myself and prayed that on-one would notice. They all waved me off as I sped like a bat out of hell round the corner and away on my old racer; Blenheim Palace, here I come!

## 18. 'Winstontaneous Combustion!'

It was like picking a bouquet of wild flowers to put on a special grave. Misplaced urgency; my excitement the very flowers themselves, all wild and whizzing in my greedy, grasping snatching of moments, as I spilled down to the slowly advancing avenued grave of good-byes to brothers and sisters who I'd probably never see again after today. Strangely, I felt it was myself I was saying good-bye to; I could no longer be that same person that I'd always been, a new one had to somehow emerge from that grave-like womb out from which so much fun and laughter had flowered. I'd already said a sad goodbye to my best College pal of all, 'Art' Tomkins, tangled-up in his testosterone monsoon without any wellies or umbrella for protection. Manhood showed no mercy and didn't piddle about with poems or any etiquette, neither did it even knock the door but instead smashed it down, killing dreams and all dreaming before frowning the sky by command to a higher, more unreachable place, horizons to further, more futile places yet and left no kisses anywhere, no warmth. I was so very alone as I pedalled my way, grey and leaden with sadness, hoping I'd not forgotten how to laugh and smile; I wasn't a boy anymore, I was here in this most treasured lane of lanes, Darnford Lane, born a man, right here at the very graveside of my childhood.

The larks were speaking from a vertical mile as I sped to the canal bridge and over, round the cottaged 'S' bend and up onto my pedals in readiness for the hill, only to find my Uncle George there on foot, laboriously pushing his bike, in no hurry to get to work whatsoever. Here was the man who, only a handful of years earlier had been a sailor serving on a minesweeper in the war, risking his life for his country which now couldn't really give a damn for him or the cabbage sandwiches which had to sustain him in his peacetime pittance of tending to the pot-holed roads. He'd been wild like me once, but right now I could see it all neat and tidy, cruel and vindictive; his dreams had all been incinerated and his dreaming, cradled mind left impotent and forsaken of anything remotely directional or wholesome. I had to plead with him to let me go so that I could catch my bus, thence to board my coach to Blenheim Palace of all unimaginable places.

Life was holding so many pains in store; barbed-wire fences meant nothing anymore, there were built-in fences galore, barbed-wired an' all! Freedom was not straightforward; it may have been for some but it most certainly wasn't for the likes of me. Every inch forward bled a little; forward thoughts left bruises and aches, left previously fit people limping and lame in a lamentation that showed that we'd lost our 'Nature' through contrivance alone. The 'Family', as with wild dogs was the very centre, place of meaning, the very, very heart; a place to return to where all love was healingly bandaged and where 'all' operated as 'one'; nothing could be more beautiful if it tried. In 'travelling', supposed 'broadening' of the mind simply buggered the mind, full stop! The only thing to register was a feeling of defiance, an overdue statement of independence with the added right to choose, being a desirable component part; animals faced similar situations when pecking-orders became numerically complex. Our supposed 'broadener' of the mind, 'travel', soon became 'Emigration', separation by oceans and continents inducing new colonisations, turning the 'possible' into the 'impossible'. No different to the long, long ago separation through galactical space when our original forefathers arrived here on this planet, which they eventually called 'Earth'. We were used to heartbreaks of this magnitude, even though 'Time' was forgiving. I wondered, somewhat sardonically, would 'Time' be so forgiving as to turn 'Emigration' into 'Migration', make 'finite', 'infinite'; show us rhythms and patterns that we never knew or even dreamed and install them into our perceptions? I had a deep feeling that she already was, but was being blatantly and cussedly ignored.

The coach was there ready and waiting when I ambled up the street in the thick of the Rugeley crowd, trying not to attract attention to my trousers. Spirits were high, everyone else was smart and smelling of soap; coloured glass beads were glinting in the sun, newly washed hair shone with rainbows and cotton dresses were delicately swishing all flowery and see-through thin. 'Art' Tomkins would have been in his element if only he could have waited ... but I daresay he wasn't doing so bad where he was. The Band had already claimed the back seats and, to my surprise, had somehow fiddled it so that the trombonist as well as the banjo player had joined the party, no doubt under the name of students who hadn't intended coming. 'Turps' Turpin was as usual bristling over with confidence, his bleached-perfect teeth flaring from their cave in his newly shampooed beard, his tanned muscly legs showing off leather sandals at one end and very tight-fitting short shorts at the other, as he brandished his gleaming cymbal. Ivor 'Vandyke' Brown was there in his gaudy dickey-bow, fiddling with his temperamental saxophone-reed and doing a few flash dashes up and down the scales while, in the opposite seat, 'Pee-wee' Peters was similarly warming-up his clarinet. It was all so vibrantly exciting, despite the bemused expressions on the faces of the couple of Lecturers who hadn't expected things to turn out quite like this. I shuddered to think of what would happen when the Band really started-up; this was just tuning-up, nothing more than that.

We were still awaiting the undisputed star of the show, 'Walt' Heron. It went without saying that Burto would be the last to board the coach, even though he only lived half a mile away; nobody expected miracles where his punctuality was concerned. Then a cheer went up as the bedraggled figure of 'Walt' was spotted galloping raggedly beside the graveyard, trumpet-case in one fist, lumpy paper carrier bag in the other. Behind him a shrieking group of others from that neck of the woods, one of them a long-ringletted, auburn haired, mouth-watering, stunningly beautiful Goddess from the Dress Designers. I wasn't the only one who quaked in my shoes whenever she appeared, over thirty of us shared the same steamy dream each night over her, yet she was boringly, domestically involved with a huge, almost seven foot ex-public school sissy of a third-year, an overfed, posher than smoked-salmon piss, a rich, characterless, talentless slob; that's what money could get you when everything else failed!

The cheers were deafening as 'Walt' boarded the coach with beads of sweat dripping from his nose, just as I'd so often seen it do at the 'Crown Inn'. He, by contrast, with the red-head's big 'jelly-baby', was virtually penniless, nonetheless a most richly talented clown of a genius, loved by every single one of us. Howls and wolf-whistles greeted the Goddess of our wet-dreams as she dutifully took her seat by the window next to her beaming-faced 'Theobald'. "Are we all here?" one of the lecturers called out, list of names in his hand and a pencil eager to tick them off. "Burto's not here yet!" Alison screeched and everyone jeered and started to sing a chorus of, 'Why are we waiting', keeping it going full blast for ten minutes before the laid-back figure of 'Burto' came unhurriedly into view, determined to do it his way right to the last cussed slow step; he could be damnably annoying at times!

The show was on the road; it was like Noah's Ark, a priceless container of all that was the very best of my life thus far; a self-dissolving capsule which would remain evermore in memory alone. It was fruitless to allow thoughts of tomorrows to spoil this immaculate of conceptions right here now being breathed, touched, experienced. Be that as it may, thoughts had their own on-off switch and operated independently, regardless of what was preferable. I felt close to everyone aboard in a real, rounded, 'family' sort of way, even the most envied 'jelly-baby' man with the red-haired beauty who we all rented for our sordid salvations. If ears really did burn when someone was talking or thinking really hard about somebody, her lovely ears would have been reduced to mere blistered worm-holes by now and 'he'd' never have known what she looked like in ear-rings! It really was an emotional experience being here, amongst 'brothers' and 'sisters', for the last time in so many cases.

This was the 'Crownin' Glory's' farewell tour and the poor driver was almost projected forward through his windscreen when the great surge of sound blasted forth from down at the back of the coach as 'Walt' led the 'Saints go Marching In'. It was the single best moment of all time and I felt pins and needles prickling my skin in an eel-like writhing down my spine; it was pure unadulterated Gold! The shock-wave must have come like a bolt out of the blue for those others in the coach who'd never heard the band before, or even knew of its existence. It was a bit late to find out now that it wasn't to your liking, particularly those that'd , from the womb been daily dosed with Cod Liver Oil, Milk of Magnesia and Classical Music played by Mantovani; but it made no difference whatsoever, most of us loved it and nothing was going to tame it now, absolutely nothing! It occurred to me that, perhaps, just maybe, Blenheim was in for a bit of a shock ... a Jazz Band. Wow, that'd really be something!

I had to admit, I'd never heard the Band play as well as this before; it was an inspired performance, well worthy of it being the ultimate farewell. I tried to work out why this might be, the sound was different, all sort of raw and primitive, sparkling crisp and open, then I knew what it was ... the piano wasn't there. 'Old Vic' had brought an old steel-strung guitar along and was here providing an even better chordal colouration. Then I spotted another difference when, true to form, a terminal artistically-temperamental tantrum by 'Vandyke' Brown, over his being too cramped to be able to impress with his saxophone, resulted in the better new sound that I was hearing. This had allowed 'PeeWee' Peters on his clarinet, the space to demonstrate why he was truly the most gifted musician in the band. Tom Crossley provided a steady stomp on a hand-made drum while, 'Turps' Turpin's cymbal penetrated and was adequate for the most part, we all knew he'd go over the top when he switched to his irresistible guttural 'Rugeley Creole'. Music didn't come naturally to 'Turps' like it did with 'Walt' who had never played trumpet better, supported on either side by trombone and banjo pro's; it was all so brilliant.

For a few it came as a relief when the driver pulled-in at a 'watering-hole' near Warwick; bladders as well as eardrums were bursting by now and the Band had done their 'thing' and were fairly blown-out and in need of a breather themselves. There was nothing left for them to prove; this trip would mark their disbandment for all; time and I felt it very poignantly in the deep-end of my own secret heart. Correspondingly, Teddy was here saying his own goodbye in the most dignified of quietnesses as I watched him struggle to drink the most insipid of milky coffees from a see-through glass cup; another bit of 'Art' from America was my guess, unsympathetic and grossly crude. Before I could tell him that I was going to miss him, he beat me to it and said ... "I shall miss you, Jim-Jim; we've spent some 'interesting' times you and I!" Words physically failed me and a brick-sized lump came to my throat each time I tried to respond. He could see my problem and quietly said ... "Don't worry, I know the feeling." I felt embarrassed and lowered my head so's nobody could see the tears welling up. Too late, one of them let me down and 'Chicory-Essence' Nigel had been watching and came concernedly prancing over like a fairy on springs and asked Teddy if I was alright, to which Teddy reassured him that, due to there being so many good-byes in the air right now, I was just feeling a bit 'sensitive', that's all, and that I'd soon get over it. They both discreetly accompanied me outside for a breath of air and I coughed the lump from my throat and apologised to them both, there was nothing else that I could do or say when my wet eyes were saying it all for me. "You're a sensitive so-and-so, Jim ... I find that really quite attractive," Nigel said coyly. "Don't ever change." "I shouldn't worry about that if I were you, Jim-Jim'll never change." Teddy grinned reassuringly and I took a long, deep breath, I couldn't stomach any more of this embarrassing, slushy, 'girly' stuff; I had to get a grip on myself before Nigel started calling me 'Jim-Jim'. If I heard it once more I swore to myself that I'd perform a mercy-killing! It didn't help my resolve one little bit when Nigel whispered; "Don't think I'm being facetious, Jim, bit I do like those trousers. From the front you've got them to look like a skirt, all tweedy; is that your idea?" "No it bloody well aint!" I groaned, a hair's breadth ahead of vomiting and blushingly took an unscheduled dash to the toilet where I frantically soaked them to their utmost limit. Wet trousers didn't worry me one little bit ... a tweed skirt most certainly did!

Back on the coach, a boisterous, bawdy sing-song spirited us the remainder of the way to the intimidatingly grandiose Palace itself. Somewhat on the peachy side of cream in colour and styled in the little-known illegitimately hybridized 'English Baroque' this sumptuous Palace was built by 'Vanbrugh' ... and of course thousands of other ragged-arsed little blokes unworthy of having names or any need of wealth or notoriety. The time being broadcast by solid gold and gone-to-seed dandelions, was just turned 1705 AD ... given the odd minute or two, and a sudden micro-climate of generosity was suddenly bursting upon the air in the form of a 'GIFT' from the 'Nation'. This was proclaimed and bestowed by the good Queen Anne upon the victorious warrior the 1st Duke of Marlborough, by way of a back-hander kind of reward for murderous services rendered in the beheading, disembowelling, raping and plundering of their sworn enemy, Louis XIV's zillion-strong armies across the Channel. Such butchery being an 'Alien' characteristic that'd been transported here to Planet Earth, not by 'Inter-Galactic Explorers', but by 'Outcasts', banished, abandoned and confused; sent by some weirdly mysterious deity back out there in the depths of space, and now, sadly established far, wide and lost throughout the Planet, continuing the mayhem madness that caused them to be sent here. They all looked up to the skies which for some reason they called 'The Heavens', and they begged and prayed for another 'Ark' to call and take them back home, having found it totally beyond them to fit-in and become in anyway part of Earth's harmonic majesty or requirements.

It was damnably frustrating; one could wait two thousand million years for an 'Ark', they always ran late, then pop behind a bush for a pee and, Bingo! ... two of the bloomin' things suddenly go trundling past! Perplexing things those 'Deities' who operated the 'Service'; it was a miracle that no-one had given up the ghost and forgotten about them completely, especially after being dumped here all that time ago. Our 'Deity' was called 'God', others knew them by various names; there were so many different ones, maybe they were all the same one; nobody seemed to know.

Whatever my feelings were regarding opulence, there was no escaping the absolute beauty that glowed all about me. I could have done with a bit of that opulence-stuff right now myself, but I doubted very much that they sold trousers here! Tumbling out from the coach onto this mesmerising architectural canvas was a most dwarfing experience; it'd never been part of the grand plan for the peasant-stock likes of me to be here at all trespassing our eyes on such alchemy of the rich. I could sense the ages-old callous indifference for we 'lesser' mortals in the air all around me; I was here by default alone, a trespasser in my feet and fingers as well as my eyes and ears. My own stalwart pride turned into a rage within and I felt a growing stubborn refusal to set foot inside the place; just how dared they have the effrontery to take my money and then rub my nose in all their greedy, insanely vulgar blessed way of life! I turned and cast my eyes over the artificial lake, I could hear the ghostly command now ... "Bring Beauty to ME; bring it right here under my nose to where my greedy eyes ... and mine alone ... may gloat over its perfection!" I cringed here under so many ghosts that Time had erased all traces of status from. Ghosts were ghosts, take 'em or leave 'em; it was 'status' that was artificial and non-existent. All ghosts were 'salt-of-the-earth' good pals that enjoyed a good scream and a laugh, poking fun at the 'Great Pretence'; every ghost knew that the skeleton of a Duke was no different from that of a slave. They found this absolutely hilarious because there remained absolutely no trace of whatever it supposedly was that elevated them to such toweringly pretentious heights. At the end of the day, the simple truth was that we were all the same, all equal!

I looked about me for signs of the dreaded 'Sandwich Inspector', but I couldn't see anything resembling one anywhere. There were certainly lots of 'paying-guests' in evidence, this place was a lucrative business with the potential to provide a revenue more prolific than acorns in an oak forest. Bitter and somewhat poisonous as they were for most creatures to swallow, pigs could always gluttonise on them until their great bellies were bursting, and with no apparent ill effects.

I couldn't help myself harking back to the absolute mess that mankind the Alien, had wrought upon this previously virgin Planet, and all because of gluttony and greed, here about me now so lavishly disguised as Beauty. It was of no comfort my feeling sickened by it and distant from it when I couldn't escape from the knowledge of being one of that Alien species myself; a throw-back indication perhaps that, back at 'Home', wherever that was, things were not so bad after all. In a flash of resolve, I quickly pulled myself together and laid the stubborn beast within me to rest and swallowed my ridiculous pride; it wasn't the kind of thing that served me well, being part of my humbled, 'apologetic' upbringing. So, with my trousers still wet, I set myself free and joined the others.

It was impossible to think of this place as being a 'home' in my two-up, two-down way of thinking; the very thought of its dwellers going to bed here, all tired and aching after a day out hunting, then sleeping, dreaming dreams like you and me. Coughing in the night, peeing in a poe, counting the cockerels crowing at first light, before staggering to the window and pulling back the curtains to see what the weather was doing, then eating toast and patting the dog. In this sense it wasn't much different to any other mundane life; bacon always smelled like bacon and burnt toast always smelled like burnt toast wherever you were or whoever you were, the similarities were countless.

It came as a bit of a surprise to learn that Winston Churchill was born here inside this Palace. So much for my having thought of him as being one of the 'People', an ordinary sort of bloke that'd done well and had risen to fame; having shown leadership, doggedness and tenacity in denying extreme-alien Hitler his longed for Cannibal English Breakfast. Some 'Ordinary bloke, why dammit, the man was 'Royal'; one of his Great Grandfathers being the 1st Duke of Marlborough ... John Churchill. Wars ran in their family every bit as noses did in mine, the distinguishing difference being that, no Queen or King ever saw fit to build us a Palace as reward for a spectacularly successful sneezing fit! I recalled seeing a cartoon entitled, 'Churchill's Ladder'. It showed three male figures, one standing on the ground having a slightly bigger man on his back and he with another even bigger man on his back. The top man had his hand in the middle man's pocket and the middle man had his in the standing one's pocket. The standing one, who was supporting them both, was the 'ordinary working man', the middle one was his gaffer, the 'middle-man' himself, while the one on top was Churchill. A fine example of the power of 'Illustration' as distinct from 'Painting' and it gave me food for thought, a far broader picture of how Churchill was perceived to be by others; powerful Art indeed.

It was virtually, but not entirely, beyond my imagination to picture the infant Churchill here, crawling and crapping about the floors, putting salt in the sugar and pepper in the snuff. Similar thoughts were occurring to 'Walt', I knew what he was picturing and sensed a response, something quite daring brewing behind his wicked grin, as we endured the monotonous spiel on the great man. While we were being herded away from the bed in which baby Winston had been born, 'Walt' clambered up onto it and enacted the part of the slobbering infant, gnawing away at the bedposts and gurgling ... "Never, never in the field of human exploitation has so much been owned by so few; urgh ... Mummy, Mummy, I've done a whoopsie!" Shrieks of laughter rang out and swept like flames along the lavishly adorned corridors, the kind of which had probably never been heard here before. 'Walt' was safely back hidden in the anonymous crowd as a concerned bemusement of officialdom feared for their very own lives, anxious that the joyful music of laughter had not permeated the living quarters of the untouchable, if indeed they were here at all anymore. Apart from the intermittent hilarious odd moment, I was generally finding this palatial confined indoctrination all a bit tedious. Endless old mug-shots in oils, not only were they of self-adoration but they tended to look like dreary repeats of the same pompous generality and would, to my mind, have been photographs had photography been around at the time. Early portrait painters for the most part, were in fact 'Photographers-in-waiting', 'Art' being something altogether different, something capable of uplifting spiritual dimensions and expectations. I counted my lucky stars that I'd not been born a Prince or a Duke; their world seemed austere, daunting and perplexing in the most unavoidably high-profile of ways imaginable and it was showing me that it was my good fortune to have been born a common villager instead of to a life, which undoubtedly, carried the most burdensome of responsibilities, and with no recognisable freedom like I knew simple freedom to be. The more I saw, the more I felt I was in a prison rather than a palace, and I couldn't wait to get back outside into the air ... even this directly hereabout seemed unreal, concocted like part of the prison itself. As for my deviously planned spot of trout poaching, I no longer had the stomach or the slightest inclination for it. I decided instead to set my village earthworms free in the palatial garden earth where they could establish an aristocratic expatriate community and have fun writing to their children back home in my village garden, letting them know how the upper-crust worms lived.

The journey back was just a huge letting-off of steam, everyone was going at it twenty to the dozen. Idle promises impossible to keep, tied tangled knots with good-byes; alchemic cacophony if ever there was and with swirling undercurrents as the shores of dark reality for some were closing-in too fast and a thoughtful hush pretended to be tiredness as it befell the coach.

## 19. 'Red Fires in the night, Green Cinders in Grasses'

This was just another raw, bloody limb dissected from the mysterious body of life; a creature now quite un-fawnlike and really quite an ogre with concealed faceted dillusions which it aloofly disregarded and kept hidden. This Life-thing was picking up pace and was more readily showing its true colours, these being of an alluring intensity and intent; a learning journey amongst obstacled heartbreaks with spaces intended for snatching elusive dreams, glowing like Gold and stitching them to our very hearts in the despairing hope that they'd remain forever. 'Life' was the most unconsidered gift to present to the most innocent flower of loving, turning a frail pink blossom into a hard apple, crabbed and bitter, or, pippined and sweet; no-one knew at that high blinding moment when lusting thoughts were pure cider, drunkards its drinkers.

Only one solitary bud remained to flower in this lounging last summer, this late bloom being the Summer School at Barlaston Hall. Some of those I'd already said goodbye to and were effectively, no longer Art Students, had enrolled for this week-long artistic nicety prior to being called-up for National Service; either this or some other vanishing trick. Amongst these was my latterly emerged, like-minded friend from the third years that was, Tom Crossley. Apart from his being the tea-chest bass-player in the Jazz Band, he'd been one of our best illustrators as well as an intriguing Artist in a broader sense. He and I had a lot in common; he was an unassuming sort of bloke, feeling his way the same as I was doing, brought-up to be made to feel less than second rate in an identical manner to that which I had been. I'd never have guessed it though, he'd obviously been an amazingly good actor throughout all the time that I knew him. Those pre-war and early post-war years had a lot to answer for, being rather more of a curse upon both of us, in the emerging new order of things.

Another of those to be showing melancholic reluctance to face the future was Teddy who, to my surprise, made me the offer of his motorbike taxi-service, an offer which I was glad of for melancholic reasons of my own. It was just like old times again and he had another 'secret' that was 'hot off the press', one which he wanted me to be the first to know about. I was reminded of a previous 'surprise' that he'd sprung on me, a rather sad one I recall, one involving my old 'too randy for his own good' friend, 'Art' Tomkins, now

'Guardsman Tomkins'. It all seemed so very long ago, so very foreign.

This was promising to be a memorable event. All of my immediate colleagues had enrolled ... with the predictable exception of 'Burto' who was otherwise engrossed. In addition, quite a gang of other, slightly more remote ex-third years had also added their names to the list guaranteeing it to be a bumper event. These included the heart-throb redhead's deposit-paid, six and a half feet of mollycoddled confectionery known as Theobald; too bad the Goddess herself wasn't coming, a late ghastly revelation which almost caused mass cancellations and the odd suicide attempt, my own included. This was partway compensated for by the inclusion of one of the more wildly outrageous, vulgarly glamorous of the ex-third years, Fanny Phelps, bohemian to the core in the most liberated and lubricated of ways, earthy and funny, just terrifyingly unnerving if she happened to glance in your direction, that's all. It was all looking really promising in fact; I couldn't have prescribed anything better for myself if I tried.

Julie announced that she was going away with her parents on their now 'annual' holiday by the sea in Cornwall, for the most part coinciding with the dates of my Summer School. This made me feel a bit less guilty for being away from her and at the same time setting me free to grow a little ... every little bit helped. The College was now vacated of life, ghosts were being ineffectively bleached and disinfected from all surfaces and the phantomlike 'Burto' was in another world, blissfully being brushed by swallows, cricketing the grass-smelling moments away, something he loved far more than any conceivable aspect of Art College 'extra-curricular activity'. I understood what he felt like, I'd felt similar feeling over cycle-racing, an unfulfilled dream that still ached, especially when I knew that I could have done well ... loving every minute of it.

Dad looked upon my idle moments with an 'Iron Age' disdain, mouthing nothing, but saying it all with his glancing condemnation. It wasn't my fault that I was caught-up, suspended between animations; solace had its place of virtue within every industried fervour. Were Christ here now, there'd be those times when he too had to stand in a bus-stop, idly having to wait for a bus that was late. Then, Teddy rolled up and Dad smiled at last, his son was not such an idler after all.

Teddy only ever drank 'proper' coffee, but Mom nevertheless raced off to make an obligatory cup of tea. To Teddy, tea was just a crumbly, mouse turd-like substance, a tannic, dark-staining textile dye derived from overgrown weeds grown primarily in Ceylon; other more obnoxious varieties showing up on mountain slopes in India and China, these ranging in taste from 'piss-like' to 'gone-off smoked fish'. His learned ignorance on the subject was wasted on us, we only drank Co-op tea, anyway.

I tried to warn him not to ask for coffee and that it would be wiser for him to stick to tea, otherwise it'd regrettably be 'Council House' coffee, the bottled stuff with chicory essence, a headache on its own, but with sterilized milk with the skin floating on top, a nightmare and a half! It was stuff like this which I felt stigmatized by, a substance which, more than any other, convinced me that moving away from the village was my best option. Beverages however, were the very last thing on Teddy's mind, he could withhold his secret no longer and he blurted, "You'll never guess, Jim-Jim ... I've been accepted into the Royal College of Art; what do you think of that!" I made him repeat it while I discreetly, 'accidentally' spilled his beverage down the drain. "Bloody hell, Teddy, that's great!" It made me think of Dad's heartbreaking story of his being one of those few accepted to study Painting at 'The Slade School' all those years ago; what a different story that was.

Barlaston Hall was a miniaturized version of Blenheim Palace, a recognisable dwelling without ostentation ... but not without ghosts of its own. A terrible bloody murder had taken place there only a few years earlier, I remembered seeing it in the newspaper at the time. Despite time's passage acting as anaesthetic, dull memories still remained and morbidly grew, as occasion favoured, from earthworm to anaconda, and with the scene of the crime having been recorded for posterity on the blood-stained white marble-slab beneath the carpet by the fireplace. Revelation of which was simply irresistible for one female student, who'd attended a previous Summer School here and had been sickendly subjected to sight of this grizzly stain on the floor which not even bleach had been able to erase. Of course, there now simply had to be a ghost of the murdered woman, one which every single one of us would, at some time or other, believe we'd seen, or heard, or felt. As for the murderous jealous husband himself, he really sent the shivers down our spines... No-one could recall what had happened to him where was he ... was he still here hiding in one of the cupboards, or perhaps, was he just another ghost to have to contend with? It didn't bear thinking about! What it did do however, was to bring the girls several trembling heartbeats closer for reasons of comfort and security, aloneness not proving to be the most desirable of states to find oneself in. I rather liked this arrangement, apart from which, I didn't like having to reveal that I was feeling a bit of a nervous wreck myself.

Our 'Artist-in-Residence' mentor, this Reginald Haggar chap, gaunt, old and gnarled as he was, turned out to be a most interesting, kindly, enthusiastic and absolutely first-rate Artist; a water-colourist with a deep, guttural, tobaccoed posh voice. One of the 'old school', a Potteries man through and through. I was fascinated by him, his poshness of voice gave the false impression that the physical process of discourse was a painful undertaking for him to endure and he grimaced his words as though they hurt from all their far corners. I felt inspirationally provoked into drawing him, each attempt looking like a caricature, which in life was what he actually was. I didn't have to try and make him look funny, in the nicest of ways, that's what he most charmingly already was. He made my drawings of him look more like cartoons and I could do nothing to alter this, much as I tried. Because of my fascination with personality and facial storytelling, I'd become thought of as something of a cartoonist, all too readily dismissed as not being serious because of this. Nothing could have been further from the truth and I'd found the most ideal vehicle in 'drawing' for furthering my delight in humorous situations, thoughts and ideas. Recognising 'character' was of vital importance to me; it was through the reading of personality and character that individuals grew, each identifiable from the next, and I therefore believed there to be a place of honour for humour and pathos also; too many things in 'Art' were bland and wart-less.

The faces which I recall Van Gogh having painted, were 'real' characters, likewise those painted by Rembrandt and Hogarth. 'Character was not the sole province of the human facial anatomy however; the Artists that I loved saw character and personality in everything, throughout anatomy, in fact throughout Nature. In trees, plants, animals, in landscape itself; honouring frailty and imperfection with a humility and dignity, recognising that 'imperfection' was probably the closest one was ever likely to get to 'perfection'. Something which, in a 'how long is longer' kind of way, simply didn't exist despite grand, bland prophestations in Renaissance and pre-Raphaelite painting; hence their abandonment of 'warts-and-all' reality in favour of a 'make-believe', sham-spiritual 'pap', a wistful thinking substitute devoid of the ability, or indeed, the advisability of being able to laugh, cry or fart.

This Reg Haggar chap was real enough, even though the music of his deliverance gave one the impression that he'd swallowed a ruptured bagpipe; he knew his stuff and we all held him in high esteem because he could back it all up with the ability to practice what he preached. He showed us masses of stuff which he projected onto a screen which, because of perpetual tobacco smoke, eventually became just another ghost of Barlaston Hall.

There were tennis courts over at the back and, as much as I'd have loved a vigorous, fun knockabout, I'd somewhat mysteriously injured my left foot and was thus reduced to a severe and extremely painful limp; something was trying to tell me to slow down a bit, it was either that or a ghost prank. Snail-pace wasn't a thing which I found easy to accommodate but, one which after I had sampled it, found it to be interestingly different and really rather nice. It felt especially good with the summer sun now so uncommonly motherly aloft in the paleness of blue where swifts were all screaming. On the lawns below where cotton dresses had eventually yielded to the wiser counsel of flimsy panties and very little else. Big 'jelly-baby' Theobald had grown tired of his bully-boy brand of tennis and was sniffing the air in a ram-like manner and was clumsily stumbling along an alluringly rancid pheromone trail, being ruthlessly seduced and reduced to beef-dripping. He'd become a source of depraved fascination and intrigue before the provocatively wicked and womanly attentions of the more-than-his-match, Fanny Phelps, who was herself like two army-sized dollops of sausage-meat in a pan, shedding her lardy excesses and intermittent spluttering and spitting, as the fat advanced to the button marked, 'spontaneous combustion'.

I sat with Tom Crossley on the hot stone steps above the lawn, engrossed in the deeper meaning of Art, Music, Literature and nubility, both of us aware of this 'other' unsubtle bit of loin-lusty cat-and-mouse that was making the earth tremble and was getting in the way of other more delicate things. Everyone else was clocking it too as Teddy came and quietly joined us, tut-tutting under his breath ... "Rather him than me!" Tom stretched and sighed ... "She'll make mincemeat of him she will, Teddy, spit him out as gristle, you'll see. If Fanny can't make a Man of that great mamby-pamby, nobody can!" "There's surely a better way of becoming a Man," Teddy groaned, adding "personally, I'd rather watch two stallions fighting ... or even badgers being baited. It's all so distasteful, don't you think?" He shuffled barefoot indoors to where he was cool and where he could contemplate the Royal College with his feet up and a 'Senior Service' writing a smoke-poem amongst his luxurious thoughts.

A gong signified that tea-time was upon us, not the most likely event to trigger off a sonnet; it really wasn't that bad and it aroused other circulations to stimulate the mind and body over more social dimensions. Fortunate for Teddy, 'proper' coffee was an optional beverage that released more tea to help satisfy my own lifelong addiction. It was all really rather summery with bowls of radishes, tomatoes, cucumber, lettuce complete with greenfly, spring onions, cheese and bread; not in abundance, but just enough to keep us alive. This frugality provoked the counter-measure of evening sausage feasts, cooked outdoors over a fire in the grounds. A group of us had earlier chipped-in while the Butcher's was still open and I accompanied Teddy on the motorbike just a couple of miles up the A34 to where we found what we were looking for. I was immediately struck by how friendly and sociable the Potteries people were, with the butcher being most accommodating to our pleas of being hungry, poverty-stricken students. During the course of events we were introduced to the delight of Staffordshire oat pancakes, which it didn't take long to discover were probably the best, most versatile basic food-item yet invented ... anywhere in the world. You could roll anything up in them, sea-food, meat, sausage, bacon, cheese, honey, jam, treacle, mashed spuds with H.P. Sauce, mashed bananas with sugar, you name it; nothing was more versatile!

With tea-time long since out of the way, the rest of the evening belonged to us and the bats which brushed us with their cool silky black umbrella-wings in their fervidly blind pursuit of moths, that had judged it safer to take to the wing now that all the birds were sleeping. Thoughts of ghosts now awakening was only half a meadow's distance away from being an aphrodisiac, distance being impossible to judge in the cindered failing light. We lit our fire and gathered closely round its spitting glow, singing student songs and vexing the first owls, denying them their discourse with the moon. I felt a small hand softly entwining my fingers before tightening its grip; it was Lucy, a bit of a tom-boy second-year potter, plainly nervous in this 'other-wordly' impending darkness and of the belief that I could protect her in some way. I was more than happy with this approximate calculation of hers because, not only could she make my bell ring and steam come hissing from my navel, but I was of a similar misconception that she could protect me in some way too. It was such a cosy, courtly charade here listening to sausages spluttering and spitting their sides with laughter in the pan, silly songs bravely telling phantoms where to go and that there were no vacancies on board any of us for the cadging of lifts, thank you very much! Meanwhile, inside the Hall, in a spooky room with a bed and a bedside lamp excitedly glowing its dim eye blind, the door of the room bolted and without a key to obstruct the view through the substantial keyhole of the old busted lock, the pheromone trail had come to its well-planned day of reckoning. The cunning old cat had finally seized upon the sacrificial mouse, in this case a sugar rat, and was in the process of mauling him to his ecstatic death. Those others not part of the sausage feast were taking turns feasting instead through the keyhole, relaying a running commentary, a form of Radio Luxembourg with an 'X' certificate, bush-telegraph fashion, and we somewhat caustically joked that there'd be another corpse that needed explaining in the morning. The wailing sounds coming from that sordid little room were banshee-like, magnified by the considerable flabby tonnage being brought to bear on the straining bedsprings. It was a seriously horrid stain on our otherwise 'romantic', fun Summer School. Let's face it, a half ton nymphomaniac on heat and a six and half foot of jellied ex-public school bullyboy baby with his testicles on fire, were never going to be likely candidates for a wild flower-spotting expedition prior to breakfast. Teddy was right, watching two stallions fight was marginally preferable, as was badger-baiting ... and had a degree or two more finesse to boot.

By darkness the Potteries landscape was dramatic, a most awe-inspiring transformation; it was now a panoramic inferno of red glowing kilns as far as the eye could see. Like a scene from the blitz, but with fired earthenware pots instead of charred human bodies. Somewhere out there amongst them was 'Wedgwood', most famous pottery of them all and, tomorrow a trip had been arranged for us to be shown around the works and to be able to see the whole process, from the wet clay right through to the finished miracle. I was so much looking forward to this, especially their most famous 'Jasper-ware' which had intrigued me since first coming across it all those years ago. I was just longing to see it crafted in all its intricacy, then being transformed by the furious might of fire into the most classically striking of pottery. From an artistic perspective, my only reservation regarding 'Jasper', was Josiah Wedgwood's insistence on 'Jasper's' forms being taken from Classical Greek, instead of allowing it freedom to explore intriguing new possibilities in design, shape and colour, without losing any artistic integrity in the process. I feel that it was 'Jasper' that was the loser as a result of the insistence. Pottery was just such an intriguing art-form, situated precariously between the domestically functional and the 'locked-cabinet' ornamental which bordered at times on the sculptural, its only common factor that of being fired. Through the various techniques involved in applying artwork, together with the textural magnificence of slips and coloured glazes, Pottery had really become an Art of Splendour; too bad its masterpieces too easily became 'smashedtopieces' when dropped ... a bit like birds' eggs.

As we were luxuriating in the balmy night air with the tired scent of the last wood-smoke wafting idly over us, still lost for words to describe the banqueted nightscape spread before us, an intimately close-by tawny owl violated the entire dream with a loud and rivetingly haunting cry, sending terror throughout the heavens and all the stars scurrying. It was so eerily clear and piecing, leaving no doubt whatsoever over who the night's owner really was.

Wide-eyed and dumfounded we listened to the sound go staining out across the vast expansive darkness; it was so commandingly beautiful and coming from such a diminutive and insignificant a life, from an existence unconsidered and so very remote from our own. Poor Lucy was rigor-mortised with fear anew and clung on to me more tightly than ever, laughing nervously as the others all spontaneously tried to imitate the cry. "It's the Barlaston ghost!" Cyril howled, setting the girls off into a pitiful whimpering, effectively bringing our starlight meditation to a close. As bodies began dispersing, Lucy let go of my hand, giving me a lightning kiss on the cheek and rushed away into the darkness to catch up with the others who were briskly braving it back to their sleeping quarters.

The old saying of how 'time flies when your having fun', really was applicable here, reminding me of another such saying about how 'the best things always came in small packages'. I concurred with both, this small package of days felt like pure Gold and was flying by too quickly. The 'Wedgwood' outing proving to be the most humbling and fascinating experience with so many modestly mesmerizing skills being displayed right across the board. I saw my 'Jasper' being created with meticulous skill in an overall abundance of taken-for-granted artistry. Pots were being turned, designs painted, lines being applied with a tiny brush around revolving pot after pot, cup after cup, plate after plate; a dexterity that you swore had grown on a tree somewhere ... one that nobody had told you about and few had ever even heard of. Being up close to those bottle-necked red-brick kilns was like being on a day-trip back to the Stone-age. It was nothing less than a miracle for us to set our eyes upon such artistic treasures that'd resulted from those red glows in the night which we'd all been so awe-stricken by.

It had been decided that what we needed to round of our week, was an old fashioned 'constitutional', a thorough good 'blow-out' to put some real, raw, fresh air back into our lungs after a week of being mostly cooped-up in lectures; and being obliged to breathe in copious amounts of tobacco smoke! A coach had been laid on to take us on a ramble in the Peak District, to Dovedale, a place where the transparent scar-tissue of a magical river wedded my own county of Staffordshire with the next door neighbour, Derbyshire; a most exquisite union here being consummated before our astounded eyes. A place where lonely hills gave birth to gurgling brooks, thence into babbling streams, to sparkling rivers tumbling over falls, cascading over rocks, swirling round boulders, becoming mirror-like on deeper pools where the young boy 'Walton', learned how to 'completely' angle with a fly for speckled Trout and floppy-finned Grayling. Lonelier hills roamed beyond the dale, a wilderness where sheep cried from somewhere lost beyond the lowering sky, the first buzzards I'd ever seen, mewed like kittens and circled high, endlessly round and round without flapping a wing. It was a world of miracles, a vanished river that'd only left its bed of stones and boulders as proof of it ever being there, having long since plunged underground beneath the 'Manifold Valley', Trout, Grayling, Crayfish an' all, subterranean-specied now ... I wonder? The river then, quite contrarily re-emerged further down the dale somewhere to confound the eye; a river indeed ... just springing from nowhere? I don't believe it! The God of Thunder lived hereabouts in cloud-lands high, in a bed-sit cave which he shared with the Devil, amongst other time-long hills where Iron Age Man made circles of stone, an early form of granite telephone-box through which to get in touch with 'home' and to beg for guidance, questioning the practicability of God's command that they go forth and multiply; stressing that this was easier said than done when marauding wolves took firstborns with greater ease than nibbling bramble berries from a briar.

The mystery of my injured foot remained, but I limped on, intoxicated by the majesty of my surroundings. This truly was a most beautiful place in a most beautiful island which had only come into being as a result of glaciers melting and fenland sinking, allowing seas from both north and south to rush in and create an island, turning nomadic wanderers into islanders. People with a finite place which, once they got used to the idea, might eventually get to be called 'home', a place with all the trappings and petty bureaucracies that permanence inevitably drifted into, together with the nastier trappings of squabbles over territory and the 'original sin' of 'greed' re-emerging and assuming control and then fighting over ownerships with pillaging, plundering and killing gone rife, never to end. It was only his previous nomadic wandering way of life that'd kept him placid; drifting into the ever changing seasons of things without owning or wanting to own anything of it. Just picking, gathering, sharing, learning; destroying nothing, just wandering on, singing, dancing, playing, forever going forth and multiplying, meeting old friends along the way, brothers and sisters all.

Ceasing to move anymore had revived and set free the beasts of Greed and Avarice to gluttonise and grovel in a lusting for Power and Domination. There simply wasn't a species anywhere to be found on planet Earth so charged with the insatiable crazed need to have all that it could see, possess all that could be possessed, rule over all that could be ruled and with the safeguard of pecking orders to ensure that the vast subservient, rather placid and feeble majority were ruled and managed through the most unimaginably fiendish methods of 'persuasion'. This strange behavioural trait existed in this 'settler' species that'd solidly settled and was weighed down with accumulated dust. He had no rhyme or reason for being here at all, unless of course his arrival was an Act of War, an army sent by a Warrior-Race to subdue the Earth, so go forth and multiply throughout it, having dominion over its entirety before, in the grand, time-old and honoured 'blaze-of-glory' manner, destroying himself and every single other living organism along with him. If this couldn't please his Gods, nothing could!

There was much revelry as our last evening sacrificially became a bedlam of bangers, beans and bread, bitter beer in bottles and a barrel, giggling girls and jazz records louder than laughter. With all hair let down, chastity belts came out from closets, their keys not properly hidden and the picking of locks not entirely forbidden. In all the poking, choking, bonfire smoking, Lucy singled me out and lingered close by, itching but afraid of where a kiss might lead, idly burning twigs on the fire, watching them, blazing her own burning desire; becoming miserable as smoke snuffed out the flame which mirrored her own self-denial. We contrived a game of hide-and-seek and agreed to let this decide our fate; she was the one that would hide, and if I found her, that was to melt all self-denial and would settle the issue, there'd be no decider. She knew that I would probably cheat if I was the one to hide, I'd make it easy for her to find me as well she knew. So I agreed to be seeker and to agree to fully ten minutes for her to hide herself, no clues allowed and no hidden rules suddenly appearing either. Of course she was just as capable of cheating as I was, but I knew that she wouldn't and I could tell that she was really quite nervous and afraid deep-down and I loved her and respected her for that. I didn't want to take any advantage from a situation so flippantly hinged around just the mere chance of being found, but she wasn't to know that I wouldn't insist on holding her to the rules ... not unless of course it was she who insisted that I did. I had to find her first and, as I consulted the velvet dark where she had melted, the immensity of the night suddenly hit me with a startling new realisation; the ten minutes were up, the game had started.

With my bell being rung and scorching steam coming hissing from my navel, I stumbled forward with all senses clouded in a testosterone blur and wishing I had torches in my toes; surely my pounding heart would give warning of my approach as, even barefoot on tip-toes I was throbbing like a tractor. The power of love's desire was sufficiently strong in both of us as to sweep all ghosts out from the sooty dark where they'd been hiding and where Lucy now was somewhere trembling with a pounding heart of her own. Raucous voices wailed beyond where bottles emptied and the barrel went down, prompting the first tender brains to fall from their prams then to warble face-down jibberish from vomit-spattered lavender borders. Starlight had no useful wattage beneath the ancient yews where blackness could hardly be blacker as I grimly groped before coming to grief over the coupled mutton of what, in one cologne-salted whiff I knew was Fanny Phelps, plus something else that had no trousers on its legs. A veritable mountain which I unceremoniously cleared and in one thunderous glass-shattering sidelong impact, wrecked a small greenhouse gathering a montage of assorted minor disfigurements in the process. Filthy language confirmed Fanny's close proximity, as well as her displeasure, under an uproar of inebriated laughter as I got to my feet and gingerly brushed myself down. I could see stars under the tree now, they were different ones from those above the tree, these were swirling haphazardly before slowly dispersing. I moved forward a few careful steps before, out from the darkness, a figure stood up draped in a white sheet and holding a torch to his face. It didn't fool me as it wobbled past smelling of beer and moaning like a knackered old bumble bee before vanishing down a fading perspective of shrieks, not one of which was the one I was searching for.

Unperturbed and with an ardour raging even harder, I persevered out from the tawny-owled umbrella of the yew and back out into the sugar-dusted constellations beneath which a darkly boxed shape dimly ghosted. I pondered a moment before remembering this to be an outside lavatory and my heart suddenly became a heartquake zone as I dithered my fingers in search of the latch. Nervously I entered, amidst a whole Jackson Pollock of splattered din that couldn't be 'sound' if it tried and I almost died when I walked blindly into two flaying, chest high, barefooted legs, immediately followed by a pandemonium of other body parts accompanied by vocal gibberish. "Is that you, Lucy?" I murmured rather stupidly, prompting a most venomous bridling of words ... "No it bloody well aint, so fuck off!" My blushes were wasted in the dark and I felt a smile itching when I matched that irritated voice with a familiar face before being unceremoniously ejected back out to a growing frustration.

Lights were on inside the Hall where the tea-totalers were browsing through books and being perfectly normal. I dismissed this as being a likely hiding-place; it was outside where all the fun was. Drawn curtains kept the lawns in darkness where chastity lay planktonic in bite-sized pieces and the fire still embracing a dull glow as the jazz repetitiously played, with no-one willing to release the stylus from its dirtied groove. Those that could drink, still drank; those that couldn't just lay around groaning and wanting to die. I still couldn't find Lucy, try as I may, she remained chaste despite being chased; surely there wasn't any fun in not being found.

My forehead had now started to throb and I could feel a proud lump as a result of my argument with a hard part of the greenhouse; the game was losing some of its appeal. I couldn't imagine Lucy choosing to hide amongst this 'seedy' obstacle course, it didn't make sense. So I pondered over the situation before feeling inclined to follow my instincts and to just saunter down along the driveway, away from the pitch-black clutter. It all became so differently soothing, I could breathe again ... and hear the silence whispering upon my skin as I left the noisy old Hall behind beyond the green-speared bushes. The air was most calming, simplifying my burning ardour down within reach of my control again. The world suddenly felt overwhelmingly massive, and my own life-force less than a pin-prick amongst it all; it was a sort of scary, lonely feeling of being what I was ... nothing.

In absolute pristine silence, I suddenly saw something, a tiny dazzling green glow of a glow-worm in the grass beside the lane; it was a moment of pure Gold. At this moment, 'it' was more 'something' than I was and I was made to feel even more of a 'nothing' when an even more magical shooting-star lit up the entire heavens in a split-second of blindingly silent light in a diminishing long trail as it ran out of existence above my head. I gasped, unable to offer any more than that; then ... Aghh! ... two tiny arms came slipping round me from behind, making the distance between having a heart-attack and shitting myself immeasurable. I spun round and there she was ... Lucy in the starlight.

She'd been following me all the time, quieter than a mouse, making sure of being in control. "I think you won that game," I whispered with a bashful smile. "Let's call it a draw!" she whispered back. For the very first time, we held each other tightly and kissed ... and kissed ... and kissed. I became so transported that I feared that at any minute, an alarm-clock would go off and awaken me from my dream ... but it didn't. There was no softer light than starlight and I could see it in her eyes; this was a moment of pure loveliness; we were not burglars of each other, just sharers and we simply smiled with our very hearts and strolled arm-in-arm dreamily beside sweet dreaming parsleys and deep-secretly nectared vegetations, looking for glow-worms; we were not playing silly games anymore.

## 20. 'Driftin' to a Shoot-out in the Old Saloon'

After Barlaston, a huge numbness came over the world with good-byes the size of cattle, which seemed to bellow far beyond the recognisable world with a sadness that was sinisterly laced with terror; nothing was dependable or fun anymore. The Art College had emptied bare to its splintery, dusty old floorboards and a final year was suddenly gaping buttonless like a busted fly in a cathedral; the second 'renaissance' had expired and was over and done with, never to be repeated. Lucy had paled back into lost memory and the realisation that I was suddenly a Man drew the substantial curtains across my former bounteous life. Julie was similarly struck with a recognition that the plan of life may, more than likely have been predetermined, a somewhat dark realisation that we gloomily shared, projecting us to the weighty conclusion that 'freedom' was for 'earthling' species only and not for we inter-galactical vagrants of a contrived and very much manufactured behaviour which butchered finer sense at the wielding of an axe, or sword, or the trigger-pulling bedlamic insanity of the holding of control over us by force alone. I wished now more than ever for the power to resist and refuse to lie down and take those things that I instinctively knew to be alien to my innate sense, no matter what it brandished to emphasise its supposed authority.

My trusty old colleague, Dave, was also in this 'flux of drift'; not so much inclined to look back over the handful of naively succulent years but, more in the direction of the one remaining, a tough old sod that'd appeared like an off-white and clipped-winged dove from a magician's hat. Being born was not so much a magical gift, but more of a curse if all liberty had been grabbed by the greediest and turned into a device of torture by the wickedest of those power-crazed monsters. Just how could we fight back if we were timid and not cankered with greed ourselves? The only thing we had which could be perceived as being subversive and therefore a threat of sorts, was Art. Art was a thing which only Artists possessed; being filthy rich and able to purchase any artifact of it at a whim, meant absolutely bugger-all and left the pompous owners still a thousand light-years from having the ability of producing it for themselves.

Dave came over to do some serious thinking and also for some serious painting as well. The Curator at Lichfield City Art Gallery had earlier approached me with a view to my holding a one-man show and I had taken him up on the proposal with the suggestion that it should be a two-man exhibition instead; he was agreeable to this. When I told Dave what I'd arranged, he bristled with excitement at the thought of exhibiting alongside his fellow artist, thus transforming summer into the most intense outpouring of painterly activity imaginable. Dad was bundling about in a kind of embarrassed excitement and was effectively defenceless in concealing his pride. The elastic of his smile had given way and his big smug grin steered about the house breaking crockery, burning toast, walking into only half-open doors, stubbing toes and the like, as something deep inside him had been released from its most miserable of prisons. It was like pure Gold touching upon us all at long last, and the artistry imprisoned for so long in him was breathing once more. Had I been his daughter instead of his son, I'd have hugged and kissed him; instead my bollocky hormones got in the way. I was helpless and I rushed up to embrace him, but before I could plant a kiss on his cheek, my nose was bleeding. Dad had bollocky hormones of his own and, unintentionally hard, had planted a fist incomplete of its full set of fingers soundly on my nose. Soft and sensitive as he was, Dad was a real Male of a man, a Woman's man pure and simple and he had no tolerance within him to accept any such 'sissy' forms of gentleness from a fellow male, least of all his nineteen year old son! I was confused, embarrassed, hurt, my bloody nose being the least of my concerns and I followed my nature and backed away knowing all too well of how simple things could go horribly wrong. Dave just stared in numb confusion, unable to recall a single moment when his own Father had raised even a finger to him. Families were different, life was different, just as Art from Art.

Live families were stranger than dead fiction; I had a younger brother but I'd hardly have ever known it. We had never been brothers in a proper brotherly sense; of course there was a considerable and explicable age-gap, as too there was an ever bigger one with my youngest sister, Rosie. Peas were dependably Peas as were Redcurrants with Redcurrants, Hedge-sparrows with Hedge-sparrows, Pigeons with Pigeons, you name it. Nothing was less dependable than the 'Human'; runts and throw-backs tore the very majesty from the species where dependability was concerned. A wild and unpredictable species, hardly ever capable of thoughtful contemplation and never without conflict and confrontation; providing timely step-off points, usually of the most trivial of sorts. All that I knew of my brother David was that he rather noisily picked his nose in bed and forever woke me up with his oblivious snoffling. "Stop picking your nose!" was the only lasting dialogue between us, and he grew to know me only as an observer of his nose-picking and nothing else. Whatever the differences were, my stranger of a brother was not prepared to give up his bed and to sleep on the camp-bed in Rosie's room in order that my fellow artist could lie in the next bed, where we could speak-out our frightening darknesses before we slept; right down to its roots, the world was hostile.

Finding normality as an emerging Artist simply wasn't normal; everything else was, but in a filmic, stop-frame, stop-start sort of way. A behavioural predictability, obnoxious to the vibrant threats of whatever it was that held we tenderling artists from the murdering mindlessness of the mass allied to misguided sovereignty amongst other such mythical elevations of supposed grandeur. Art didn't exist until it had been made, and that was the very precise point where it ceased to exist anymore, so transient was its most precious moment of existence. It only lived during the process of its making before becoming eternally dead, unable to move or to change colour, shape, texture. From whence it came was a mystery; was it from the paint, the brush, or was it from the hand that held the brush ... or the arm that held the hand that held the brush; where was it?

Wherever or whatever, Dave and I were out in tenderly young sun pedalling the stuff amongst where speckled

Thrushes were rapturously proclaiming and other jewel-like whistlings rose out from thickets and tangled fists of thorns and sedges; 'Art' was everywhere, unimagined. Trying to pluck tiny feathers, tiny leaves of it and to paint it to glorious death on a page of time was magically futile and blessed wasteful in a holiness close to criminality. This was for me so compellingly marvellous, a sensational invisibility of relationships felt and never properly found. Just what did it feel like to be that Thrush in the tree, having chosen this moment amongst moments for whistling those phrases so special to itself; to whom and for what reason other than the moment of time being 'Art' itself. Just like the mysterious joyful itches that waited behind my fingers for me to sing them free for everything around to have and to share for no reason other than the moment of madness itself and a grand 'thank-you' to the touching light for making existence at all.

Trees round the field were each one different from the next, each one alive and embracing the light and air within differently shaped timbered bosoms; separate poetry on individually expressing limbs, each with an invisible life force energising somewhere within. Just what did 'life' look like? Could it be kept in a jar like a tadpole; could it be seen, touched, smelled or tasted; just what was it? Was it an electricity, rented from a power-station in the sky like a flower-flame on a candle burning light into the dark? Nothing was ever more than Life; everything else was nothing. 'Art' was the only thing that I knew which could take me closest to finding my way of understanding the magical mystery of 'Life', and I had a growing suspicion that 'Life' was 'God' and that 'God' was 'Life', to be loved and honoured wherever it existed. The searching for an understanding and an expression of it was best served by the process of Art as a living incompletion.

The fascination of what seemed more akin to poetry where old iron, not possessing of the 'magical sap' was concerned, found a place of holiness within me regardless of it being dead. Life itself, together with its passage through time's eternity, was a sculptural calligraphy of poetic conversation with something which was probably nothing at all. Iron railings twisted and worn, broken down beyond use and left, forgotten yet possessing of beauty too, whatever that was. If only they could but grow like rusted iron conversations of poetry, like trees, huge and magnificent into the sky. Alas, dead things didn't grow but slipped back quietly into the ether, a slow passage of undeniable beauty nonetheless, austere and dumb; cold, decayed and dead. There was no 'in-between'; there was life and there was death with nothing separating them ... unless it was life that was in between two other dark forces that we had no perception of. I concluded that, 'Life' was all that there was ... all else wasn't.

All that we had to show for our excursion into artistic activity was a few lines and smudges mostly on paper and without evidence of having journeyed spiritually further afield. I wished and prayed for the miracle of being able to absorb the entirety of my worshipful fascination and for it to reveal itself in the little power-buds which were made live through touch alone and for my paintings, upon the softest of touches, reveal their inner sounds and smells. Alas; what I wanted was a dream too far, but it did show me the challenge which 'Art' represented, a wall for forever bashing one's head against in the search for a more complete expression.

Bread and cheese with rings of pickled beetroot relieved Mom of the headache of knowing what to provide for a vegetarian. Her solution, had I not breathed down her ear, would have been to cut the fat from the mutton and dish-up the lean, suffice that the old sheep, itself being of vegetarian ways, made the eating of its mutton, kind of 'vegetarian' as near as dammit. I shared her frustration, if not her logic, over the concept of a 'handed-down' form of vegetarianism, having myself been brought up on rabbit meat, with the rabbit itself being vegetarian ... same as a cow. Pigs and cockerels were just ravenous vacuum-cleaners and would eat whatever came their way, as too the pike and the perch which I rated as being the finest of subtly tasting foods, neither of them being too fussy over what passed through their pearly-gates; usually though it was another fish. Being a vegetarian seemed to me to be about the same as being a Jehovah's Witness, both of them fine provided they didn't interfere with my dietary preferences or my freedom in coming to my own logical conclusions over anthropological and spiritual issues. I didn't interfere with them and I didn't want them to interfere with my own way of thinking either.

More down to earth, outside their new bungalow in Darnford Lane, the village Vicar's daughters came out to greet me and my new friend. I had, over the latter part of my schooldays, grown up with Heather, the elder of the two, somehow managing to resist her having my virginity as a bead in her lustrous necklace. For Dave, as far as women went, he simply hadn't a clue, yet here he was frothing and foaming with an alien force raging and burning inside him. Instantaneous infatuation had shattered his best bone china and had been so rude as to break wind in the frailest and featheriest of inner sanctums of his beloved Brahms and Beethovens; his bollocks were barking like dogs in a betrayal far beyond his experience. The moment had changed him from being the dreamy deep-thinker that I'd hitherto known, into something no longer as dependable as Oak, but closer to

Aspen; vulnerable, whimsical, cross-eyed, cross-legged bloody useless ... apart from making baskets and rocking-chairs of course!

Even a Hornet didn't sting like love did. This was a sting, for the very first time like as that by an entomological monster as big as an airliner and with a stinging mechanism longer than two allotment gardens. The body's entire chemistry got completely rearranged, beside being ravaged, and the heart was tested to its very ultimate limits, all senses suddenly turned to compost! I'd already had my first proper sting and had grown to come to terms with what it essentially was that separated male from female and had to admit that nothing, absolutely nothing at all, burned so blisteringly or more ravenously than the prospect of turning that which separated the genders into a bridge and never ever tire of crossing it! Heather was stunningly beautiful; she had a fine, dark downiness over her bare limbs and had black lustrous hair and heavy-framed 'bay-window' spectacles which accentuated her marvellous eyes, setting her apart from other young women. She was a woman through and through, had been since the age of her first double-figures and her beauty terrified me whenever her mesmerising eyes preyed in my direction. I knew when I was beaten and I instinctively knew that I'd never survive should I allow myself to become her mirror for looking into. That's why I contrived an aloofness which fooled her into believing it to be indicative of total disinterest, overacting that effectively fooled us both. Had we ever yielded to the truth we'd have no doubt become parents. This precisely was the realistic terror that splashed over the rocks beneath that heaven-high bridge that separated her female from my male.

I watched disdainfully as Dave's Adam's-apple did clownish press-ups in this throat; it was somewhat sad to see him so instantly reduced to a gibbering idiot right here before my astounded eyes. I was relieved two-fold that it wasn't Heather that'd stung him, but her younger sister May. Artistic things meant the whole world to this lovely ecclesiastical family, young artists were even more interesting, hence the closeness that existed between them and me. A sudden fearful realisation swept through me; we were in danger of losing sight of our artistic goals and a whole lot more besides, so I reacted by reminding Dave that we had important work to do and that we were being sidetracked. 'Goddess' eyes were fixing me condemningly from behind their dusky green panes and I realised that I hadn't reacted a moment too soon. Dave wasn't overly co-operative when I seized yet more initiative and waved goodbye and started heading away up the hill, with him clumsily walking backwards behind me, utterly smitten and feverish from his first love-sting. He wasn't going to forgive me in a big hurry for intervening in the way which I had, but I had my own virginity to think about too and I knew danger when I saw it.

We settled down beside the hedge in a lush wild meadow overlooking a vast, sighing soft vale cradling Lichfield and other ghostly places away to the right, where Burton-on-Trent was lost in a hazed flatness. Inspired by blinding infatuation, Dave painted a small miracle which was as marvellous as anything ever painted by an English 'romantic' landscape artist. For me it wasn't the big landscape so much as the textural variety of what that landscape consisted of; I was searching for the voices of individual things, the grasses that shimmered and danced like a green sea with wonderful, finely structured Thistles, Foxgloves and Dog-daisies. Life-buds everywhere, miniscule, magnificent and meaningful, every little particle, part of the most joyful experience. This was what I was steadily being lured into pursuing, an 'another-ness' that I could sense and feel, something that didn't just sit there waiting to be adored and copied. No green wash would ever convince me that it knew best when multitudes of various things spoke-out separately and with a choreography where Butterflies danced and Larksong spilled like sugar from the sun. The intensity of my listening to that which constituted 'silence' was deafeningly audible by its very begging to be understood. 'Art' and 'Nature' were inseparable; I was Art and it was Nature, Nature was Art and it was me. Every little flower, feather, leaf; every whim of air tickled to movement invisible yet dancing the grasses in a ballet gigantic in all its insignificance; all of it was Art all of it was Nature. How could anyone want more than this, just how could they? Here was pure Gold in abundance; just how could they want more? Yet they did!

Our few fleeting days were highly productive and the hidden nutrients went deep and secret into our blood. Dave was, for the first time, in love and was ensnared in a loyalty and devotion of letter writing; his brilliance as an Artist rose to flower and to flow because of that chance serendipitous moment which touched him on that day of summer in Darnford Lane. It was just his heart that was broken when we learned, like a bolt out of hell, that the vicar had taken up Ministry in New Zealand and that the family had emigrated to that one place furthermost from our reach. Cycling past their empty house each day tore holes in my heart in a way that I never believed possible, and my poor old college-mate had suddenly become a 'Man', broken and hurt, revealing to me with a sadness touching grief that he'd lost his virginity with May, as she too had with him. I couldn't believe what I was hearing, I was almost envious, not because of him and her, but Heather and myself; it would only have taken one tiny kiss or touching of fingers and the whole world would have completely changed; oh, how mysteriously doth the Lord go about his 'nine-to-five'!

Our final year was all too soon breathing down our necks and squashing our eyeballs to the glass. Julie and I were still as 'one', but I sensed a change of sorts, one which sent a cold shiver through me. I couldn't pin-point it with any accuracy, but she'd not been the same since returning from their holiday in Cornwall when I detected a certain murmur of unfaithfulness going about its chemistry, and so, I accordingly backed off and left her with space, hoping and praying that she'd come rushing back to me. Worrying over her was the very last thing I needed at this time. We were both uneasy seeds in our shells; if we were dandelions, love would drift away, if we were daffodils love would surely stay.

Time, though pretending to be young, was already showing signs of ageing. My new-found friend of my late Second Year, Tom Crossley, had simply vanished from the scene and been plucked and bundled-up into the disguise of a soldier. He was undergoing the crude process of dehumanisation, uniformed in a governmental, behind-the-scenes sort of way superfluous to Nature's design. 'War' wasn't in any way part of our Artistic education; in truth we hadn't entirely been educated at all, but had used available space to educate ourselves as surviving creatures in something way beyond our control or imagination. Others too had been flushed down that same horrid hole that Tom Crossley had, and the College now seemed like a morgue, having no laughter or no music; a kind of no-man's land caught up in a fragmenting dash to metamorphosise into something sinisterly manufactured, superfluous and hostile. Suddenly being at the top of the pecking order was not the pinnacled holy place it had promised to be, only ignorance had been bliss and it made me realise just what a fortuitous and miraculous 'renaissance' that previous year had been, how completely unrepeatable and unimaginable it had proven; I was just proud to have been part of it and would remember it for the rest of my days, no matter what.

Having always been productive Artists, Dave and I were well on the way with the preparation of our forthcoming exhibition. Framing was proving to be more of a problem than the producing of artwork was, neither of us having the money for such things. It was Dad who came to the rescue in the simplest, most basic ways addressing the problem by using strips of wood which he used in his job; it was roughly two inches by a quarter of an inch, cut to length, sanded and painted white so's to conceal the knots and grains which were considered to be distractions. It was a solution, no more than that, beggars couldn't be choosers. With this to focus my mind, Julie had all the space she needed to sort out her priorities and I was sufficiently distracted into not losing too much sleep over her although, noting how she too wasn't losing sleep over me wasn't without its pain. Dave was himself still under a veil of similar sadness and we talked our hurts away, like two old men debating their ailing whippets prior to risking racing them. I aired my suspicion that Julie's holiday in Cornwall was the source of our problem; something had happened down there in all that 'fun-in-the-sun' and had changed her in a way which I no longer recognised. Much to my pain, I guessed what 'it' was and started to curse myself for brushing aside all those opportunities with other beautiful girls at College; I'd burned more bridges here than I had smoked fags, not that I could be regarded as a smoker, but I had 'done' the odd packet of five here and there. Together, Dave and I created a false bravado and were projecting 'Art' into the role of 'mistress' in the absence of there being a 'balancing' female human force to make us 'perfect' and to bring a lovelier purpose about our lives.

I'd become aware of many tantalisingly new sparkling eyes as I tore about Lichfield Streets trying not to become undermined by memory. Julie's and my own togetherness had for some time now been somewhat inspirational in High School womanly circles, and news of our 'whatever-it-was' had spread and a new 'market' situation was seemingly rife about me. It was her realisation of this emerging new tide that prompted Julie to get a hastily contrived message to me stating that she wanted to see me, leaving me feeling that I had nothing more to lose ... other than my life. It was weird seeing her, we were like recently-made strangers, seeking an oblivion of sorts to distract us from fundamental chemistried rearrangements; she was on a mission. The place she had chosen for this oblivion was none other than the back seat of her Dad's Morris Oxford Saloon which was cocooned beneath a heavy tarpaulin beneath a corrugated lean-to at the back of their cottage. In such darkness there could for her be no betrayal of eyes, although I had for many years eaten carrots and was strongly suspected of being related to both Owls and moles; I could in fact see in the dark, it just took a little longer that's all, that's how good carrots were!

Her Mom and Dad were currently being intoxicated at the mercy of the 'Black and White Minstrel-Show' on television as we stealthily crept inside this love-cocoon and silently locked its door. It all smelled like only the interior of a car could and was icily cold to the touch ... nothing else was though. I very soon found out why I had been brought here; this was a grand testosterone and saliva festival to end all such festivals and, as my carrots got to work and my eyes slowly started to see, bare limbs were ghosting tightly about me. We were like two giraffes in a ferret-pen, heavenly hell if ever there was. In these contortionistic cramped conditions came infuriating realisation of double knots in my shoe-laces and with fly-hole buttons shooting off like bullets because of the stresses wrought upon their ageing cotton when trousers refused to slip over shoes. I knew beyond any doubt what was being expected of me if only I could achieve that vital surplus of closeness. Despite these frustrating, seemingly insurmountable obstacles, I was determined for our relationship to either go out with a bang or, even better, to remain intact because of one. This was my moment, either the beginning or the glorious end. I was way past dreaming anymore, deaf to the squeaking springs. "I want you Now I want you inside!" she groaned; I was in a tortuous lunge when I saw through the dribbling condensation, a torches eye and a ghost-face, squashing against the glass as an angered voice spanning a generation screamed, "Julie is that you in there? I want you both inside, d'you hear. I WANT YOU INSIDE!" "Yes, Daddy!" Julie squeaked in the sweetest of dishonesty as she brutally disregarded my predicament in her panic to restore a 'normality' which would hopefully have her coming out of this smelling like roses, and for me to remain brazen and bold as the briar from which she had so innocently shed a petal. We both had sweat profusely dribbling from us and were dishevelled beyond repair, as was the back seat of the Saloon! We both felt terrible. It would have been the most opportune of moments to have eloped and started a family somewhere, but no, her irate Dad had left the kitchen door open and the yard light on; there was no escape.

I had buttons in the wrong holes, others missing. I felt the scrutiny of too many eyeballs the size of medicine balls while Julie, cool as a cucumber, shoved her nose in the air and explained that she'd been faced with the problem of ending our relationship, and out of sheer desperation, had chosen the car as being the most ideal sort of place, where we could do some serious 'talking'. The poor man hadn't heard a word of it, he was staring at me in abject disbelief. His mouth fell open and a dribbly droplet splashed out onto the carpet as his wife found it necessary to leave the room in despair. The heat of the room was evaporating yet more steam from my clothing, making me look like approaching bad weather, in addition to which I was bloodily scratched and severely love-bitten. The only thing I wanted to do in all desperation, was to say goodnight, but I knew that I'd fail for the second time in minutes to get my leg over, that sod of a fixed-wheel bike of mine was uncooperative at the best of times! My body was reluctant to get the message and my blood still boiled in the wrong place, making the prospect of continuous rapid pedalling a torture to even think about. The fact that I was still 'Virginus Intactus', despite having come so perilously, ecstatically close to making it the most unforgettable memory, was a hell beyond hell to behold, triggering off inconsolable weeping at the realisation that it effectively marked the end of our relationship. With salty tears now washing away the salty sweat, I caught a last glimpse of Julie's sweaty locks as she vanished. My Gold had all slipped through the hole in my pocket ... not so much 'perspired alchemy', but 'alchemy expired'.

## 21. 'Concept of Aliens after an Exhibition'

There was no escaping the feeling of heartbreak which I felt; keeping it a secret from Mom was impossible and it broke her heart too. Dad went into a respectful silence and thoughtfully watched from the sidelines, as too did Fay, unlike my brother Dave. He wickedly sniggered his throat sore, finding my catastrophic transition from slushy high romance down to grief-gloomy grovelling a side-splitting comedy to beat anything that his 'Beano' had to offer, triggering him off into picking his nose again, a nasty little habit of his which I thought I'd broken him of, especially the bit where he wiped it onto the patterned wallpaper beside his bed in a show of new defiance! Sharing the room at all was bad enough, but it was made much more of a pain when it happened to be my painting studio, with a work desk, two drawers full of treasures, secret love letters and photographs, all of which had his thumb-prints liberally squidged all over them. The other drawer was full of artifactual riches ... mouth-organs, a busted wristwatch, bike-bits, socks, badges, stuff like that which, for David, was as jam to a wasp. My desk-top had my sketchbooks, notebooks of ideas, preliminary illustrations and layouts for College projects, unfinished poems, an assortment of pens, rubbers, sharpeners, a candlestick, a box of matches and an ashtray. I had an easel, always with something 'not to be touched' on it and, all ledges and shelves were crowded with jars of brushes, some soaking in white spirit, some in water; jars of pencils, charcoal sticks and Conte-crayons; bottles of turps, linseed oil, tubes of paint everywhere and wet paintings propped against anything that was available. The situation was no good for either of us, both of us deaf, both of us dumb to each other, with five years and a whole lot of other stuff separating us.

Having a window that opened wide was a God-send, even when freezing fog came swirling in. Breathing-in turps fumes was quite normal for Dad, it was virtually all that he ever breathed, and so he expected both David and myself to cope with it like 'men' ... he couldn't tolerate 'cissies'. What annoyed David more than anything else was the fact that I invariably worked into the late hours on my pictures, often well into the early hours, a pattern which worsened over the last Christmas. I had received a box of two hundred Senior Service cigarettes, a most unexpected present from Teddy, one which I felt obliged to indulge in out of respect and gratitude, if nothing else. The window was now essential to our survival and remained wide-open no matter what God or the Devil threw at it, and my brother was now competing with me for the light which only 'it' provided when, with his saved-up pocket money, he sent away for an ex-admiralty telescope, a monster of a thing in a heavy wooden box. He grabbed the space where my easel was and fought for the window-ledge itself for resting the huge brass thing on. The fledglings were rapidly outgrowing the nest, made even worse when a short-wave, crystal-set type of receiver arrived together with what seemed like half a mile of wire, which he explained was its aerial which needed the window as well. So, with tangles of wire and a forever nose-picking, hunchbacked astronomer cum train-spotter cum peeping-tom forever blocking access to my work-area, I got around to concluding that the growing-up process was a rapidly degrading, shitty affair, and with an increasingly frequent feeling that, being born was more likely to have been a punishment rather than a gift from the Almighty!

Had it not been for our Lichfield Spring Exhibition, there'd have been nothing to prevent me for free-falling all the miserable way to impacting against the ultimate wall of reckoning, the National Diploma itself. Even though our Exhibition's lengthy preparation and the Show itself had provided me with a life-saving distraction, the pain of losing Julie refused to be diluted out of my system. I lost count of the amount of times that I had to endure being told ... "There are plenty more fish in the sea!"... a weird consolation offered to me as a philosophical, comforting elixir for the heart. Fish? ... what the bloody hell had fish got to do with it? Maybe I was in the process of 'evolving' into a fish-gorging Gannet ... or, on reflection, maybe a 'Shag' might have been a more appropriate species!

Such had been our preoccupation, neither Dave or I were aware that, running concurrently with our own Show, another Exhibition at London's Victoria and Albert Museum was celebrating Graphic Design throughout Midlands Art Colleges. We were rather pleasantly surprised to be shown quite a lengthy review of it in a newspaper, with the reviewer waxing lyrical over the standard of work on show. It came as even more of a surprise to discover that we'd both got write-ups; Dave for his illustrations to a book about old, broken-down people in a hospital, while I was being praised for my illustration to the macabre Russian work, 'The Coffin Maker'. The College had come off really favourably and could really start to feel good about itself, while for us it'd made the last five years not such a waste of time after all, with the thought that it wasn't every day that we could read of our work being on view in the 'V & A' of all prestigious places.

As for our own Exhibition, such a body of work on display filled me with mixed feelings; a part of me was sort of embarrassed, part proud. I was always shy and dreadfully self-conscious over the raising of my profile whenever I climbed those spiralling stairs up to the gallery, afraid of anyone associating me with the pictures and trying my best to look like just another viewer. It surprised me how well attended it was and I prayed and kept my fingers crossed that Julie wouldn't suddenly show up and spoil it all. Dave put my mind at rest over this concern when, on browsing through the Visitor's Book, spotted her signature with the word 'Wonderful' and a kiss. I looked at him and slowly shook my head in a gesture of confused resignation. "Don't let it worry you, Jim," he said in a low, compassionate voice, knowing what I was feeling, then going on to say ..."Just look around you, you've managed to do most of this work 'despite' her, not 'because' of her; just you remember that." I waved my arms in exasperation and sighed; "'Despite', 'Because', what's it all matter? I still miss her all the way down to my boots!" There was a brief stunned silence, then Dave leaned forward somewhat impishly and whispered ... "There's plenty more fish in the sea!" I spun round, grabbed hold of the Visitor's Book and threw it at him with all my might ... just as a little bespectacled and trilby-hatted man with a notebook and a pencil popped-up out of nowhere, like something out of Alice in Wonderland. "Are you the two artists?" he asked somewhat nervously, with Dave on the hop and hissing with pain and rubbing his head where the book had hit. Blushing, we sheepishly admitted to him that we were the two in question, whereupon he shook our hands and introduced himself ... a Reporter from the County newspaper.

To make things worse, or probably better, a whole class of teenage schoolkids came suddenly bursting upon the scene with their harassed teacher trailing and doing her best to implore a 'reverence' upon them, but to little avail. "Hey, look at this!" one of them shouted out; "That's 'Old Tom', that is ... cor, aint it just like him!" They were looking at my painting of a much-loved old man that walked the city streets and begged love as well as scraps to eat and drink from kindly souls with hearts big enough to be thankful for their own good fortune. They clamoured around it, instantly relating themselves in a broader, deeper sense to the Exhibition. It was a beautiful moment for both Dave and myself, as we watched them excitedly dash from painting to painting, looking and talking over faces and places familiar to them. Silence had no purposeful place here, it was just perfect the way it was, 'nature' itself and it made the whole laborious preparation of it all worthwhile in a deeply satisfying way. Before leaving, the schoolteacher came and apologised for all the kerfuffle and thanked us for having provided such a stimulating experience for all concerned, herself included. "Thank YOU," I said ... "this is what Art is for ... it's for sharing!" As they all left, hotly followed by the Reporter, a familiar voice from the past, one which I recognised, rang out. "You smooth talkin' bastard!" I turned and was confronted by a dark-grey suited figure on crutches and with a leg in plaster ... 'Art' Tomkins! I almost sucked my last dying breath with shock and raced across to hug him, almost toppling him back down the hard, cold spiralling stairs. "Guardsman Tomkins!" I bawled, wincing with pain as he shook my hand and grinned gleefully at the cracking sounds that it made. I didn't bat an eyelid and asked ... "What the bloody hell have you been up to for Christ's sake; you'll not be getting that leg-over in a big hurry!" "Guards Independent Para', if you don't mind," he corrected me, going on to say how he was now doing parachute-jumps from aeroplanes in full kit, and that this was the result. "Get a sudden crosswind and you don't hit the deck like you'd planned to ... you're soon in Shit-Street!" "Welcome to our Shit Street Exhibition," I said, in an overwhelming muddle of deep-rooted feeling for this, my staunch, stolid old running-mate. It was like a Brother returning from the darkness, hungry to discover vital roots in establishing a discreetly invisible stability. We'd got lots to talk about and this wasn't the time.

One of the most proud paintings I had on display was one which I had been commissioned to paint for my old school Headmaster back in the village; the lovely, far-sighted

Mister Nichols, 'Old Nickel' as we more commonly knew him. The painting was to commemorate his retirement from the profession which he so dearly loved. I most readily wanted to paint this very personal of 'thank-yous' on canvas, something which I couldn't afford, inspiring me into using the next-best thing in the circumstances ... a farm sack. I took a good deal of time in choosing the very best sack available, a heavy and tightly-woven one with the word 'Libbys" boldly painted on both sides. A fortuitous find in a junky sort of antique shop provided me with a dog-eared gilt frame for which I constructed a rude stretcher upon which I stretched my sack, glue-sized it then gave it two coats of white lead primer. When it was ready it had a real 'primitive' feel about it, a Kalahari Bushman sort of canvas upon which I painted the most peaceful of things that I felt appropriate, a 'Pissaro'-like, foliage-flickering of blossoming trees, a place that he knew; this very Art Gallery itself, hidden amongst celebrating foliage. For me, this had been a very emotional undertaking; had it not been for this marvellous man I'd have never gone to Art School in the first place, and now I was giving something back. He had no idea what was going on, or that this painting was specially for him; I'd marked it 'On Loan', and it would be presented to him at the end of the exhibition. The two styles of painting on display were very complementary; Dave's style was that of the most meticulous, academic, expansive landscapes in watercolour, while mine, by contrast, was somewhat looser, somewhat 'urgent', vigorous, in a more tactile, textural search for 'atmosphere'. It all exemplified why Art should be taken as a serious and not frivolous subject and why, mastering the art of walking prior to that of running was so vitally essential. There were no short-cuts; only from miniscule pips did apple trees grow; from their soft-budded fingers did blossoms show, only then came sweet apples and the sparkling cider flow. Dave and I shared similar feelings over most things, neither of us judged the value of anything just by its price-tag. The biblical concept of 'giving without counting the cost', had etched itself deeply into my God-given values and I had grown to understand what was meant by 'cost'. Nothing was as valuable a gift as that which had cost in time, skill, love and commitment. I felt this way over my paintings and drawings; nothing gave me more joy than that of giving something which had cost me the most in what it was that I most truly was. This for me was far more beautiful, a sharing which I hoped eventually would prove 'Art' to be spiritually above and beyond monetary transactional 'prostitution' and all its false Gods as well as false measure. If someone really loved what I was doing, to present it to them, was for me, pure Gold, perfect Alchemy!

True value I felt, should have been equated with 'Time'. Time for me being just as valuable as time was to anyone and everyone else, and the monetary value of that time being of equal worth. For excellence in all its forms to be free of price-tags and instead, valued for worth in human terms and not by Gold, mined by Colonised slaves, or by diamonds dug from Earth's very bowels by hopelessly plundered people starving. Everything went on existing despite the requirement of a monetary measure which bred covetousness and inevitable plague-like greed, which thence required brutality and force to maintain its permanence and falseness as a measure by which to 'control'. Poverty was never the most likely of things to elevate a 'nothing' at the bottom of the pile into becoming a 'something' at the top of it; we'd got ourselves a contrived status quo-ad infinitum kind of arrangement, which only the dream of Revolution might address ... and even then, only temporarily before the whole wretchedly sad disease took hold again, due to its most incurable of addictions.

Impossible to define as the concept of 'worth' was, its existence was undeniable despite forever veiled in ambiguities. 'Excellence' was never enough on its own to be of any use as a measure of worth; similarly, 'Beauty' had no cast-iron guarantee either; some beautiful things could be priceless, while other equally beautiful things could be worthless. 'Rarity' was a factor involved, as too was 'Demand', something which was just as likely to devalue by the very popularising of any given thing. 'Size' seemed like a fairly dependable factor, 'big' being beautiful sort of thing, but we all knew that the best things always came in small packages and the difference between 'Big' and 'Too Big' turned all logic on its head. This resulted in a dilemma which bred mistrust, my own suspicions bringing into question as to precisely who or what it was that was doing the measuring and orchestrating the whole bizarre complexity of it all above and beyond my own and everyone else's evaluation of worth.

It wasn't quite such a mystery once logic had got to work in identifying that it was all to do with 'Control'; the having of it over that of 'being controlled'. Money was still doing the talking, just as it was with this bureaucratically, political oddity called 'Democracy', for so long and so subtly being fastened about our minds like a blinkered harness, with all emphasis being cunningly steered towards this magic thing known as 'The Vote'; something which was unquestionably, by the very having of it, proof suffice that the 'people' could now have things according to their choice in a 'most-votes-wins' kind of arrangement. What a load of bollocks! The monster that held the whip would never let go of it no matter what was concocted; 'Control' was all that mattered. We had been led to believe that we now had a system whereby we had a say and could choose, it sounded like perfect freedom ... unfortunately, the part of the menu that attracted us was never available. The Bill of Fare had already been pre-selected by some behind-the-scenes beast of control, resulting in the maddening outcome of having no place, no space whatever, for the voicing of your opinions or preferences. Of course there never could be, it was never intended that you ever should; the barbed-wire of bureaucracy was always there to keep you precisely where you'd always been. Money would always, always stay where money had always been ... they weren't that daft!

This was an increasingly frantic and stressful time; the weeks were skidding by faster than the days. There wasn't time for complaining now and any grievances there may have been were usually those of our own making. There never had been time for slacking as we had repeatedly been warned; some had taken heed of this perfectly good advice, some had to a large degree disregarded it and were now coming to the boil in a growing state of panic. Some students quite naturally worked more slowly than others and had always appeared to be struggling without them being lazy in any way; it wasn't their fault and they had my sympathy. Examinations were strange, unpredictable things; final exams being the strangest ones of all. A bad dose of nerves at the wrong time had the ability to turn a final exam into a living nightmare, immobilising the creative ability into a state of rigor mortis-like deep-freeze and with the thaw coming too late to be of any use. This was why it was so important to have worked hard and to have produced an abundantly impressive portfolio of work, together with an equally impressive sketchbook as well as a highly crafted, hand-written and hand-bound Thesis which explored in depth, some thematic aspect within the range of one's study. There was always a remote, outside chance of being awarded your Diploma, despite having had a bad exam, provided all those other things spoke adequately for themselves, but there was no guarantee of this.

Having had the extra pressure of an Exhibition to prepare artwork for, I wasn't short of drawings and illustrations to swell my portfolio and my sketchbook was bursting at the seams. More importantly than that, all the hard work that it entailed was now proving to be worth its weight in Gold in addressing whatever demands the forthcoming National Diploma was going to present. I just had to remember to turn up, I smugly joked in private moments of my feverish nerves; I took nothing for granted. The nervous energy in the form of electricity being generated over this time could profitably have been wired to the national grid and put to use, as too, all the gas being released could be piped and pressurized into cylinders ... just a couple of silly ideas ahead of their time! "Thank God that's all that they were!" I sighed with relief, suddenly fearing this silliness to be more of a prophecy than a frivolous letting-off of steam. Bizarre ideas came with increasing frequency and always had a 'practical' side when analysed, the nervous gas-thing being one such example. I could find it entirely feasible for the gasses produced by each individual person, to be contained and stored in some way prior to being used in addressing that person's energy needs. There would be greater attention given to 'high gas' foodstuffs so's to ensure that, by farting alone, each person could be expected to provide energy for his or her own cooking, heating, lighting and washing. Each person would, by law, be required to wear a 'precision', surgical garment to which was attached an inflatable bag, etc., etc., Whilst being beyond the bounds of decency, it wasn't impossible; all it took was some tyrannical 'Hitler' that was hooked to the idea of a humanity that had to pay for its upkeep ... he, no doubt, being excused the indignity!

A far less frivolous idea was that of, on successful completion of the National Diploma course, we should be invited onto a Grand Celebratory Year of exploring other aspects of Art from a purely experimental angle. A kind of creative 'messing about with Art' sort of thing, designed to broaden our artistic perceptions and to reinvigorate artistic expectations. There'd be a deferment of National Service in the hope of it being abolished in the meantime, something which our magical 'Democratic Vote' should have already done for us, and for humanity to move forward into the civilization which it mouthed but hadn't as yet discovered how to practice.

The year of 1957 was ripening way beyond it's Winter and was foliating and flowering well into its late Spring, my fifth and final one at the College. It didn't seem like it had taken more than five minutes to get to this point. I was but a colt when I started this ... 'Aspiring Alchemist's Gymkhana-cum-Novices Gold Cup' thing, and I was now an aspiring stallion ripe for racing and other pleasantries associated with being in the saddle and jumping obstacles with ease, all whipped-up in the thrill of the chase. The final furlong was but a bend away, one which I was already rapidly going round with a colossal growing realisation of just where and what I most truly was as I felt all grandiose dreams purge out from me, insisting upon me as they fled that, men who had themselves fled from bullets of wars were not cowards, just lovers of life, wanting to go on living, go on loving, courting beauty, sowing seeds and reaching a grave without regrets to spoil their resurrection into a more heavenly dream yet to awaken ... instead of being stood blindfold before a wall and shot!

Little Larks still went about their rejoicing, having slept their nights crouched beneath shrouded grasses above which blew black, bleak winds wearing busted pearl necklaces of rain strewn haphazardly beyond the bounds of worth and with hungry foxes prowling, sniffing for the frailest scent of Lark breath. How different were the poles in this cycle of hours; from all the glowing sewing of the needled night's grass-smelling shroud, to an elevated place of pure dazzling blue light beyond dark-patched clouds. A place where vixens couldn't reach and where outspread wings flirted and held hands, entwined feathered fingers with invisible swirling, whirling whims of winds from where to pour out their very souls and with no keyboard, drums or three-pin plug anywhere in sight!

Blessed with the ability to learn and referred to as being the 'Beast of Reason' like no other creature aboard planet Earth had so been labeled, Man's golden inheritance had sadly soured down to something more resembling an unwanted gift which had become a burden around his neck. The 'gift of reason' had in fact been rendered impotent and cunningly stolen from his grasp by none other than his own kind. This uniquely wonderful gift had been blessed upon us like as a 'Lantern unto our Feet', a guiding light to keep us safe from straying into darkness and becoming lost; the 'light of reason' being the most dependable of illuminations. However, try to reason as we may, with all power assuredly remaining where power had always been, the 'magic lantern' dimmed, plunging us into the darkness at the mercy of the bullying bigots of Holy Orders. Their armies forever on plundering, debaucherous orgies of blood-letting, while proclaiming that it was only they, blessedly they who were the light that we should blindly follow, and to trust in the power of their reasoning, to succumb and be governed by it. From 'Beast of Reason' to 'Creature of Habit'; too apathetic and far too afraid to question or to reason anymore.

Sad to say, there wasn't a single other species upon the planet that's behaviour was so utterly contrived and manufactured, and whose evaluation of worth was so artificial and transparent. Neither was there a species so overwhelmingly destructive, callous and uncaring; a wrecker of all the things it claimed to love, including itself and the very planet upon which its survival as a species depended. When wild creatures killed, they did so for food; when mankind killed it was for a multitude of the most vile of reasons to do with lusting over something or other. It could be over the greed for territorial possession, for gold or diamonds, precious metal deposits of that black gold known as 'oil'. He killed for his religion, pompously appointing himself 'God' so's to sanitize and condone his wrong doings. Even in leisure he did it for pleasure, calling it 'sport', and took delight in chasing some poor, inedible creature and outnumbering it by more than hundred to one, before finally tearing it to pieces in the most horrid of murders. The 'Sport of Kings' they called it ... 'Love of Kings' being more to do with syphilis, according to the painter Hogarth, who was an expert on these matters! Some things changed, but other things never did, hence the title 'Creature of Habit'.

No; it was these little Larks that most truly belonged here, this was their home-eternal. Man's home alas, was out there somewhere unknown deep within the timeless heavens, light-years beyond where Larks went to whistle. Man's true majesty lay in the fact that he would eventually find that place from whence he had been transported, and he would, through his gift of science and mathematics, complete the circle and, in a craft like that which brought him here, return whether he was welcome there or not, but he would most assuredly return to that place called 'home' and discover the bones of his long-lost forefathers. This was the reason why, search as he may, no time-old fossils here on earth could ever record his ever being here prior to the 'Age of Dinosaurs'. He'd come a very long way since being 'put to the test', and now he was well into the penultimate stage prior to this, his 'Final Exam'.

Despite the down-side, we were and are, the most amazing species; so potentially miraculous despite our having eyes to see that've been made blind through ignorance resulting from greed. We are the most formidable alien ... we Homo Sapiens, at odds with every single thing upon this newfound outpost with the Galaxy. Seemingly 'indigenous' humanoid species had, prior to our invasion, existed as wanderers, at harmony and apparently in tune with all other life around, and with Holy reverence being shown to Mother Earth in all her bountiful, beautiful provision. They were 'wild' animals of a spiritual and nobler kind. Others long before them, majestic and miraculous had existed on great land masses long since swallowed beneath oceans in uproar as a result of Planet Earth's own bilious intestinal reorganisation following cataclysmic impact by Asteroids which came close to shattering the planet to fragments with their incalculable force of impact, which wiped out the dinosaurs and plunged the planet into Dark Ages which triggered Ice Ages and preceded the settlement of Earth by this, mostly pale-skinned invader.

The inescapable realisation that every single thing was different from each other was really bugging me; I simply couldn't get my mind round the fact that variety was infinite with every individual flora and fauna so completely different from the next, yet miraculously inter-related and at balance; with the exceptions of Homo Sapiens, who stuck out like a sore thumb in his demonstration of being unavoidably at odds with everything, including his own kind. For a Lark to be a Lark and a Hawk to be a Hawk, a Kingfisher a

Kingfisher or a Jay a Jay, was a miracle beyond comprehension; the differences were startling, while the similarities were there too. Each of them had the characteristic of being birds with feathers, beaks, wings, aerial dexterity and separate languages. Differences were more different than similarities were similar; I simply didn't have the capacity to imagine such wealth of differences, which spoke volumes when the 'Human' was busy cloning his monosyllabic opinion upon the earth, elevating 'Habit' up into plague-like proportions. Being 'different' was a threat to his mentality; safety lay in numbers, sameness was 'Holy'. Periodic fashions alone would ring-in the permitted differences, with Sheep serving as the role-models in safeguarding the reins of control and the desirable manipulation and management of mass. Not even the tiny Ants did live like this, and the only reason why Sheep did was because Man had herded and imprisoned them and had made barriers of impenetrable thorns and stones in his grabbing of land, and had farmed-away a Sheep's freedom to roam; cloning them down into flocks, just as he was with his own children. This was not the behaviour of 'Earthlings', but 'Aliens'; out of sync. with the rest of things.

My quest for reason was itself without end and I could no more swallow something without question than I could kill something without question. This intriguing web of a thing called 'Art' was what it was that'd inspired me to the bewildering Alchemy of knowing and my resultant ignorance was in such a tangle that I couldn't tell the difference between a haemorrhoid and an asteroid. What I did know with a degree of confidence was that both were piles of some sort. The very idea that piles of rock were hurtling about the heavens in a willy-nilly, anarchic fashion, kinda killed some of the awesomeness of God's music: surely if he was that clever, so overwhelmingly in charge, he could have, in effect 'netted' them so's to prevent them from inflicting disaster on His Master-design.

In my deeper search for reason, the seemingly outrageous idea had occurred to me that, perhaps the 'vehicle' which brought Mankind to this planet may have in fact been a 'controlled, manned Asteroid', an intergalactical mobile-home in effect, one of unimaginable, darkening proportions as it orbited the earth several times before skilfully using the Great Ocean as a cushioned landing strip, forming a vast continent as it eventually settled to rest, having caused tidal waves of such catastrophic dimensions as to swallow entire continents and wipe out species upon species and with the violation of earth's surface being of such magnitude as to crack it like an earthenware pot and bleed-out the fiery volcanic magma all along the fractured lines, demonstrating just how perilously close the planet came to total oblivion.

What was a mere final National Diploma Exam compared with the magnitude of the questioning of what I really was? I was an offspring apparently; a child of an un-earthly invader, part of a colonisation that didn't seem to have worked, and whose brief measured earthly history had consisted virtually entirely by wickedness measurable more by spilled blood than anything else, and with 'World Domination' being its ultimate goal. It concocted answers that suited, long before the questions had been asked, and forever proceeded along blind avenues of preference rather than reason, a surrealism pure and simple. All that 'Surrealism' was, was a 'Solution by Magic', a whimsical disjointing of things, a 'fun-way' of expressing the maddeningly impossible frustration of never being able or capable of discovering the answer to the ultimate question; a glorious giving up of trying, for reasons of not belonging.

Mankind everywhere needed his Gods to whom he could pray and have all fears soothed away. The Universe out there was, and is, without Beginning or End, a concept beyond our capacity to understand; only our Gods could offer comfort over the confrontation of this impossible-to-grasp truth of truths. And, what was God? To my grovelling, snoffling, truffle-hunting intellect, 'God' was in fact the furthermost distant hand-me-down of timeless memory; it wasn't a 'person', it was in fact, the entire Universe, a living bodily organism of which we were the most macro-miniscule parts of parts. 'God' was everywhere and 'God' was everything and we, we all of us were part of 'God'.

Little Larks knew what we didn't know, so too did Ladybirds, dusty Moths, Dormice, blue Butterflies, Wrens and silvery dace in sparkling brooks, together with a million trillion other tiny vessels in which the magical river of life flowed. All knew the majesty holding us close upon its beating heart. In every little Acorn were the squawking cries of Jays, the grunting of Swine, the colour of clouds and the sweet scent of Gorse in flower; there was even more than that ... in just a single Acorn lost amongst such a vast equality of things. The reason why 'Earth' functioned as a diversely balanced organism prior to the arrival of an Alien, was simply because everything was equal and at perfect balance with reasons for things and seasons for things; systems perfectly fitting and functioning within systems fitting and functioning within other systems fitting and functioning ad infinitum. A spanner in the works, that's what we were and what we still are; aspiring Alchemists lost of any sense of belonging, because of the belief that 'Gold' alone could provide the measurement of worth where everything prior to this conclusion had been of equal worth, worthless, yet of great wealth of beauty, of magnificence and of glory.

## 22. 'Last Bus to Nowhere'

There was something rather haunting about the bike ride I made to see my old pal 'Art' Tomkins, now Guardsman Tomkins, B.A. (Busted Ankle!). It revealed a vivid picture of my own 'Paradise Lost' and touched deep inside, right through to my trembling jelly. There was no escaping the sweet, sad memories of Julie and I almost choked when I cycled within a hundred yards or so of her cottage. These were unmistakable feelings of loneliness; I'd have given anything to just turn the clock back a few years and relive the abundance of joy that'd held me so warmly over the last precious years. The truth of the matter was that I wasn't a boy anymore; I blame it all on my Dad's demob-suit for accelerating my passage through to manhood, worst of all, I was still wearing the bloody thing, interspersed by occasional lightweight flannel trousers which were threadbare and holey in no time at all. That confounded demob-suit was indestructible, a living relic of the Second World War, in which I served my time as a young child, being blitzed and bombed bereft of the reasoning which caused it; or the reasoning behind the assumption that, through mass-murder, anything lastingly good could emerge at all.

'Art' had chosen to be a professional soldier. He had freely offered himself up to be a tool of war and, try as I may, I still couldn't understand why, when it was plainly obvious that what he most dearly wanted to have was a willing woman, and he was equally willing to marry the first one to make him a father. I had no doubts whatsoever over his ability to be a most marvellous Dad, and I daresay a good, loyal and hardworking husband too. He'd come from the very warmest of loving families; a fun loving and laughter filled household with a bollock-licking pacifist of a terrier-cross mongrel called 'Laddie'. I always loved being there amongst them and 'Art' and I had, in the past, sat painting through his bedroom window, a snowscape with an abandoned green vegetable delivery van broken down in the middle of it.

That was then; now was so very different. I know that I was growing up by the way I could look back upon times that broke my heart to shreds and left me in a bewilderment of isolation. My legs pedalled and my 'Dunlop Road-Race' tyres spoke upon the tarmac over which 'Art' and I had left our rubber when boyhood inched into youth and was getting its first testosterone eruptions to boost us into wanting to conquer the world.

My twentieth year, still a virgin as well as an alien; I still had only one single heart to break, how many times it could be broken remained the great mystery of life. I had no idea as to whether a heart was weakened or, possibly strengthened by being broken; it was all perilous guesswork. Gazing about me, there were so many old people that seemed to have survived, and so I just slipped into neutral and waited. There was no such neutral where a fixed-wheel bike was concerned; continuous pedalling was like continuous heart-beating. Going too fast into the corner of Weston Road resulted in my pedals hitting the ground violently and the bike, with me astride it, bucked over onto the wrong side providing me with a timely reminder which I could learn from, lending to the idea that, giving bikes gears was a step in the wrong direction, a bit like giving a tramp a sofa when staying in tactile control was the prime essential of factors; you free-wheeled at your peril.

'Art' was a proud man with his white-plastered and written-on lower leg up on a chair; he was still my very best mate of all time. His ivoried grin was more real than a tree and I just resignedly shook my head and grinned back. How very different were we all as people; whatever it was that rang his bells, didn't ring mine in the same way, yet we shared an undeniable brotherly kind of bonding. His Mom and Dad were so very proud of him being a Guardsman, it made them glow to think of their beloved son standing on guard-duty in his shiny-buttoned, scarlet uniform and with a black bearskin on his head outside Buckingham Palace; getting his leg pissed-up by royal Corgies and his immaculate image on a million postcards. All that bull-shitty grandeur was missing when I sat beside him in the front room of their council house; me there in my hand-me-down 'indestructible', he in a navy dressing gown and a plastered leg, sitting there beside an ashtray mountain of stubs. We talked of the good times we'd spent, relived old memories and generally up-dated ourselves on things which were bearable to speak of; I had hardly dared to venture into what awaited me regarding compulsory military service. I was a gentler animal that 'Art' ever was, but I knew that I had a deeply secret core of steel and a belief in my ability to, at the very least, hold my own. I really believed that I could win, no matter what the odds; 'Art' had discovered this to his cost in the past, adversity was more my friend than ever it was his. Living-down an inherited choosing to be an 'ordinary nobody', positioned somewhere safely between second to last and second to first, had been a curse and not a blessing, the scars of which would never properly go away. After this point, I never saw my friend again; this was a proper 'goodbye', not of design, but of circumstance.

There was hardly any room left in this 'old life'; I could clearly see the wall at the end of this stage of life coming ever closer. It had no windows for me to peep through and steal a glimpse of what lay in store beyond that last concluding hectic week of my five years in coming, National Diploma of

Design examination. Nerve-racked as I most clearly was, I was nevertheless up for it with a confidence coming from determination alone. I hadn't realised until these very crucial moments of my life that, the reason for my wanting to succeed so badly, was for Dad, for him alone. I wasn't the 'Artist of the family' as he had described me as being ... he was, and always would be the 'Artist of Artists' in my mind. He hadn't a hope in hell of ever succeeding when poverty had thrown him into the 'workhouse', even after he'd won the most coveted scholarship of studying painting at London's most highly prestigious, 'Slade School. All of that went out of the window and instead of studying Art in the most enviable of places, he was thrown to farm work at the very lowest of places. He'd become a 'slave' no less, to a wealthy landowner farmer, an absolute philistine of an Englishman, the sort of which England was so lavishly provided. Dad's bed was a mildewed stinking damp pile of hay in a shed, he was fed on the left-over scraps which even the farm dogs turned their noses up at. He was a pile of skin and bones when he could have been at 'The Slade', coffeeing in cafes and indulging in Art amongst Artists.

I had a lot to prove and was embittered with resentment over why my own species had been worse than cannibalistic over its kind by using, abusing, depriving and denying prior to exploiting them for the rest of time. This being at least as bad as cannibalism, unspeakably vile as the practice was, at least it was honest! The strange thing about cannibalism was that it echoed a kind of functional behaviour in predatory wild animals, in that it ate its own kind, albeit in more of a 'dog-eat-dog' than a 'hawk-eat-hawk' sort of way, as opposed to oppressing them, as did those now claiming to be 'civilised'. Whether or not their cannibalism used selective methods by sorting out those amongst them that were weak or injured, or maybe just old or perhaps had broken laws in some obscure way which rendered them 'pot-bound'! It was hard to find any reasoning whatsoever and all of it was alien to my logic and I was tempted to sign everything that I drew or painted, 'This is the work of an Alien', but I knew that it'd be taken as being the work of a madman instead. So I bided my time until the day when I would paint images of what I believed madness to be and to qualify it by showing the void that existed between 'it' and what had always existed at perfect balance and harmony upon this stolen planet.

I suppose that this was what 'Surrealism' was largely to do with; some may say it was the addressing of madness with madness, but it reinforced my belief that Art was the most powerful force to emanate from Man. Unlike science, Art was free and could echo the personality of its creator, as well as to visually explain the inexplicable. Science was precise in its methodical pursuit of factual, evidential accuracy; when it resorted to guesswork it ceased to be Science and became 'Surrealism'. 'Art' could never be precise, that was what was so exhilarating about it. When it attempted to be factual, all that it was doing was deluding itself and was copying something that already existed; either that or it pretended, just like a magician pretended, creating illusions with such trickery as to making things seem real. To be Science at all, it needed to be factually accurate and precise, together with the most impeccable integrity. Having 'theories', exciting as they may be in relieving the frustration in a 'rebellious-outburst' kind of way, were fantasies pure and simple, totally devoid of proper scientific base. Theory 'Evolution' being the most mammoth myth of them all, not only setting-back science light-years, but to betray an entire people in their own wholesome searching for understandings, fine, delicate, spiritual and majestically imprecise. 'Similar' was never enough when it was 'Same' that you were searching for!

I had no idea whatsoever as to how or why I found myself to be forever reasoning in this way; this 'life-thing' was proving to be complex, a growing puzzle which absolutely no-one around me showed the slightest interest in whatsoever. Sitting in solitude on the canal bank had, in earlier, more tender years, provided me with another ear and another heart to listen to the 'great asking' within my own soul; and here I was and here 'it' was, doing it all again. Imprecise as my need was, I felt that I needed to be with 'God'. I was here out of nothing and out of nowhere, here on the canal bank with my mind as complex as a dandelion clock, complex as feather-systems, leaf systems, scale systems or any other systems in a myriad of magical systems. Here I was with majesty as abundant in myself as in anything else; I being the only thing that needed to question it. Why? What? How? was what I always asked of the water, as I gazed blurredly down into it, to the upside-down sky where the water became still while I went sailing away on the great ship of the canal bank. "It's a journey," the water said. "It's all a journey ... everything is a journey ... nothing isn't. Make your journey well, be the very best that is within you to be, settle for nothing less; discover what you are in solace; resist!"

My time of reckoning had arrived; 'The National Diploma of Design' bore no resemblance to its earlier component part, the 'Intermediate' Examination. What we now confronted was a painfully concluding and on-going culmination and assessment of the various disciplines spanning the last three years, which included 'History of Art', 'History of Costume', meticulous copies and illustrations with handwritten text, lightly bound and beautifully presented. In addition to this there had to be a bursting-at-the-seams sketchbook, hand-bound and abounding in 'delights', a portfolio containing all the design projects we'd undertaken; a hand written and fully illustrated Thesis of about a dozen pages, all put together in the most craftsmanlike example of the Bookbinder's art. If that wasn't enough, there was the 'live' Examination itself which addressed both our 'Main' subject and our 'Additional' subject. As an 'Illustrator', this involved being given the chapter of a book of which I had to provide four illustrations, all of which had to be reproduced in two-colour letterpress, typeset, printed and bound. My 'Additional' subject was no less daunting and in my own case involved the Art of Lettering; decorative, creative hand-lettering supplemented with Calligraphy all gilded to look like a page from the 'Book of Kells' or the 'Lindisfarne Gospels'. Whilst not being able to see its relevance in a modern world, I could still recognise its beauty and the aspirational sense of high Poetry which it represented. It was all so very nerve-racking, regardless of how well prepared we were or how confident we may have felt; all of it was made worse by there being strict time deadlines and no recourse to reference material of any sort. Being 'shagged-out' at the end of this felt more like having been colonically-irrigated orally ... with a fireman's hose!

I wasn't the only one that felt exhausted and adrift in a sense of lostness; it was easier to see now how people yielded to the process of ageing, some quicker than others as though being more willing or less willing to make a fight of it. 'Living' was all now being piled up, boxed and labelled on towering shelves in a bureaucratically straight-jacketed, insurmountable wall, all the rest of the way ahead. It should all have been fun like childhood had been, even though for the most part its skies had been full of deafening metal planes with bellies full of bombs and with guns itching and festering on wings and poking out from blistered lumps. We were all gipsies of sorts, hunters and gatherers to a large extent; we didn't need bits of paper telling us what to do.

There should never have been a 'rich' or a 'poor', and all those bits of paper were making absolutely sure that things would forever remain divided as they now were. 'Heroic Outlaws', that what we should have been, making fires from those pompous signs which said, 'Keep Out!', 'Private, Trespassers will be Prosecuted'. We should have been free to roam, to tickle Trout in brooks, catapult Pheasants at roost, stalk Deer with bows and arrows in forests throughout a land that was ours as equally as it was anyone else's. Such was the stuff of romantic improbability which was still at liberty to plague my uncomfortably dissatisfied mind prior to my having to earn a token coinage in order for me to rent my standing-space on Earth; either that or starve to death, options not being an option for the poor!

The future stood up big and brutal, dark and foreboding whilst offering no clue as to what it held in store. Paradise had breathed its last breath and had taken a full nineteen years before deciding to fail me at this point in time, just two months short of my twentieth birthday. I glanced across at Dave and could see a man that was twenty years older in the space of days; next to him, 'Burto' was glazed, dazed and numb, others looked even worse; this was what shit did when it hit the fan ... I'd often wondered what it looked like! Our lecturers took on the characteristics of midwives and, with loving compassion, comforted us into the hauntingly empty days of waiting which now lay ahead.

After sleeping on it, I didn't feel too despondent about my own exam. I'd known that it wasn't going to be easy right from the start and to start worrying about it now served no purpose at all, what's done was done! Sleeping on it hadn't eased Dave's mind any and he had serious doubts about his own performance, others were similarly gloomy while, by contrast, Burto had adopted a kind of laid-back smugness, through his having remained true to 'playing-it-safe' and putting his trust in remaining a 'minimalist' to the end with yet another of his forward defensive strokes. To be 'not out, nought' being preferable to that of being caught on the boundary whilst going for a big Six!

We all said our goodbyes, hugged and shook hands as our insides broke apart. Lecturers warmly thanked us for our contribution to their own lives and somewhat chokingly bade their farewells and well-wished us on our separate ways. Art College was over, it was gone forever, just a memory now.

I sat in the upstairs back seat of the Midland Red double-decker for my very last time, a packet of five 'Park Drive', a box of matches and a broken heart. I choked on my tears as I smoked, head drooped and no 'Art' Tomkins sitting beside me. If that wasn't pure 'Gold' that I was leaving so tragically behind me, then there was no such thing as 'Gold' and 'Aspirations' and 'Alchemy' were nothing more than arms that were too short to reach for that marvellous 'Golden' apple that you wanted to steal.

End

This book is a work of non-fiction based on the life experiences and recollections of the author. In some cases names of people have been changed to protect the privacy of others.


ISBN: 978-1-912804-00-9
CIP catalogue record for this book is available from The British Library
Published by Bridgen Unabridged
Printed in Great Britain by Biddles Books Limited, King's Lynn